本书受北京外国语大学卓越人才支持计划支持

中国刑事诉讼法简明讲义

Handbook on Chinese Criminal Procedure Law

郑曦 著
Zheng Xi

图书在版编目(CIP)数据

中国刑事诉讼法简明讲义=Handbook on Chinese Criminal Procedure Law：英文/郑曦著.—北京：北京大学出版社，2022.10
ISBN 978-7-301-33406-5

Ⅰ.①中⋯ Ⅱ.①郑⋯ Ⅲ.①刑事诉讼法—中国—教材—英文 Ⅳ.①D925.2

中国版本图书馆CIP数据核字(2022)第185366号

书　　　名	中国刑事诉讼法简明讲义
	ZHONGGUO XINGSHI SUSONGFA JIANMING JIANGYI
著作责任者	郑　曦 著
责任编辑	邹记东　张　宁
标准书号	ISBN 978-7-301-33406-5
出版发行	北京大学出版社
地　　　址	北京市海淀区成府路205号　100871
网　　　址	http://www.pup.cn
电子信箱	law@pup.cn
新浪微博	@北京大学出版社　　@北大出版社法律图书
电　　　话	邮购部 010-62752015　发行部 010-62750672
	编辑部 010-62752027
印　刷　者	北京鑫海金澳胶印有限公司
经　销　者	新华书店
	787毫米×1092毫米　16开本　14.75印张　320千字
	2022年10月第1版　2022年10月第1次印刷
定　　　价	48.00元

未经许可，不得以任何方式复制或抄袭本书之部分或全部内容。
版权所有，侵权必究
举报电话：010-62752024　电子信箱：fd@pup.pku.edu.cn
图书如有印装质量问题，请与出版部联系，电话：010-62756370

PREFACE

Fighting against crimes is a basic requirement for maintaining social stability, but it must be carried out within the framework of the rule of law, especially by restricting state power and protecting human rights, which brings the need of being regulated by the Criminal Procedure Law. The Criminal Procedure Law is one of the most important departmental laws in China. Since its content mainly involves two aspects of state power restriction and human rights protection, it is also called the "mini-constitution".

In China's legal education system, the course of criminal procedure law has always been required for all law school students and occupied an important position in China's unified qualification exam for legal professions. With the deepening of China's reform and opening up, the international exchange of legal education has become increasingly prosperous. An increasing number of Chinese students go to study in law schools abroad, while a larger amount of foreign students come to China to study Chinese law, including China's Criminal Procedure Law.

The Law School of Beijing Foreign Studies University, where I work, has LLM students from all over the world for many years. Every year, I teach them China's Criminal Procedure Law course in English to help them understand the criminal justice system in China. However, I found it difficult to find a suitable textbook on China's Criminal Procedure Law written in English. Although some scholars have published such textbooks, these textbooks are either too complicated and challenging for LLM students, or they have not been renewed according to the latest revision of related laws. Given the issues discussed above, the intended audience for this volume includes foreign LLM students and any foreign friends who are unfamiliar with China's Criminal Procedure Law, and the book aims to provide an easy-to-understand and systematic handbook of China's Criminal Procedure Law.

In line with these objectives, this book is divided into eight chapters according to the system of China's criminal procedure. Chapter One introduces the legislation and revision of China's Criminal Procedure Law, as well as basic knowledge such as types of cases, litigation stages, and basic principles. Chapter Two reviews the special state organs for criminal proceedings and their respective jurisdictions. Chapter Three discusses the participants in the criminal proceedings and the protection of their rights. Chapter Four includes the restriction and deprivation of the freedom of criminal suspects and defendants. Chapter Five introduces China's pre-trial procedures, including specific procedures such as case filing, investigation, and prosecution. Chapter Six introduces China's trial procedures, including the first instance, second instance, review of death sentences and trial supervision. Chapter Seven details the punishment execution system for convicted criminals. Finally, Chapter Eight discusses the special procedures for criminal proceedings, including incidental civil action procedure, procedures for juvenile criminal cases, procedures for public prosecution cases where parties have reached settlement, procedure for trial in absentia, confiscation procedures for illegal income in cases where the criminal suspects or defendants escape or die, and procedures for involuntary medical treatment of mental patients legally exempted from criminal liabilities.

The publication of this book was greatly helped by the Law School of Beijing Foreign Studies University and Peking University Press. I am very grateful for the financial support provided by the Law School and the great effort which has been put into the publication process of Mr. Yang Lifan and Ms. Zhang Ning of Peking University Press. Due to the limitation of my own research, there are inevitably some errors in this book, and comments and advice from readers are welcomed.

Zheng Xi
April 7, 2022

CONTENTS

CHAPTER ONE   An Overview of Criminal Procedure in China 1

   1. Legislation and Amendment Process of the Existing Criminal
      Procedure Law 3
   2. Types of Cases 9
   3. Litigation Stage 11
   4. Litigation Principles 11

**CHAPTER TWO   Special Organs for Criminal Proceedings and
                     Their Jurisdiction** 15

   1. Investigation Organs 17
   2. Public Prosecution Organs 22
   3. People's Courts 26
   4. Executing Organs 30
   5. Jurisdiction System 32

CHAPTER THREE   Participants in Litigation and Their Rights 41

   1. Criminal Suspect and Relevant Defense System 43
   2. The Defendant and Relevant Defense System 50
   3. Victims and Their Rights 54
   4. Witnesses and Their Rights 57
   5. Other Litigation Participants 58

**CHAPTER FOUR   Restriction on and Deprivation of Freedom of
                    Criminal Suspect and Defendant** 63

   1. Forced Appearance 65

  2. Bail ··· 67

  3. Residential Confinement ··· 72

  4. Detention ··· 76

  5. Arrest ·· 81

CHAPTER FIVE   Pre-Trial Phase ·· 89

  1. Case Filing ··· 91

  2. Investigation ·· 100

  3. Prosecution ·· 125

CHAPTER SIX   Trial Stages ··· 141

  1. First Instance ··· 143

  2. Second Instance ·· 157

  3. Review of Death Sentences ·· 165

  4. Trial Supervision ·· 171

CHAPTER SEVEN   Execution ··· 181

  1. Death Sentence With Immediate Execution ······························ 183

  2. Punishment Against Liberty ··· 188

  3. Punishment Against Property ·· 199

CHAPTER EIGHT   Special Procedure ····································· 201

  1. Incidental Civil Action ·· 203

  2. Procedures for Juvenile Criminal Cases ······························· 209

  3. Procedures for Public Prosecution Cases Where Parties Have Reached Settlement ··· 215

  4. Procedure for Trial in Absentia ······································ 220

  5. Confiscation Procedure for Illegal Income in Cases Where the Criminal Suspect or Defendant Escapes or Dies ···························· 222

  6. Procedures for Involuntary Medical Treatment of Mental Patients Legally Exempted From Criminal Liabilities ································ 225

CHAPTER ONE

AN OVERVIEW OF CRIMINAL PROCEDURE IN CHINA

The Criminal Procedure Law is the basic legal source for criminal proceedings in China. Since enacted in 1979, the Criminal Procedure Law has been revised for many times and has formed a system with a relatively complete structure and Chinese characteristics.

1. Legislation and Amendment Process of the Existing Criminal Procedure Law

1.1. Pre-Criminal Procedure Law

At the early stage of the founding of the People's Republic of China, in 1951, the Central People's Government formulated and promulgated the Provisional Organic Regulations of the People's Courts and the Provisional Organic Regulations of the Supreme People's Procuratorate Office of the Central People's Government. These Regulations established the functions and powers of the courts and the procuratorate office, and stipulated that the people's courts adopted procedural systems of open trial, disqualification and defense in trying criminal cases.

In September 1954, the First National People's Congress adopted the Constitution, the Organic Law of the People's Courts and the Organic Law of the People's Procuratorates, stipulating the principles and systems of criminal procedure. In December of the same year, the National People's Congress also promulgated the Regulations on Arrest and Detention, stipulating the systems of Arrest and Detention.

1.2. Enactment of the Criminal Procedure Law of 1979

As early as 1954, the Commission of Legislative Affairs under the Standing Committee of the National People's Congress drafted the first version of the Criminal Procedure Law. After the Third Plenary Session of the Eleventh Central Committee of the Communist Party of China, the task of enacting the Criminal Procedure Law was put on the agenda with the acceleration of the construction of democracy and the legal system. After repeated amendments and deliberations, the Criminal Procedure Law was formally adopted on July 1, 1979, and had been in force since January 1, 1980. At this point, the first criminal procedure code of the People's Republic of China was formally born.

This Criminal Procedure Law of 1979 was divided into two parts, "general provisions" and "specific provisions". It consisted of four parts, 17 chapters and 164 articles. It basically adopted the ex-officio-doctrine-based litigation structure from the civil law system, absorbed the principles and systems of criminal procedure established at the early stage of the founding of the People's Republic of China, and had played an important role in punishing criminals in a timely manner, effectively protecting the legitimate rights and interests of citizens, maintaining public order, ensuring reform and opening up, and ensuring the smooth progress of economic construction.

1.3. The 1996 Amendments to the Criminal Procedure Law

With the continuous development of China's reform and opening up as well as the cause of socialist construction, especially the gradual formation of a socialist market economic system, profound changes had taken place in all fields of social life in China, and criminal offences had also taken on new characteristics and trends. Some of the provisions of the Criminal Procedure Law of 1979 had been unable to adapt to changes thereof. Objective needs and the strong appeal of the theoretical and practical sectors had prompted the amendment of the Criminal Procedure Law to be formally placed on the legislative agenda.

On March 17, 1996, the Fourth Session of the Eighth National People's Congress deliberated and adopted the Decision on Amending the Criminal Procedure Law of the People's Republic of China. The amended Criminal Procedure Law came into effect on January 1, 1997, with 225 articles increased from the original 164 articles. Except for the articles of the incidental civil action, the time period and service of process, and the death sentence review, significant additions and revisions had been made in other parts of the Criminal Procedure Law, which had made the criminal procedure system a big step forward in the direction of legalization and democratization. Aiming at the defects in the Criminal Procedure Law of 1979 and the problems existing in judicial practice, this amendment concentrated on solving a number of problems that had not been solved for a long time and that were difficult to solve, such as pre-investigative detention for suspects, exemption from prosecution, and handling of doubtful cases. As for the guiding ideology, it no longer emphasized one-sided fighting against crimes, but emphasized the combination of fighting against crimes and protection of human rights, and strengthened the protection of the litigation rights of victims, criminal suspects and defendants in terms of specific systems and procedures. Based on China's reality, this amendment also absorbed the achievements of foreign legislation and the criminal justice norms of the United Nations, such as the principle of presumption of innocence, the involvement of lawyers in the investigation stage, the addition of summary procedures, and the civilized execution of death penalty. It strengthened the protection of the legitimate rights and interests of victims, gave victims the status of litigants, affirmed the rights of victims to apply for disqualification, lodge a complaint and appoint agents to participate in the proceedings, and at the same time expanded the scope of private prosecution lodged by victims, stipulating that if they have evidence to prove the existence of criminal facts but the public security organs or the people's procuratorates did not pursue the criminal suspects for criminal liability, victims might directly initiate private prosecution in the people's court.[1] It absorbed the reasonable pattern of adversarial proceedings, and made significant modifications to the mode of trial.

1.4. The 2012 Amendments to the Criminal Procedure Law

Compared with the 1996 amendments to the Criminal Procedure Law, the 2012 amendments to the Criminal Procedure Law have greatly increased the number of articles and made significant progress in the content. In terms of quantity, the total number of articles had increased from 225 to 290. In terms of content, there were not only adjustments to the original procedural system, but also construction of the new procedural system. The amended Criminal Procedure Law of 2012 was not only practical, but also forward-looking in the system. Its main highlights are as follows:

(1) Incorporation of "Respect and Protection of Human Rights"

China had already incorporated "respect and protection of human rights" slight into the Constitution when the Constitution was amended in 2004. To this end, the Criminal Procedure Law of 2012 added a new provision in Article 2,

---

[1] Article 170 of the Criminal Procedure Law of 1996.

requiring "respect and protection of human rights". This provision not only conformed to the mainstream value of the society, but also highlighted the progress of human rights protection in our country. It can be said that this is the most dazzling flash point of the 2012 amendment to the Criminal Procedure Law.

(2) Improvement of the Evidence System

The adjustment of the evidence system in the 2012 amendments was very comprehensive: First, the concept of evidence had been changed from "theory of facts" to "theory of materials". Second, in terms of the types of evidence, documentary evidence and physical evidence were separated into independent types of evidence, the "expert conclusion of forensic identification and evaluation" was changed to "expert opinion", and new forms of evidence such as "identification and investigative reenactment transcripts" and "electronic data" were added. Third, the principle of voluntary confession had also been confirmed, stipulating that "It shall be strictly prohibited to force anyone to commit self-incrimination."① Fourth, the burden of proof was clarified and the standard of proof was revised. Fifth, the scope of the exclusion of illegal evidence and the procedure of exclusion was stipulated, so that the legal framework of exclusion of illegal evidence was established in China. Sixth, the amendments clarified the protective measures for witnesses to testify in certain cases, and included issues such as subsidies, salaries, bonuses and other benefits of witnesses into the scope of such protection measures. In addition, the amendments also provided for the conversion and application of physical evidence, documentary evidence, audio-visual materials, electronic data and other evidentiary materials collected in the course of enforcement of administrative law.

(3) Major Adjustments to Compulsory Measures

In terms of arrest, the Criminal Procedure Law of 2012 refined the conditions for arrest, and improved procedures for the arrest examination and approval, established a post-arrest detention necessity review mechanism. It required that the arrested person should immediately be transferred to a detention center for custody. In terms of residential confinement, the Criminal Procedure Law of 2012 adjusted the applicable conditions, enforcement venue, content to be examined, and applicable surveillance methods. The new law also

---

① Article 50 of the Criminal Procedure Law of 2012.

provided for measures such as notifying family members, defense by the defense counsel, and procuratorial supervision. In addition, the new law clarified that the term of residential confinement at designated places of residence should be deducted from the term of imprisonment. With respect to release on bail pending trial, the new law adjusted the examination of bail and stipulated the obligations of the accused released on bail. The new law also provided for matters such as the determination, custody and refund of bails.

(4) Strengthening the Protection of the Right of Defense

The Criminal Procedure Law of 2012 further improved the defense system and strengthened the protection of lawyers' rights. In the section of "Basic Principles", the new law clarified the principle of protecting the exercise of the defense right, expanded the scope of legal aid, advanced the time of defense to the investigation phase, and absorbed and improved the lawyers' rights to meet the suspect and review case files provided by the Lawyers Law of the People's Republic of China. The new law refined the articles on imposing the liability for perjury on lawyers and established special protection procedures for imposing such a liability on lawyers, and provided the defense counsel with remedies for obstructing the performance of the defense duty.

(5) Improving Investigation Measures

Investigation measures affect the investigation efficiency of investigation bodies, and are also related to the protection of criminal suspects' rights, which is an important topic in the area where power and rights engage. The amendments incorporated technical investigation into the scope of adjustment of the Criminal Procedure Law, and clarified the scope of application, subject and term of such investigation. The amendments established an audio and video recording system of interrogation to curb the extortion of confessions by torture and other illegal activities for obtaining evidence. In addition, the amendments stipulated the right to file complaints or accusations against violations of laws by judicial authorities and their staff.

(6) Reshaping Trial Procedures

The Criminal Procedure Law of 2012 made corresponding adjustments to all trial procedures, and the most significant change was the reconstruction of summary procedures. The amendments expanded the scope of summary procedures, adjusted its form and time limit of trial, and emphasized the right of parties and the duty of prosecutors to appear in court in cases of public prosecution. With respect to procedures at first instance, the amendments improved the system of appearance in court by witnesses and forensic identification and evaluation experts, implemented the system of transferring the entire case files to people's courts, and added regulations on pretrial meetings. Meanwhile, the amendments expanded the scope of parties that could lodge incidental civil actions, and clarified that incidental civil actions could be mediated. In the procedure of second instance, the amendments clearly stipulated remanding a case with unclear facts for a new trial should be limited to one time. It also stipulated the principle of no increase in punishment for remanded cases, and made sure the principle of no increase in punishment on appeal could be fully implemented. With respect to procedures for the review of the death sentence, the amendments increased the participation of the defense counsel in the review of the death sentence, and emphasized the procuratorial supervision of such cases. With respect to retrial procedures, the amendments refined in detail the reasons for retrial, requiring prosecutors to appear in court in cases of trial.

(7) Establishment of Special Criminal Procedures With Chinese Characteristics

The amendments, for the first time, had added a special procedure to the Code. It stipulated, in four chapters, the procedure of criminal proceedings for juveniles, the procedure for public prosecution cases where parties have reached settlement, the confiscation procedures for illegal income in cases where criminal suspects or defendants escape or die and the procedures for involuntary medical treatment of mental patients legally exempted from criminal liability.

(8) Improvement of Enforcement Procedures

The amendments provided for community corrections and clarified their objects. At the same time, the amendments improved the system of temporary execution of sentences outside an incarceration facility, expanded its objects and clarified its application procedures. In addition, the procuratorial supervision of penalty enforcement activities by the procuratorial authorities had been strengthened.

1.5. The 2018 Amendments to the Criminal Procedure Law

Since the 18th National Congress of the CPC, the Central Committee of the CPC has carried out several reforms in the field of criminal justice. On October 26, 2018, the Standing Committee of the National People's Congress adopted the decision of amending the Criminal Procedure Law, adjusting 18 articles of its original ones and adding 18 new articles, with the total number of articles increasing to 308. The purpose of this amendment was to respond to the amendments made to the Constitution and the Supervision Law, as well as to solve the problems of constitutional compliance and connection between the law and the Constitution, and to upgrade the relevant achievements of judicial reform to legal provisions in a timely manner. Therefore, the amendments mainly involved three aspects: the connection between the supervision procedure and the criminal procedure, the construction of the trial in the absentia system, and the adoption of the system of leniency for guilty pleas and punishment acceptance and the expedited criminal trial procedure.

2. Types of Cases

Cases in criminal proceedings can be divided into two categories: cases of public prosecution and cases of private prosecution. A criminal case is normally a case of public prosecution, and a public prosecution is initiated by the people's procuratorate. The cases of private prosecution refer to those which are brought to the people's courts by the victims themselves or their close relatives in accordance with the law. This kind of cases do not need to be filed for investigation by the public security organ or the people's procuratorate, and should be filed and tried by the people's court against the litigants directly. Article 19 of the Criminal Procedure Law provides that: "Cases of private prosecution shall be directly accepted by the people's courts." According to Article 210 of the Criminal Procedure Law, cases of private prosecution include the following three categories.

2.1. Cases to be Handled Only Upon Complaint

To be handled only upon complaint means that a case shall be handled only upon complaint by the victim or his/her legal representative. According to the provisions of the Criminal Law, there are four types of cases to be handled only upon complaint: cases of insult or defamation, violent interference in the freedom of marriage, abuse and embezzlement. As if these four types of criminal cases are minor, the circumstances of the cases are relatively simple, and the facts of the cases can be ascertained without investigation, it is suitable for the people's court to directly accept such cases.

2.2. Minor Criminal Cases for Which the Victims Have Evidence to Prove

According to the relevant judicial interpretations of the Supreme People's Court, these cases include the following eight types: cases of intentional assault (minor injury), cases of illegal trespass of residence, cases of infringement of freedom of correspondence, cases of bigamy, cases of abandonment, cases of production and sale of fake and inferior goods, cases of intellectual property rights infringement, and cases that may be sentenced to a fixed-term imprisonment of not more than three years under Chapters IV and V of the Specific Provisions of the Criminal Law.

Not only the circumstances of this kind of cases shall be minor, but also the facts are obvious and the identity of the defendant is clear. Also, the victims have evidence that can prove the true circumstances of the cases, so there is no need to resort to the powers of the investigative organs for investigation, and it is suitable for the people's court to directly accept such cases.

2.3. Cases of Which the Victims Have Evidence to Prove That the Defendants Should Be Pursued for Criminal Liability According to Law Because Their Acts Have Infringed Upon the Victims' Personal or Property Rights, Whereas the Public Security Organs or the People's Procuratorates Do not Pursue for the Criminal Liability of the Defendants

This kind of cases fall within the scope of cases of public prosecution in nature. To become a case of private prosecution, it must meet three conditions: first, the victim has evidence to prove guilty; second, the defendant has infringed upon victim's personal or property rights and shall be pursued for criminal liability; third, the public security organ or the people's procuratorate does not pursue for the criminal liability. The purpose of such provisions is to strengthen the restriction on the case-filing and jurisdictional matters of the public security organs and the procuratorial organs, to protect the legitimate rights and interests of the victim and solve the problem of "difficulty to lodge a complaint" existing in the judicial practice.

3. Litigation Stage

Generally speaking, the criminal procedure can be divided into five stages according to the order of its progress: case filing, investigation, prosecution, trial and execution. The investigation stage includes the implementation of the investigation and the conclusion of the investigation or supplementary investigation which is required in some cases. The prosecution stage includes the decision of the procuratorial organs on whether to initiate a public prosecution or not after examination, and private prosecution initiated by the victim. The trial stage includes the procedures of first instance, second instance, death sentence review and trial supervision.

After the adoption of the Supervision Law, the Criminal Procedure Law has also been amended accordingly. For suspected criminal cases handled by the supervisory organs, the litigation goes through three stages in criminal procedure, namely, prosecution, trial and execution.

In addition, for some special cases, the Criminal Procedure Law provides for special procedures, including the procedure for juvenile criminal cases, the procedure for public prosecution cases where parties have reached settlement, the procedure for trial in absentia, the procedure for confiscating illegal income in cases where the criminal suspects or the defendants escape or die, and the procedure for involuntary medical treatment of mental patients legally exempted from criminal liability.

4. Litigation Principles

The basic principles of criminal proceedings are stipulated by the Criminal

Procedure Law, which run through the whole process of criminal proceedings or the main litigation stages, and are the basic principles that the public security organs, the people's procuratorates, the people's courts and the litigation participants must abide by in criminal proceedings.

In the international arena, the prevailing principles of criminal proceedings include the principle of public prosecution, the principle of separation of prosecution from trial, the principle of presumption of innocence, the principle of fair trial, the principle against forced self-incrimination, and the principle of prohibition of double jeopardy. These principles have been established in the domestic legislation of various countries and have been affirmed in many international conventions. They not only are the summary of the long-term experience of criminal procedure legislation and judicial practice in various countries, but also meet the demands of common value in various countries in criminal procedure. Although there is no clear stipulation on these principles in our current domestic legislation, many concrete system designs still embody them.

In our country, the basic principles of criminal proceedings are clearly stipulated by the Criminal Procedure Law. The basic principles of criminal proceedings stipulated by Chapter I of the Criminal Procedure Law form a complete system. These principles are interrelated and mutually reinforcing, and the realization of each of them presupposes the proper implementation of the other principles, and undermining one of them would affect the implementation of the other principles. Specifically, there are the following basic principles in criminal proceedings in our country: **a.** investigation power, procuratorial power and judicial power are exercised by the designated organs in accordance with the law; **b.** people's courts and people's procuratorates exercise their functions and powers independently in accordance with the law; **c.** reliance on the masses; **d.** taking facts as the basis and law as the criterion; **e.** all citizens are equal in the application of law; **f.** division of work responsibility and mutual collaboration and restraint; **g.** people's procuratorates exercise legal supervision over criminal proceedings in accordance with the law; **h.** citizens of all ethnic groups have the right to use the spoken and written languages of their own ethnic groups in the proceedings; **i.** public trial; **j.** criminal suspects and defendants have the right to obtain defenses; **k.** the defendants or suspects shall not be found guilty without being judged by the people's courts in accordance with the law; **l.** litigation rights of litigation participants shall be protected; **m.** exemption of criminal liability in accordance with the statutory circumstances; **n.** the Criminal Procedure Law has jurisdiction on foreign nationals in terms of criminal liability in accordance with the law; and **o.** leniency for guilty pleas and punishment acceptance.

It is worth mentioning that the 2018 amendments to the Criminal Procedure Law added the principle of leniency for guilty pleas and punishment acceptance into the part of basic principles, stipulating that criminal suspects and defendants who plead guilty voluntarily, admit the corpus delicti they are accused of and are willing to accept punishment may be dealt with leniently in accordance with the law. For this, corresponding procedures are provided for all stages of criminal proceedings, for example: **a.** For the approval or decision of arrest, the information on the guilty plea and punishment acceptance by criminal suspects or defendants shall be taken as factors for consideration of the possibility of social danger. **b.** When interrogating criminal suspects, investigators shall inform suspects of the legal provisions on guilty pleas and punishment acceptance. **c.** If suspects voluntarily plead guilty, such pleas shall be recorded and transferred with the cases to the people's court, and the relevant information shall be specified in the prosecution opinions. **d.** If suspects plead guilty and accept punishment, the people's procuratorate shall make a decision within ten days if the conditions for the application of expedited procedures are met; the said time limit may be extended to fifteen days if the suspect is punishable by fixed-term imprisonment of more than one year. **e.** If suspects voluntarily plead guilty and agree to the sentencing proposals and the application of procedures, they shall sign an affidavit on guilty pleas and punishment acceptance in the presence of their defense counsels or on-duty lawyers. If suspects are blind, deaf or dumb, or are mental patients who have not completely lost the ability to recognize or control their conduct; or if the legal representatives or defense counsels of juveniles of suspected crimes dissent, the signing of such an affidavit is not needed. **f.** If suspects plead guilty and accept punishment, the people's procuratorate shall make sentencing proposals on principal penalty, accessory punishment, whether the probation applies, etc., and transfer the affidavit and other materials along with the case. **g.** If defendants plead guilty and accept punishment, the chief judge shall inform defendants of their litigation rights and legal provisions on guilty pleas and punishment acceptance, and examine their voluntariness and the authenticity and legitimacy of the contents of the said affidavit. **h.** For cases involving guilty pleas and punishment acceptance, the people's court shall generally adopt the charges and sentencing proposals charged by the people's procuratorate when rendering a judgment in accordance with the law, except under the following circumstances: the defendant's acts do not constitute a crime or the defendant should not be imposed criminal liability upon; the defendant pleads guilty and accepts punishment against his/her will; the defendant denies the corpus delicti they are accused of; the crime charged in prosecution is inconsistent with that found in the trial; the people's court believes the sentencing proposals are obviously improper; the defendant or the defense counsel raises an objection to the sentencing proposals, the people's procuratorate may adjust its sentencing proposal; the people's procuratorate does not adjust its sentencing proposal or the sentencing proposal is still obviously improper after adjustment, the people's court shall make a judgment in accordance with the law.

CHAPTER TWO

SPECIAL ORGANS FOR CRIMINAL PROCEEDINGS AND THEIR JURISDICTION

Special organs for criminal proceedings in China include public security organs, procuratorial organs, courts, and many others. They perform their respective functions and powers in criminal proceedings in accordance with the provisions of jurisdiction.

1. Investigation Organs

1.1. Public Security Organs

Public security organs are the social order protection organs of our country. They are constituent parts of people's governments at all levels, armed security administrative forces and criminal judicial forces, and the special organs in charge of social security and domestic safety. In terms of nature, public security organs are different from people's procuratorates and people's courts. The former belong to administrative organs, while the latter belong to judicial organs.

(1) Organizational System of Public Security Organs

At the central level, the State Council shall establish the Ministry of Public Security, which shall be responsible for leading and directing the work of public security throughout the country, and shall, in accordance with the relevant agreements, jointly combat transnational and cross-border criminal activities in cooperation with the International Criminal Police Organization (INTERPOL) and foreign police organs. Local public security organs at all levels shall be established according to administrative divisions. Public security departments (bureaus) shall be set up at the level of a province, autonomous region or municipality to direct and administer public security work in the whole area thereof; public security offices (bureaus) shall be set up in districts, autonomous prefectures and municipalities; public security bureaus shall be set up in counties, county-level cities and autonomous counties; and public security sub-bureaus shall be set up in municipal districts of municipalities. As needed, police stations shall be set up in the subdistrict offices of large and medium-sized cities and in towns and townships subject to counties. They are dispatched agencies of public security organs at the primary level and shall perform some of the duties of primary public security organs.

In addition, the Ministry of Public Security and local public security organs may, according to their work needs and upon the approval of the State Council, set up special public security organs in some special departments or entities. Special public security organs established in our country mainly include the Anti-smuggling Bureau under the General Administration of Customs and in all customs offices directly under the General Administration of Customs, as well as the public security organs set up in the railway, forestry, civil aviation and other systems.

The public security organs at higher levels may directly command the investigation and other operational activities of those at lower levels and may use investigation forces at lower levels to participate in the investigation of cases conducted by public security organs at higher levels. The public security organs of different regions and systems shall not be subject to each other and they constitute a cooperative and collaborative relationship in the process of case handling. Article 83 of the Criminal Procedure Law provides that, where a public security authority executes detention or arrest of a person in a different place, it shall notify the public security authority at the place of residence of the detainee or arrestee, and the public security authority at the place of residence of the detainee or arrestee shall provide assistance.

(2) Functions of Public Security Organs

In criminal proceedings, the public security organs exercise the power of investigation, and they are the most important investigation organs. Except for the cases directly accepted by the people's courts, the cases investigated by the supervisory committees, and the cases filed for investigation by the people's procuratorates, state security organs, prisons and military security organs, the vast majority of criminal cases shall be investigated by the public security organs.

In criminal proceedings, the main functions and powers of public security organs are:

A. Power of case filing. According to Article 109 of the Criminal Procedure Law, a public security authority or a people's procuratorate which discovers any facts of a crime or a criminal suspect shall file a case for criminal investigation according to its jurisdiction.

B. Power of investigation. The public security organs are the principal investigation organs in criminal proceedings. During the course of investigation, the public security organ shall have the power to interrogate the criminal suspect and question the witness according to law. The public security organ shall have the power to conduct inquest, examination and search, and shall have the power to seize physical evidence, documentary evidence, audio-visual materials, electronic data and other evidence, inquire about and freeze deposits, remittances, bonds, stocks, fund shares and other property, organize forensic identification and evaluation, identification, and investigative reenactments, take technical investigation measures, and execute wanted orders.① It has the right to take compulsory measures against the criminal suspect, such as forced appearance, bail pending trial and placing him/her under residential confinement. The public security organ shall have the power to hold an active criminal or a major suspect in detention.② As to a criminal suspect who meets the conditions for arrest, it may apply to the procuratorial organ for approval of arrest. As to a criminal suspect who is arrested upon approval of the people's procuratorate or upon decision of the people's procuratorate or people's court, the public security organ shall have the power to make arrest.③ The public security organ shall have the power to make a decision to conclude the investigation of a case if the statutory conditions are met.④ In addition, in special procedures, the public security organs also have some functions and powers, for example, for a juvenile suspect or defendant who has not had a defender, a people's court, a people's procuratorate, or a public security authority shall notify a legal aid agency to assign a lawyer to defend him/her⑤, examine whether the settlement is reached voluntarily and legally, and preside at the preparation of a settlement agreement; ⑥ prepare a written opinion on confiscation of illegal income or involuntary medical treatment and transfer it to a people's procuratorate.⑦

---

① See Chapter II, Sections 2-9 of Part II of the Criminal Procedure Law.
② Articles 66, 80, and 82 of the Criminal Procedure Law.
③ Articles 87 and 90 of the Criminal Procedure Law.
④ See Chapter II, Section 10 of Part II of the Criminal Procedure Law.
⑤ Article 278 of the Criminal Procedure Law.
⑥ Article 289 of the Criminal Procedure Law.
⑦ Articles 298 and 303 of the Criminal Procedure Law.

C. Power of execution. This includes the execution of criminals sentenced to criminal detention, deprivation of political rights, or deportation. Where a convict is sentenced to fixed-term imprisonment but the remaining term of the penalty is not more than three months before the convict is delivered for execution, the sentence shall be executed by a Detention Facility which is a subordinate department of public security organs.[①]

1.2. Other Investigation Organs

Other investigation organs mainly refer to state security organs, military security agencies, prisons, the China Coast Guard and anti-smuggling departments of the customs. In the criminal proceedings they participate in, these investigation organs shall divide their responsibilities for their respective work with the people's procuratorates and the people's courts, coordinate their efforts and check each other. Where it is necessary to arrest a criminal suspect, the arrest shall be subject to the approval of the appropriate procuratorial organ. After the investigation has been concluded, if it is necessary to initiate a public prosecution against the criminal suspect, a written recommendation for prosecution shall be prepared, which shall be transferred, together with the case file and evidence, to the procuratorial organ for examination and decision.

(1) State Security Organs

The state security organs are state security protection forces of the country and component parts of the people's governments at all levels. Article 4 of the Criminal Procedure Law stipulates that, state security authorities shall, in accordance with the law, handle criminal cases regarding compromising state security and perform the same functions as those of public security authorities.

(2) Military Security Departments

The military security departments are the political security organs of the Chinese People's Liberation Army and are not part of the public security organs. They form their own administrative and professional systems and are not subject to the leadership of public security organs. In accordance with Article 308 of the Criminal Procedure Law, the security departments of the armed forces shall have the authority to investigate criminal cases that occur within the armed forces. In

---

① Article 264 of the Criminal Procedure Law.

criminal proceedings, the security departments of the armed forces may exercise the functions and powers of public security organs such as investigation, detention, preliminary examination and execution of arrest as prescribed by the Constitution and laws.

(3) Prisons

A prison is an organ of the State for executing criminal punishments and the main place for carrying out effective judgments made by the people's courts and for carrying out reform through labor for prisoners. In accordance with Article 308 of the Criminal Procedure Law, crimes committed by convicts within a prison shall be investigated by the prison.

(4) China Coast Guard

In 2013, the State Council reorganized the State Oceanic Administration, which carried out law enforcement on the sea in the name of the China Coast Guard, and uniformly commanded and dispatched the coast guard team to carry out law enforcement activities on the sea. In 2018, the Third Session of the Standing Committee of the 13th National People's Congress decided to transform the coast guard team under the leadership and management of the State Oceanic Administration into armed police forces and establish the general coast guard corps of the Chinese People's Armed Police Force. When the Criminal Procedure Law was amended in 2018, a provision was added in Article 308, which read: "The China Coast Guard shall perform the marine right protection and law enforcement functions and exercise the authority to investigate criminal cases that occur at sea."

(5) Anti-Smuggling Departments of the Customs

Since 1998, China has set up investigation departments for crimes of smuggling in the Customs at all levels, which are specially responsible for investigating the cases of crimes of smuggling. For example, the Customs General Administration has set up an anti-smuggling bureau which is responsible for investigating smuggling cases, while the Customs at a lower level has sub-bureaus (branches) which are responsible for investigating smuggling cases. These investigation departments enjoy the same powers as the public security organs in their investigation activities, and have the same litigation status as the public security organs.

2. Public Prosecution Organs

In our country, the procuratorial organs are the only public prosecution organs, and exercise the power to prosecute cases of public prosecution on behalf of the State. All criminal cases, except those of private prosecution, must be prosecuted to the people's courts by the people's procuratorates and require procurators to appear in court to support the public prosecution.

2.1. Organizational System of Procuratorial Organs

In accordance with the provisions of the Organic Law of the People's Procuratorates, the people's procuratorates are divided into: **a.** the Supreme People's Procuratorate; **b.** the local people's procuratorates at all levels; and **c.** the military procuratorates and other special people's procuratorates.

(1) The Supreme People's Procuratorate

The Supreme People's Procuratorate is the highest procuratorial organ of China, which located in Beijing, the capital of China. Its main duties are: to direct the work of the local people's procuratorates at various levels and of the special people's procuratorates; to exercise procuratorial authority over major criminal cases throughout the country; to lodge a protest in accordance with the procedure of judicial supervision if any definite error is found in effective judgments and rulings of the people's courts at various levels; to interpret issues relating to the specific application of laws and decrees; to formulate regulations, rules and measures for procuratorial work.

(2) Local People's Procuratorates at Various Levels

Local people's procuratorates include that: the people's procuratorates at the provincial level, including the people's procuratorates of provinces, autonomous regions and municipalities; the people's procuratorates at the districted city level, including the people's procuratorates of municipalities directly under the jurisdiction of provinces or autonomous regions, the people's procuratorates of the autonomous prefectures, and the branches of the people's procuratorates of provinces, autonomous regions and municipalities; the primary people's procuratorates, including the people's procuratorates in counties, autonomous counties, cities not divided into districts, and municipal districts. People's procuratorates at the provincial or districted city level may, according to the needs of the procuratorial work, with the consent of the Supreme People's Procuratorate and the relevant departments at the provincial level, and upon approval of the standing committees of the people's congress at the same level after requests are submitted thereto, set up people's procuratorates in the specific regions within their jurisdictions as local offices. The people's procuratorates may, according to the needs of the procuratorial work, set up procuratorial offices in prisons, detention houses and other places to exercise some of the functions and powers of the people's procuratorates dispatching them, and also conduct circuit procuratorate of the aforesaid places.①

(3) Special People's Procuratorates

Special people's procuratorates in China include railway transport procuratorates and military procuratorates of the Chinese People's Liberation Army. Railway transport procuratorates include branches of railway transport procuratorates and primary railway transport procuratorates. Military procuratorates are the special organs for legal supervision established in the Chinese People's Liberation Army and exercise procuratorial authority with respect to crimes committed by active military servicemen in violation of their duties and other criminal cases.

With regard to the leadership system, the procuratorial organs of our country practice a dual leadership system. On the one hand, people's procuratorates at various levels are created by the people's congress at the same level to be responsible to and supervised by the people's congress at the same level; on the other hand, the Supreme People's Procuratorate directs the work of people's procuratorates at various local levels and of the special people's procuratorates, and people's procuratorates at higher levels direct the work of those at lower levels, and may directly participate in or direct case-handling activities of the procuratorates at lower levels. The daily work of each people's procuratorate shall be under the unified leadership of its chief procurator.

People's procuratorates at all levels set up procuratorial committees, which

---

① Articles 13, 16 and 17 of the Organic Law of the People's Procuratorates.

shall be presided over by the chief procurator, to discuss and decide on major difficult cases and other major issues. Members of the procuratorial committees shall be appointed and removed by the standing committees of the people's congresses at the corresponding levels. Chief procurators, deputy chief procurators and persons-in-charge of all functional departments generally are members of the procuratorial committees. The procuratorial committee shall apply the system of democratic centralism and apply the principle that the minority is subordinate to the majority in discussions and decisions on issues. If the chief procurator disagrees with the opinion of the majority, the matter may be reported to the standing committee of the people's congress at the corresponding level for decision.

2.2. Functions and Powers of Procuratorial Organs

In criminal proceedings, people's procuratorates mainly exercise the following functions and powers:

(1) Case Filing and Investigation Power

In accordance with Article 19 of the Criminal Procedure Law, where, in performing its statutory duty of supervision of legal proceedings, a people's procuratorate discovers that any justice functionary commits a crime of false imprisonment, extortion of a confession by torture, illegal search, or any other crime that infringes upon a citizen's rights or damages the fair administration of justice by taking advantage of his/her functions, the people's procuratorate may open an official investigation into the crime. Where a case regarding a serious crime committed by any staff member of a government authority by taking advantage of his/her functions under the jurisdiction of a public security authority needs to be directly accepted by a people's procuratorate, the people's procuratorate may open an official investigation into the case upon decision of the people's procuratorate at or above the provincial level.

During the course of investigation, the procuratorial organs are entitled to the following functions and powers: to interrogate a criminal suspect, inquire a witness or victim, to carry out inquest, examination or search, to seize material and documentary evidence, to organize forensic identification and evaluation and identification, to collect and obtain material evidence, documentary evidence, audio-visual materials and other evidence from the relevant entities and individuals, to take compulsory measures against the criminal suspect, such as issuing a warrant to compel the appearance of the criminal suspect, obtaining a guarantor pending trial, placing the suspect under residential confinement, detaining or arresting him/her, and to carry out supplementary investigation into the case transferred for prosecution after the investigation has been concluded.①

(2) Power to Public Prosecution

At the stage of examination before prosecution, the procuratorial organs are entitled to the following functions and powers: Any case requiring initiation of a public prosecution shall be subject to the examination and decision of a people's procuratorate; ② Where state property or collective property has suffered any loss, a people's procuratorate may initiate an incidental civil action along with a public prosecution; ③ Where a supplementary investigation is necessary, the people's procuratorate examining a case may return the case to the public security authority for supplementary investigation or conduct investigation itself instead.④

During the stage of trial, the procuratorial organs are entitled to the following functions and powers: send procurators to appear before court to support the public prosecution, question the defendant, question a witness, a forensic identification and evaluation expert, read out a statement of a witness who is not in court, an expert opinion of an identification or evaluation expert who is not in court, transcripts of crime scene investigation, and other documentation serving as evidence in court, adduce physical evidence before court, and debate with opposing parties etc.⑤

(3) Power to Supervise Litigation

According to the Constitution and the Organic Law of the People's Procuratorates, the people's procuratorates are the state organs for legal supervision. The supervision of the procuratorial organs over criminal proceedings runs through the whole process of proceedings. They exercise legal supervision over the investigative activities of the investigation organs, the judicial activities

---

① Article 164 of the Criminal Procedure Law.
② Article 169 of the Criminal Procedure Law.
③ Article 101 of the Criminal Procedure Law.
④ Article 175 of the Criminal Procedure Law.
⑤ Articles 189, 191, 194, 195, and 198 of the Criminal Procedure Law.

of the people's courts, and the execution of criminal punishments by the executing organs to determine whether they are lawful. Specifically, if a public security organ believes there is an error in the decision to file or not file a case, it shall have the power to request the public security organ to make corrections; review the application of the public security organ, state security organ, military security organ, prison or any other investigation organ for arresting a suspect and decide whether or not to approve the arrest; supervise the investigation activities of the investigation organ and, if any violation of law is found, give a notice to make corrections; give opinions on the correction of any violation of law committed by a people's court during the trial process; lodge a protest under legal procedures with respect to any misjudgement made by a people's court; supervise the special procedures such as involuntary medical treatments; and exercise supervision over the execution of a judgment or ruling during the execution stage.①

3. People's Courts

According to Article 128 of the Constitution and Article 2 of the Organic Law of the People's Courts, the people's courts are the judicial organs of the state. According to Article 3 of the Criminal Procedure Law, people's courts are responsible for trial and sentencing. According to its Article 12, no person shall be found guilty without being judged so by a people's court in accordance with the law. Thus, the people's courts are the only special organs that have the authority to try a case and adjudicate a person guilty in criminal proceedings.

3.1. Organizational System of People's Courts

According to the Organic Law of the People's Courts, the organizational system of people's courts is composed of the Supreme People's Court, local people's courts at various levels and special people's courts. Meanwhile, the law provides that the Supreme People's Court may set up circuit courts, which are parts of the Supreme People's Court and the judgments and rulings made by the

---

① Articles 80, 113, 171, 209, 232, 276, and 307 of the Criminal Procedure Law.

circuit courts are deemed as those made by the Supreme People's Court itself.

(1) The Supreme People's Court

The Supreme People's Court is the highest judicial organ of the state and is located in Beijing, the capital of China. The Supreme People's Court shall supervise the trials of the local people's courts at all levels and the special people's courts; cases of first instance under its jurisdiction as prescribed by the law and deemed by itself to be under its jurisdiction; appellate cases judged and ruled by the higher people's court, retrial cases filed in accordance with the trial supervision procedures; may explain the issues on the specific application of law in the trial work.①

(2) Local People's Courts at Various Levels

Article 13 of the Organic Law of the People's Courts stipulates that the local people's courts at various levels are divided into higher people's courts, intermediate people's courts and primary people's courts.

The higher people's courts include: **a.** higher people's courts of provinces; **b.** higher people's courts of autonomous regions; and **c.** higher people's courts of municipalities directly under the Central Government. The higher people's courts shall have jurisdiction over the following cases: **a.** cases of first instance under their jurisdiction as prescribed by law; **b.** cases of first instance for which requests are submitted by people's courts at lower levels for trial; **c.** cases of first instance of which the jurisdiction is designated by the SPC; **d.** appellate cases judged and ruled by the intermediate people's courts; **e.** retrial cases filed in accordance with the trial supervision procedures; and **f.** death penalty cases for which requests are submitted by the intermediate people's courts for approval.②

The intermediate people's courts include: **a.** intermediate people's courts of municipalities directly under the jurisdiction of provinces or autonomous regions; **b.** intermediate people's courts of autonomous prefectures; and **c.** intermediate people's courts established according to prefectures in provinces or autonomous regions. The intermediate people's courts shall have jurisdiction over the following cases: **a.** cases of first instance under their jurisdiction as

---

① Articles 16 to 18 of the Organic Law of the People's Courts.
② Articles 20 and 21 of the Organic Law of the People's Courts.

prescribed by law; **b.** cases of first instance for which requests are submitted by primary people's courts for trial; **c.** cases of first instance of which the jurisdiction is designated by the people's courts at higher levels; **d.** appellate cases judged and ruled by the primary people's courts; and **e.** retrial cases filed in accordance with the trial supervision procedures.①

Primary people's courts include: **a.** people's courts of counties and autonomous counties; **b.** people's courts in cities not divided into districts; and **c.** people's courts of municipal districts. Primary people's courts shall try cases of first instance, except as otherwise prescribed by law.②

(3) Special People's Courts

Special people's courts are established in addition to the above-mentioned ordinary courts, including military and maritime courts, intellectual property courts, financial courts, etc.

People's courts at higher levels supervise the cases tried by those at lower levels. The Supreme People's Court supervises the cases tried by the local people's courts at different levels and by the special people's courts. The supervision by people's courts is not achieved through providing guidance for specific cases. People's courts at all levels shall try cases independently in accordance with their functions and powers. A people's court at a higher level shall not deal with any case that is being tried by a people's court at a lower level. The people's courts at lower levels shall not submit cases to the people's courts at higher levels for examination and approval before making judgments. The people's courts at higher levels shall exercise supervision by maintaining the correct judgments and rulings of the people's courts at lower levels and correcting their wrong judgments and rulings through the procedures of second instance, trial supervision and review of death sentences.

In accordance with the Constitution and the Organic Law of the People's Courts, the Supreme People's Court is established by the National People's Congress and is responsible to and reports its work to the National People's Congress and its Standing Committee. The Standing Committee of the National People's Congress supervises the work of the Supreme People's Court. Local

---

① Articles 22 and 23 of the Organic Law of the People's Courts.
② Articles 24 and 25 of the Organic Law of the People's Courts.

people's courts at different levels are established by the people's congresses at the corresponding levels and are responsible to and report their work to the people's congresses at corresponding levels and their standing committees. The standing committees of local people's congresses at different levels supervise the work of people's courts at the corresponding levels.

3.2. Functions and Powers of the People's Courts

The functions and powers of the people's courts in criminal proceedings can be divided into two categories, namely, judicial power and other functions and powers vested to ensure the exercise of judicial power.

The judicial power of the people's courts mainly includes: **a.** Directly accept cases of private prosecution and handle them according to specific circumstances. The people's court shall decide to hold a court session to hear the case, or persuade the private prosecutor to withdraw the case, or rule to dismiss a private-prosecuting case. **b.** After examining a public prosecution initiated, a people's court shall decide to hold a court session to hear the case if the charges in the indictment are based on clear facts. **c.** Entitled to render a judgment according to the facts and law on whether the defendant is guilty or innocent, whether the charges in the indictment are serious or minor, or whether he/she is subject to punishment or exemption from punishment. **d.** Entitled to render rulings or decisions on the procedural issues and part of the substantive issues; and **e.** Entitled to hear the case, to which the confiscation procedure or the involuntary medical treatment procedure or other special procedures apply and render rulings.[①]

The people's courts enjoy other functions and powers to ensure the exercise of judicial power, mainly including: **a.** Deciding to arrest the defendant and taking compulsory measures such as force his/her appearance before court, releasing him/her on bail pending trial and placing him/her under residential confinement; **b.** in the course of a court trial, investigating and verifying evidence and, when necessary, conducting inquest, examination, seize, impound, forensic identification and evaluation, inquiry and freeze the property; **c.** compelling witnesses to appear in court and impose penalties; **d.** imposing

---

① Articles 19, 186, 200, 300 and 305 of the Criminal Procedure Law.

necessary penalties on participants in proceedings and bystanders who violate the court order; **e.** collecting and dealing with illicit money, goods and their proceeds, executing some judgments and rulings, and examining and verifying and rendering rulings on certain issues arising in the execution; and **f.** putting forward judicial proposals to relevant departments.①

4. Executing Organs

According to the different characteristics of various punishments and the different functions of various executing subjects, the executing organs may be classified into three different categories, namely, the execution delivering organ, the executing organ and the execution supervising organ.

4.1. Execution Delivering Organs

The execution delivering organs refer to the organs that deliver the effective judgment and the criminal to the relevant organs for execution of criminal punishment under legal procedures. The people's courts are the judicial organs of the State as well as the organs that deliver the effective judgments for execution. The people's courts shall deliver them to different executing organs for execution in accordance with the contents of effective judgments and the different execution methods of punishments. In accordance with the relevant provisions of the Criminal Procedure Law and the Interpretation by the Supreme People's Court Concerning the Application of the Criminal Procedure Law of the People's Republic of China, legally effective judgments and rulings shall generally be delivered for execution by the original people's court of first instance.

4.2. Executing Organs

In addition to the people's courts, prisons, juvenile reformatories, detention centers, etc., the executing organs shall also include public security organs, community correction organs, the employer of a criminal and the grass-roots

---

① Articles 66, 193, 196, 199, 271 and 272 of the Criminal Procedure Law.

organizations at the place of the criminal's residence.

In accordance with the different execution methods of effective judgments and the different functions and powers of the executing organs, the types of punishments executed by these executing organs are as follows: the people's courts are responsible for the execution of innocence, exemption from criminal punishment, fine, confiscation of property and incidental civil action judgments as well as the immediate execution of death sentences; prisons and reformatories for juvenile delinquents are responsible for the execution of life imprisonment and fixed-term imprisonment, in addition to this, prisons are also responsible for the execution of judgments on death sentences with a two-year suspension; although the detention centers are not the executing organs, in order to reduce the burden of escort and save resources, the criminals with a remaining term of imprisonment of less than three months may be executed by the detention centers on their behalf; public security organs are responsible for the execution of deprivation of political rights and criminal detention.

In addition, Article 269 of the Criminal Procedure Law stipulates that: A convict who is sentenced to supervision without incarceration, is granted probation or parole, or temporarily serves a sentence outside an incarceration facility shall be subject to community correction, which shall be executed by a community correction institution.

4.3. Execution Supervising Organs

The people's procuratorates are the state legal supervision organs and exercise legal supervision over criminal proceedings in accordance with the law. Execution is an important stage of criminal proceedings, and of course the people's procuratorates are also the supervisory organs of criminal execution. In this regard, "Execution", Part Four of the Criminal Procedure Law, has a number of articles clearly stipulating about it. For example, Article 263 provides that: Before delivering a convict for execution of a death sentence, a people's court shall notify the people's procuratorate at the same level to send prosecutors to supervise the execution. Articles 266, 267, 273 and 274 provide that the people's procuratorates shall exercise supervision over such circumstances as decisions on temporary execution of a sentence outside an incarceration facility, commutation or parole, and that a criminal commits a crime again during execution of a sentence. Article 275 provides that, where, during execution of criminal sentences, a prison or any other executing authority deems a sentence erroneous or a convict files a petition against his/her sentence, the prison or other executing authority shall transfer it to a people's procuratorate or the original trial court for handling. Article 276 also provides that, people's procuratorates shall supervise the legality of execution of criminal sentences by executing authorities and, if discovering any violations of law, shall notify executing authorities to make corrections.

5. Jurisdiction System

Jurisdiction in criminal cases refers to the division of functions and powers of the special state organs in accepting criminal cases in accordance with the law. For the purpose of the Criminal Procedure Law, jurisdiction refers to the division system whereby the public security organs, the people's procuratorates and the people's courts, etc., file and accept criminal cases in accordance with the provisions of the law, and whereby the people's courts try criminal cases of first instance within the system of people's courts.

Jurisdiction in criminal proceedings includes two aspects: first, the scope of functions and powers of the people's courts, the people's procuratorates and the public security organs in directly accepting criminal cases respectively; second, the scope of functions and powers of the people's courts in trying criminal cases of first instance.

The former is to solve the problem of division of functions and powers of the people's courts, the people's procuratorates and the public security organs in directly accepting criminal cases, i.e., the case filing jurisdiction or the functional jurisdiction. The latter is to solve the problem of division of functions and powers of the people's courts at all levels, of the people's courts at the same level, and between the ordinary people's courts and the specialized people's courts, in hearing criminal cases of first instance, i.e., trial jurisdiction. Trial jurisdiction is further divided into jurisdiction by level, jurisdiction by region, designated jurisdiction and special jurisdiction.

5.1. Jurisdiction in Case Filing

The jurisdiction in case filing refers to the scope of functions and powers of the special state organs in directly accepting criminal cases. The jurisdiction in case filing aims to solve the problem that which type of criminal cases shall be accepted by the public security organs and which others shall be accepted by other organs.

Article 19 of the Criminal Procedure Law generally prescribes the scope of case filing jurisdiction of the people's courts, the people's procuratorates and the public security organs:

(1) Criminal Cases Directly Accepted by the Public Security Organs

Paragraph 1 of Article 19 of the Criminal Procedure Law provides that: "Investigation of criminal cases shall be conducted by public security organs, except as otherwise provided for by law." This mainly refers to the vast majority of criminal cases other than those directly accepted by the people's courts, investigated by the people's procuratorates themselves, and investigated by the supervisory committees. Exceptions of the law refer to the criminal cases investigated by the state security organs, military security organs, prisons and the China Coast Guard as provided for in Articles 4 and 308 of the Criminal Procedure Law.

(2) Criminal Cases Directly Accepted by the People's Procuratorates

According to Article 19 of the Criminal Procedure Law, where, in performing its statutory duty of supervision of legal proceedings, a people's procuratorate discovers that any justice functionary commits a crime of false imprisonment, extortion of a confession by torture, illegal search, or any other crime that infringes upon a citizenship's rights or damages the fair administration of justice by taking advantage of his/her functions, the people's procuratorate may open an official investigation into the crime. Where a case regarding a serious crime committed by any staff member of a government authority by taking advantage of his/her functions under the jurisdiction of a public security authority needs to be directly accepted by a people's procuratorate. The people's procuratorate may open an official investigation into the case upon decision of the people's procuratorate at or above the provincial level.

(3) Criminal Cases Directly Accepted by the People's Courts

The term "criminal cases directly accepted by the people's courts" refers to cases brought by litigants that are directly filed with and tried by the people's courts without going through the filing and investigation of cases by the public security organs or the people's procuratorates, and without going through the initiation of public prosecution by the people's procuratorates. This type of criminal cases is called private prosecution cases in criminal proceedings. Article 19 of the Criminal Procedure Law provides that: "Cases of private prosecution shall be directly accepted by the people's courts." This provision clearly indicates that criminal cases directly accepted by the people's courts are limited to cases of private prosecution. The term "cases of private prosecution" refers to cases the victims themselves or their close relatives bring to the people's courts. According to Article 210 of the Criminal Procedure Law, cases of private prosecution include the following three types of cases:

First, cases to be handled only upon complaint. Handling only upon complaint means that a case shall be handled only upon complaint by the victim or his/her legal representative or close relatives. According to the Criminal Law, there are four types of cases to be handled only upon complaint: **a.** cases of insult or defamation as stipulated in Section 1, Article 246 of the Specific Provisions of the Criminal Law; **b.** ases of violent interference with freedom of marriage as stipulated in Section 1 of Article 257; **c.** ases of abuse as stipulated in Section 1 of Article 260; and **d.** cases of embezzlement as stipulated in Article 270.

Second, minor cases cases in which the people's procuratorate has not initiated a public prosecution but the victims haveevidence to prove. These types of cases include: **a.** cases of intentional injury (minor injury); **b.** cases of illegal trespass into residence; **c.** cases of infringement of freedom of correspondence; **d.** cases of bigamy; **e.** cases of abandonment; **f.** cases of production and sale of fake and inferior commodities (except those seriously harming social order and the national interests); **g.** cases of infringement of intellectual property rights (except those seriously harming social order and the national interests); and **h.** other minor criminal cases under Chapters IV and V of the Specific Provisions of the Criminal Law, where the defendants may be sentenced to less than a fixed-term imprisonment of three years.

Third, cases in which the victims have evidence to prove that the defendants should be pursued for criminal liability according to law because their acts have infringed upon the victims' personal or property rights, whereas, the public security organs or the people's procuratorates do not pursue for the criminal liability of the accused.

(4) Cases Investigated by the Supervisory Commission

According to Article 11 of the Supervision Law, it shall conduct investigations of duty-related violations and crimes such as suspected corruption, bribery, abuse of power, neglect of duty, power rent-seeking, tunneling, practice of favoritism and falsification, as well as the waste of state assets. Article 34 of the Supervision Law stipulates that, where the people's court, people's procuratorate, public security organ, auditing organ or any other state organs discover in work any clue to suspected corruption, bribery, neglect of duty, malfeasance in office, or any other duty-related violations or crimes committed by any public official, it shall transfer such a clue to the supervisory organ, and the latter shall investigate and handle it in accordance with the law. Where the person under investigation is suspected of not only serious duty-related violation or duty-related crime but also any other violation or crime, the supervisory organ shall take the lead in conducting investigation, and other organs shall provide assistance.

5.2. Trial Jurisdiction

Trial jurisdiction refers to the scope of authority of the people's courts to try the criminal cases of first instance, which includes the division of authority among the people's courts at different levels, among ordinary people's courts and specialized people's courts, and among the people's courts at the same level in trying the criminal cases of first instance.

According to Article 176 of the Criminal Procedure Law, where a people's procuratorate deems that the facts of a criminal suspect's crime are clear and that evidence is solid and sufficient, and that the criminal suspect shall be subject to criminal liability, it shall make a decision to initiate a public prosecution; and, according to the provisions on trial jurisdiction, initiate a public prosecution to a people's court and transfer the case file and evidence to the people's court. Therefore, cases in which a people's procuratorate initiates a public prosecution shall be in conformity with the scope of cases to be tried and heard by the people's courts at the corresponding levels. Therefore, the procuratorial authority that initiates the public prosecution shall be determined according to the trial jurisdiction.

According to the Organic Law of the People's Courts, in addition to the Supreme People's Court which is the highest judicial organ of the State, there are local people's courts at different levels, military courts and other special people's courts. Local people's courts at different levels are further divided into: primary people's courts, intermediate people's courts and high people's courts. Accordingly, the trial jurisdiction of criminal cases is divided into jurisdiction by level, jurisdiction by region, designated jurisdiction and specialized jurisdiction.

(1) Jurisdiction by Level

Jurisdiction by level refers to the scope of authority of the people's courts at different levels in trying the criminal cases of first instance.

A. Criminal cases of first instance under the jurisdiction of primary people's courts. Article 20 of the Criminal Procedure Law provides that "a primary people's court shall have jurisdiction over ordinary criminal cases as a court of first instance, except those under the jurisdiction of the people's court at a higher level as provided for by this Law." It can be seen that a primary people's court is the lowest level jurisdiction for ordinary criminal cases of first instance, and in principle, the primary people's court shall have jurisdiction over ordinary criminal cases.

B. Criminal cases of first instance under the jurisdiction of intermediate people's courts. Article 21 of the Criminal Procedure Law provides that "an intermediate people's court shall have jurisdiction over the following criminal cases as a court of first instance: **a.** a case regarding compromising state security or terrorist activities; and **b.** a case regarding a crime punishable by life imprisonment or the death penalty."[①]

**C. Criminal cases of first instance under the jurisdiction of high

---

① Articles 291 and 299 of the Criminal Procedure Law.

people's courts. Article 22 of the Criminal Procedure Law provides that "a higher people's court shall have jurisdiction over criminal cases which are significant in a province (or an autonomous region or municipality directly under the central government) as a court of first instance."

D. Criminal cases of first instance under the jurisdiction of the Supreme People's Court. Article 23 of the Criminal Procedure Law provides that "the Supreme People's Court shall have jurisdiction over criminal cases which are significant in the entire nation as a court of first instance."

The above are the provisions of the Criminal Procedure Law regarding the jurisdiction of the people's courts at all levels over criminal cases of the first instance, so the people's courts shall comply with and implement such provisions when accepting and trying criminal cases. However, the circumstances of criminal cases are very complicated. Due to the impact of subjective and objective factors, the trial of the people's courts may also encounter some problems which are difficult to solve. Therefore, jurisdiction by level must be flexible to meet the needs of certain special situation that may arise in the trial practice and to ensure correct and timely handling of cases. Therefore, Article 24 of the Criminal Procedure Law provides that "when necessary, a people's court at a higher level may try a criminal case under the jurisdiction of a people's court at a lower level as a court of first instance; and when a people's court at a lower level as a court of first instance deems that a criminal case is significant or complicated and needs to be tried by a people's court at a higher level, it may request that the case be transferred to the people's court at the next higher level for trial." These are flexible provisions made by law regarding jurisdiction by level.

(2) Regional Jurisdiction

Regional jurisdiction refers to the division of authorities between the people's courts at the same level in the trial of criminal cases of first instance.

A. Jurisdiction of the court at the place of crime. Article 25 of the Criminal Procedure Law provides that "a criminal case shall be under the jurisdiction of the people's court at the place of crime. Where it is more appropriate for the case to be tried by the people's court at the place of residence of the defendant, the case may be under the jurisdiction of the people's court at the place of residence of the defendant." This provision indicates that, in

China, there are two principles for determining the regional jurisdiction of criminal cases: the place of crime and the place of residence of the defendant. However, the status of the two principles in regional jurisdiction is not juxtaposed; the place of crime is the basic principle for determining the regional jurisdiction, and the place of residence of the defendant is the supplementary principle for determining the regional jurisdiction.

In principle, a criminal case shall be under the jurisdiction of the people's court at the place of crime. The place of crime mentioned here includes the place where the act of crime occurred and the place where the result of crime occurred, and is generally understood to include the place of preparation for crime, the place where the act of crime was committed, the place where the result of crime occurred and the place where the illicit money and goods were disposed of.

B. Jurisdiction of the court at the place of residence of the defendant. If it is more appropriate for the criminal case to be tried by the people's court at the place where the defendant resides, then that court may have jurisdiction over the criminal case. A criminal case involving a unit crime shall be under the jurisdiction of the people's court at the place where the crime was committed, however if it is more appropriate for the people's court at the place where the unit defendant is located or registered to try the case, that court may have jurisdiction over the criminal case. The place of residence of the defendant mentioned here includes the place of household registration and place of residence of the defendant. What is "more appropriate" depends on the circumstances of the case and the defendant. For example, the case occurs at the common border of two areas, the jurisdiction of the place where the crime is committed is not clear, making it difficult to determine the competent court of the place of crime; the public indignation against the defendant is greater in the place where the defendant resides, and the local people strongly demand that the case be tried in the place where he resides, and so on.

C. Priority and referral in jurisdiction. In judicial practice, there are often cases in which the defendant commits a crime within the jurisdiction of several people's courts, so that the people's courts of several places where the crime is committed may all have jurisdiction over the cases. In order to solve this problem, Article 26 of the Criminal Procedure Law clearly stipulates: "Where two or more people's courts at the same level all have jurisdiction over a case, the case shall be tried by the people's court which first accepts the case. When necessary, the case may be transferred for trial by the people's court at the principal place of crime."

5.3. Designation of Jurisdiction

Article 27 of the Criminal Procedure Law provides: "A people's court at a higher level may designate that a people's court at a lower level to try a case over which jurisdiction is unclear, or designate that a people's court at a lower level to transfer a case to another people's court for trial." In accordance with the Interpretation of the Criminal Procedure Law, where a people's court at a higher level designates a people's court to exercise jurisdiction, it shall serve the written decision on designated jurisdiction upon the designated people's court and other related people's courts before the trial. After the people's court that originally accepted the case receives the written decision from the people's court at a higher level designating another court to exercise jurisdiction, it shall no longer exercise jurisdiction. For a case of public prosecution, the people's procuratorate that initiates the public prosecution shall be notified in writing, and all the case files shall be returned, and the parties concerned shall be notified in writing. For a case of private prosecution, all the case files shall be transferred to the people's court designated to exercise jurisdiction, and the parties concerned shall be notified in writing. When necessary, people's courts at higher levels may designate other people's courts at lower levels to handle cases over which a people's court at the lower level has jurisdiction. For a case remanded by the people's court of second instance to the people's court of first instance for retrial, where the people's procuratorate, after withdrawal of the prosecution, refiles a public prosecution with the people's court at a level lower than the original people's court of first instance, the people's court at the lower level shall report the relevant situation to the original people's court of second instance level by level. The original people's court of second instance may, in light of the specific circumstances, decide to transfer the case to the original people's court of first instance or any other people's courts for trial.

5.4. Special Jurisdiction

Special jurisdiction refers to the division of work within the scope of acceptance of the criminal cases of first instance between special people's courts as well as between special people's courts and ordinary people's courts.

In accordance with the provisions of the Organic Law of the People's Courts, China establishes military courts and other special people's courts. At present, special people's courts have been established to accept criminal cases, including military courts and railway transport courts. Criminal cases under the jurisdiction of military courts are mainly those crimes as committed by active servicemen or permanent military staff in violation of military duties as prescribed by Chapter X of the Specific Provisions of the Criminal Law. Criminal cases under the jurisdiction of railway transport courts are mainly those that are investigated by public security organs within the railway transport system, such as criminal cases endangering or sabotaging railway traffic and safety facilities, criminal cases committed on trains, and criminal cases in violation of rules, regulations or caused by negligence of duty by railway workers, which lead to serious consequences.

CHAPTER THREE

PARTICIPANTS IN LITIGATION AND THEIR RIGHTS

The protection of the rights of criminal suspects, defendants, victims and other participants in the proceedings in criminal proceedings reflects the spirit of "respecting and protecting human rights" stipulated in the Constitution.

1. Criminal Suspect and Relevant Defense System

1.1. Concept Distinction Between Criminal Suspect and the Defendant

"Criminal Suspect" and "the Defendant" are two terms used to describe persons who are criminally accused for suspected crimes. In a case of public prosecution, the person accused is called a "criminal suspect" before the prosecution is brought to court by a people's procuratorate, or "the defendant" after the prosecution is brought to court by the people's procuratorate. In a case of private prosecution, after the private prosecutor has brought the private prosecution to court, the person prosecuted is called "the defendant".

1.2. Litigation Status of Criminal Suspects and the Defendant

First, criminal suspects and the defendants are litigants in criminal procedures and enjoy the right to defense.

Second, criminal suspects and the defendants have a direct interest in the outcome of the cases and are accused parties in criminal proceedings.

Third, criminal suspects and the defendants are also important sources of evidence. Statements and exculpations of criminal suspects and the defendants are types of statutory evidence. The law strictly prohibits the extortion of confessions by torture, the collection of evidence by threat, enticement, deception, or other illegal means, or the forcing of anyone to commit self-incrimination, in order to ensure that the confessions of criminal suspects and the defendants are voluntary.

1.3. Litigation Rights of Criminal Suspects

Criminal suspects enjoy a wide range of litigation rights in criminal proceedings. According to the nature and function of these litigation rights, they can be divided into defensive rights and remedial rights.

On the one hand, criminal suspects enjoy defensive rights. The term "defensive rights" refers to the litigation rights enjoyed by the criminal suspects against the charges and offsetting the effects of their charges. Such rights mainly include: **a.** citizens of all nationalities shall have the right to use their native languages in litigation;① **b.** the criminal suspects shall truthfully answer the questions of the investigators, but have the right to refuse to answer questions irrelevant to the case;② **c.** the suspects may enjoy the help from their defense lawyers.

On the other hand, criminal suspects are also entitled to remedial rights. Remedial rights refer to the litigation rights of criminal suspects to request a special state organ to review, change or cancel the actions, decisions, or judgments made against them by another special state organ. Such rights for suspects mainly include: **a.** Right to apply for reconsideration. A party or his/her legal representative shall have the right to request the disqualification. Against a decision that dismisses a request for disqualification, the party or his/her legal representative may apply for reconsideration once.③ **b.** Right to file accusations. Litigation participants shall have the right to file accusations against judges, prosecutors, and investigators who infringe upon their procedural rights or inflict personal insult on them.④ **c.** Right to apply for change or termination of compulsory measures. A criminal suspect or defendant or his/her legal representative, close relative, or defender shall have the right to apply for modifying a compulsory measure; a criminal suspect or defendant or his/her legal representative, close relative, or defender shall have the right to require termination of a compulsory measure taken by a people's court, a people's procuratorate, or a public security authority when the term of the compulsory

---

① Article 9 of the Criminal Procedure Law.
② Article 120 of the Criminal Procedure Law.
③ Articles 29 and 31 of the Criminal Procedure Law.
④ Article 14 of the Criminal Procedure Law.

measure expires.①

In addition to the above litigation rights, criminal suspects also enjoy a series of procedural protections. Such rights mainly include: **a.** it shall be strictly prohibited to extort confessions by torture, gather evidence by threat, enticement, deceit, or other illegal means, or force anyone to commit self-incrimination;② **b.** they shall not be subject to compulsory measures taken by investigators such as illegal arrest, detention, bail and residential confinement;③ **c.** they shall not be subject to illegal search or seizure by investigators and other investigation actions; and so on.

1.4. Litigation Obligations of Criminal Suspects

According to the Criminal Procedure Law, criminal suspects shall bear the following litigation obligations: **a.** being under compulsory measures such as forced appearance, bail, residential confinement, detention and arrest, when the statutory conditions are met; **b.** being interrogated, searched, detained, etc., by investigators; and **c.** answering investigators' interrogation truthfully.

1.5. Relevant Defense System for Criminal Suspects

Defense refers to the litigation activities in which the person accused and his/her defender refute the charges against the person accused, present facts and reasons in favor of the person accused, demonstrate that the person accused is innocent or the crime is minor, or shall be given a mitigated punishment or be exempted from punishment, protect the procedural rights of the person accused and protect the lawful rights and interests of the person accused.

The right to defense is an exclusive litigation right granted by law to criminal suspects and the defendants, that is, criminal suspects and defendants defend themselves against the charges in order to protect their lawful rights and interests. It occupies a core position in all litigation rights of criminal suspects and the defendants.

---

① Articles 97 and 99 of the Criminal Procedure Law.
② Article 52 of the Criminal Procedure Law.
③ Article 117 of the Criminal Procedure Law.

(1) Types of Defense Enjoyed by Criminal Suspects and the Defendants

There are three types of defense in criminal proceedings in China:

A. Self defense. It refers to the criminal suspects and the defendants refute, defend themselves, and explain against the charges. The right to defend themselves and the State's right of prosecution come into being at the same time. Once a citizen is accused and enters into criminal proceedings, he/she will automatically enjoy the right to defend himself/herself and conduct the defense mentioned above.

B. Defense by others through appointment. It refers to the situation in which a criminal suspect or the defendant appoints a lawyer or any other citizens to act as defender and assists him/her in defending. The Criminal Procedure Law adheres to the principle of autonomy of will in choosing defenders, i.e. whether to appoint defenders and to appoint whom as defenders shall be decided by the criminal suspects and the defendants at their sole discretion. From the perspective of legal provisions and judicial practices, there are only four restrictions: first, defenders can only be chosen from the persons who can act as defenders according to the law; second, in the investigation stage, a criminal suspect can only appoint lawyers as his defenders; third, the number of defenders appointed shall be two at most; fourth, a defender shall not defend for two or more accused persons in the same case.

C. Defense by legal aid. It refers to the situation that criminal suspects and defendants do not appoint defenders, but legal aid agencies designate lawyers to defend them under statutory circumstances. The Criminal Procedure Law was amended in 2018 to add the on-duty lawyer system. Article 36 stipulates that: Legal aid agencies may station on-duty lawyers at the people's courts, jails, and other places. If a criminal suspect or defendant does not appoint a defender, nor does a legal aid agency designate a lawyer to defend him/her, an on-duty lawyer shall provide the criminal suspect or defendant with legal assistance including but not limited to legal advice, recommendations on the selection of procedures, application for the modification of compulsory measures, and offering opinions on the handling of the case. A people's court, people's procuratorate, or jail shall inform a criminal suspect or defendant of his or her right to a scheduled meeting with an on-duty lawyer, and facilitate the scheduled meeting between the criminal suspect or defendant and an on-duty lawyer.

(2) The Scope of Defenders

The scope of defenders shall mean who may be appointed by a criminal suspect or a defendant to act as his/her defenders.

The following persons may serve as defenders: lawyers; persons recommended by a people's community or the employer of the criminal suspect or the defendant; guardians, family members and friends of the criminal suspect or the defendant. At the same time, the following persons shall not serve as defenders: a person serving a criminal sentence, or on probation for a suspended sentence or parole; a person whose personal freedom is deprived of, or restricted in accordance with law; a person who is without capacity or with limited capacity to conduct defense; a staff member of a people's court, a people's procuratorate, a public security authority, a state security authority, or a prison; a people's assessor; a person with an interest in the outcome of the case; a foreign national or a stateless person. In addition, when the Criminal Procedure Law was amended in 2018, a provision was added to Article 33, which reads: A person who is expelled from a public office or whose practicing license as a lawyer or notary is revoked shall not serve as a defender, except that the person is the guardian or a close relative of the criminal suspect or defendant.

(3) Defense Right Enjoyed by Criminal Suspects

A criminal suspect shall have the right to defend himself/herself or with the assistance of his/her defenders. In a case of public prosecution, a criminal suspect shall have the right to appoint a defender from the day when the criminal suspect is interrogated by an investigation authority for the first time or from the day when a compulsory measure is taken against the criminal suspect; during the period of investigation, a criminal suspect may only appoint a lawyer as a defender. When an investigation authority interrogates a criminal suspect for the first time or takes a compulsory measure against the criminal suspect, it shall inform the criminal suspect of his/her right to appoint defenders. A people's procuratorate shall, within 3 days after receiving the case file transferred for examination and prosecution, inform the criminal suspect of his/her right to appoint defenders. If a criminal suspect in custody requests for appointing a defender, the case-handling authority shall convey such a request in a timely manner. For a criminal suspect in custody, his/her guardian or close relative may appoint a defender on his/her behalf. After accepting appointment of a criminal suspect, the defender shall inform the authority handling the case in a timely manner. In a case of private prosecution, defenders can be appointed at any time. During the period of investigation, the defense lawyer may provide legal assistance to the criminal suspect, file petitions and accusations on behalf of the criminal suspect, apply for modifying the compulsory measure, find out the charges against which the criminal suspect is suspected of and relevant case information from the investigation authority, and offer opinions. A criminal suspect shall have the right to be defended by a lawyer designated by a legal aid agency, and to refuse the defender to continue defending him/her and to appoint another defender to defend him/her under statutory conditions.

(4) Litigation Rights and Obligations of a Defender in the Investigation Stage

A defender shall enjoy the litigation rights in accordance with the law, and the assumption of his litigation obligations is an important guarantee for the defender to carry out defending activities smoothly. Therefore, the Criminal Procedure Law and the Lawyers Law clearly stipulate the litigation rights and obligations of defenders.

A defender shall enjoy the following rights during the investigation stage:

A. The right to occupational protection. Defenders shall be protected by the laws of the State when performing their duties in accordance with the law. The personal rights of a defender shall not be infringed upon in the practice of law.

B. The right of meeting and communication. A defense lawyer may meet and communicate with a criminal suspect or defendant in custody. As permitted by the people's court or people's procuratorate, a defender other than a defense lawyer may also meet and communicate with a criminal suspect or defendant in custody. When a defense lawyer files a request for a meeting with a criminal suspect or defendant in custody on the basis of the lawyer's practicing license, a certificate issued by the law firm, and an attorney or an official legal aid document, the jail shall arrange a meeting in a timely manner, no later than 48 hours after the request is filed. At a meeting with a criminal suspect or defendant in custody, a defense lawyer may learn relevant case information and provide legal advice and other services, and from the day when the case is transferred for examination and prosecution, may verify relevant evidence with the criminal suspect or defendant. A meeting between a defense lawyer and a criminal suspect or defendant shall not be monitored.①

C. The right to provide and express defense opinions in accordance with the law. During the period of criminal investigation, a defense lawyer may provide legal assistance for a criminal suspect, file petitions and accusations on behalf of a criminal suspect, apply for modifying a compulsory measure, learn the charges against a criminal suspect, relevant case information from the criminal investigation authority, and offer information. During the examination and approval of an arrest request, a people's procuratorate may interview a witness and other litigation participants and hear the opinion of a defense lawyer; and, if a defense lawyer files a request for presenting an opinion, shall hear the opinion of the defense lawyer. Where, before the investigation of a case is closed, the defense lawyer files a request for presenting an opinion, the criminal investigation authority shall hear the opinion of the defense lawyer and record it. A written opinion of the defense lawyer, if any, shall be attached to the case file.②

D. Other rights. Defenders and litigation representatives may request disqualification and apply for reconsideration according to the provisions of this chapter. Litigation participants shall have the right to file accusations against judges, prosecutors, and investigators who infringe upon their procedural rights or inflict personal insult on them. A defense lawyer shall have the right to keep confidential the conditions and information regarding a client known in the practice of law.③

In addition, the defender shall bear a number of litigation obligations, including conscientiously fulfilling his/her duty, defending in accordance with the law and keeping secrets.

---

① Article 39 of the Criminal Procedure Law.
② Articles 38, 88 and 161 of the Criminal Procedure Law.
③ Articles 14, 32 and 48 of the Criminal Procedure Law.

2. The Defendant and Relevant Defense System

2.1. Litigation Rights of the Defendant

After the public prosecution is brought to court by a people's procuratorate, the status of the person prosecuted will be changed from a criminal suspect to the defendant, and he/she still enjoys a series of litigation rights, including defensive rights and remedial rights.

On the one hand, the defendant enjoys defensive rights. They mainly include: **a.** The right to use their native languages in court proceedings. **b.** The defendant was entitled to receive a copy of the indictment at least 10 days before the court session. **c.** The right to participate in court investigation: The defendant has the right to participate in court investigation, make statements regarding the facts of the crime accused by the people's procuratorate, question the witnesses and forensic identification or evaluation experts, hear the records of testimony of absent witnesses, the experts' opinions, the records of inquests and examination and other documents of evidence, which are read out or played in the court, and express opinions on the above-mentioned written evidence; they have the right to apply for summoning new witnesses to appear in court, obtaining new material evidence, applying for a new expert evaluation to be made, and another inquest to be held. **d.** The right to participate in court arguments: The defendant has the right to participate in court debates, express his/her opinions on the findings of facts and the application of law, and may debate with the prosecuting party. **e.** The defendant has the right to present a final statement before the court. **f.** The right of counterclaim: The defendant in a case of private prosecution has the right to raise a counterclaim against the private prosecutor.

On the other hand, the defendant is entitled to remedial rights. They mainly include: **a.** The right to apply for reconsideration. The defendant has the right to apply for disqualification of procuratorial personnel, judges, court clerks, forensic identification or evaluation experts and interpreters, and if he/

she is not satisfied with the decision on rejection of his application for disqualification, he/she has the right to apply for reconsideration. **b.** The right to file accusations. The defendant has the right to file charges against judges and procurators whose acts infringe upon his/her procedural rights or inflict personal insult on him/her. **c.** The right to apply for modification or termination of compulsory measures. The defendant in custody has the right to apply for modification of the compulsory measures; and has the right to request termination of the compulsory measures taken by a people's court, a people's procuratorate or a public security authority when the term of the compulsory measures expires. **d.** The right to file petition. With respect to a people's procuratorate's discretionary non-prosecution decision, the defendant has the right to present a petition to the people's procuratorate; with respect to a legally effective judgment or ruling made by a people's court at any level, the defendant has the right to present a petition to a people's court or a people's procuratorate. If the petition meets the statutory conditions, the people's court shall retry the case. **e.** The right of appeal. With respect to a judgment or ruling of first instance made by a local people's court at any level, the defendant has the right to appeal in writing or orally to the people's court at the next higher level, which causes the commencement of the procedure of second instance.

In addition to the above litigation rights, the defendant also enjoys a series of procedural protections. There are mainly the followings: **a.** A person shall not be found guilty if he has not been judged as guilty by the people's court in accordance with law. **b.** An open, independent and impartial trial shall be held by the people's court. **c.** In the process of criminal proceedings, a person shall not be subject to interrogation by judges or procurators by extortion of confessions by torture, threat, enticement, deceit or other illegal methods, and shall not be compelled to commit self-incrimination, and illegal evidence shall be excluded. **d.** When the people's court of second instance hears a case appealed only by the defendant, it may not aggravate the criminal punishment on the defendant, etc.

2.2. Litigation Obligations of the Defendant

In accordance with the provisions of the Criminal Procedure Law, the defendant shall bear the following litigation obligations: **a.** To be under compulsory measures such as forced appearance, bail, residential confinement, detention and arrest, when the statutory conditions are met; **b.** To appear in court and accept a court trial on time in accordance with law; **c.** To observe the discipline of the court and to obey the directions of the judges; **d.** To perform or render assistance to the enforcement of valid judgments and rulings.

2.3. Relevant Defense System for the Defendant

(1) Right to Defense of the Defendant

The defendant shall have the right to defend himself/herself or with the assistance of his defenders. Defenders can be appointed by the defendant at any time. The people's court shall, within 3 days as of the date of acceptance of a case, inform the defendant of his/her right to appoint a defender. If the defendant in custody requests for appointing a defender, the people's court, people's procuratorate and public security authority shall convey such a request in a timely manner. For the defendant in custody, his/her guardian or close relative may appoint a defender on his/her behalf. The defender shall, after accepting appointment by the defendant, inform the authority handling the case in a timely manner. In cases of private prosecution, defenders can be appointed at any time. The defendant shall have the right to be defended by a lawyer designated by a legal aid agency under statutory conditions, have the right to refuse the defender to continue defending him/her and to appoint another defender to defend him/her.

(2) Litigation Rights and Obligations of a Defender of the Defendant

The defender of the defendant enjoys the following litigation rights:

A. The right of occupational protection. The representation or defense opinions presented in court by a lawyer shall not be subject to legal prosecution, however, except speeches compromising the state security, maliciously defaming others or seriously disrupting the court order.[①]

B. The right of meeting and communication.

C. The right of having access to case files. A defense lawyer may, from the day when the people's procuratorate examines a case for prosecution,

---

① Article 37 of the Lawyers Law.

consult, extract, and duplicate case materials. As permitted by the people's court or people's procuratorate, a defender other than a defense lawyer may also consult, extract, and duplicate such materials.①

D. The right of obtaining evidence. A defense lawyer may gather information regarding a case from a witness or any other relevant entities or individuals with the consent thereof, and may also apply to the people's procuratorate or people's court for gathering or submission of evidence or apply to the people's court for notifying a witness to testify before the court. A defense lawyer may gather information regarding a case from a victim or his or her close relatives or a witness provided by a victim with the consent thereof and permission of the people's procuratorate or people's court.②

E. The right to provide and express defense opinions in accordance with the law. A people's procuratorate shall, when examining a case, interrogate a criminal suspect, hear the opinions of the defender or on-duty lawyer, the victim, and the victim's litigation representative, and record their opinions. The written opinions, if any, of the defender or on-duty lawyer, the victim, and the victim's litigation representative shall be attached to the case file. After determining the opening date of a court session, a people's court shall notify the people's procuratorate of the opening time and place of the court session, summon the parties, notify the defenders, litigation representatives, witnesses, identification or evaluation experts, and interpreters, and serve the summons and notices no later than three days before the court session is opened. Before a court session is opened, the judges may call together the public prosecutor, parties, defenders, and litigation representatives to gather information and hear opinions on trial-related issues, such as disqualification, a list of witnesses to testify in court, and exclusion of illegally obtained evidence. A victim, a plaintiff and a defender in an incidental civil action, and a litigation representative may, with the permission of the presiding judge, question a defendant. The public prosecutor or a party or the defender or litigation representative thereof may, with the permission of the presiding judge, question a witness or an identification or evaluation expert; may request the court to call a person with expertise to appear before the court to offer an opinion on the

---

① Article 40 of the Criminal Procedure Law.

② Article 43 of the Criminal Procedure Law.

expert opinion of an identification or evaluation expert. During a court session, a party or the defender or the litigation representative thereof shall have the right to request that new witnesses be summoned to appear in courts, that new physical evidence be submitted, or that new forensic identification or evaluation or crime scene investigation be conducted. With the permission of the presiding judge, the public prosecutor or a party or the defender or litigation representative thereof may present opinions on the evidence and merits of a case and debate with opposing parties. The Supreme People's Court reviewing a death sentence shall arraign the defendant and, if the defense lawyer files a request for presenting an opinion, hear the opinion of the defense lawyer.①

F. Other rights. A defender or close relative of a defendant may, with the consent of the defendant, file an appeal for the defendant.② A defender shall have the right to obtain legal documents relevant to his/her exercise of the right to defense, such as copies of the indictment of the people's procuratorate and copies of the judgments or rulings of the people's court, etc.

In addition, defenders of the defendant shall assume litigation obligations such as conscientiously fulfilling their duties, making defense in line with law, presenting partial evidence, keeping secrets and observing litigation disciplines.

3. Victims and Their Rights

3.1. Scope and Characteristics of Victims

A victim refers to a person whose personal, property or other rights and interests are infringed upon by a crime. The scope of victims can be divided into the broad sense and the narrow sense. In the narrow sense, a victim refers to the person who participates in the proceedings as an individual in a criminal case prosecuted by the people's procuratorate on behalf of the country, and exercises the function of prosecution together with the people's procuratorate. In the broad sense, victims also include the following two types: **a.** Victims who file criminal actions in private prosecution cases. They are called private prosecutors. **b.** In

---

① Articles 173, 187, 191, 194, 195, 197, 198 and 251 of the Criminal Procedure Law.
② Articles 187, 202 and 227 of the Criminal Procedure Law.

criminal actions, victims who suffered material losses as a result of the defendant's crime. They have the right to file incidental civil actions and are called plaintiffs of incidental civil actions.

The victim has the following characteristics: **a.** As the person who suffered from the crime, the victim has a direct interest in the outcome of the case. **b.** Based on the demand of enabling the defendant to receive a lawful retribution, the victim has the desire to actively participate in the litigation process and influence the outcome of the judgment. **c.** As a party to the litigation, the victim has approximately the same litigation status as the defendant, and also has many corresponding litigation rights with the defendant's. **d.** Although the victim has the litigation status as a party to the case, he/she is generally a person who has knowledge of the facts of the case, and his/her statements are one of the sources of statutory evidence.

3.2. Litigation Rights of Victims

In accordance with the provisions of the Criminal Procedure Law, in addition to the litigation rights also enjoyed by other parties concerned, victims also enjoy some special litigation rights.

The main litigation rights also enjoyed by the victims and other parties concerned include: **a.** Litigation participants shall have the right to file accusations against judges, prosecutors, and investigators who infringe upon their procedural rights or inflict personal insult on them. **b.** Under any of the certain circumstances, a judge, prosecutor, or investigator shall voluntarily disqualify himself/herself, and a party or his/her legal representative shall have the right to request the disqualification. Against a decision that dismisses a request for disqualification, the party or his/her legal representative may apply for reconsideration once. **c.** A victim may present a statement regarding a crime alleged in the indictment to question a defendant or to question a witness or an identification. The public prosecutor and a defender shall adduce physical evidence before the court for the parties to identify, and a statement of a witness who is not in court, an opinion of an identification or evaluation expert who is not in court, transcripts of crime scene investigation, and other documentations serving as evidence shall be read out in court. A judge shall hear the opinions of the public prosecutor, parties, defenders, and litigation representatives. A victim shall have the right to request that new witnesses be summoned to appear in courts, that new physical evidence be submitted, or that new forensic identification or evaluation or crime scene investigation be conducted. **d.** With the permission of the presiding judge, the public prosecutor or a victim or the defender or the litigation representative thereof may present opinions on the evidence and merits of a case and debate with opposing parties. **e.** A party or his/her legal representative or close relative may file a petition with a people's court or a people's procuratorate against an effective sentence or ruling. **f.** Citizens of all nationalities shall have the right to use their native languages in litigation, etc.①

The special litigation rights enjoyed by the victims mainly include: **a.** A victim or his/her legal representative or close relative in a case of public prosecution or a party or his/her legal representative in an incidental civil action shall have the right to have a litigation representative from the day when the case is transferred for examination and prosecution. A people's procuratorate shall, within three days from the date of receiving the case file transferred for examination and prosecution, inform a victim and his/her legal representative or close relative and the parties and their legal representatives in an incidental civil action of their right to have litigation representatives. **b.** A victim shall have the right to report a crime which infringes upon his/her personal or property rights or accuse a criminal suspect of such a crime to a public security authority, a people's procuratorate, or a people's court; if it believes that there are no facts of a crime or the facts of a crime are obviously minor and require no criminal investigation, it shall not open a case but shall notify the accuser of the reasons for not opening a case, against such a decision, the accuser may apply for reconsideration. A victim expresses to a people's procuratorate the opinion that a public security authority fails to open a case that shall be otherwise opened for criminal investigation, the people's procuratorate shall require the public security authority to state the reasons for not opening a case. **c.** Where a people's procuratorate decides not to initiate a public prosecution for a case with a victim, it shall serve a written decision upon the victim. Against the decision, the victim may, within seven days after receiving the written decision, file a

---

① Articles 9, 14, 29, 195, 198 and 252 of the Criminal Procedure Law.

petition with the people's procuratorate at the next higher level for initiation of a public prosecution. The people's procuratorate shall inform the victim of its decision after reexamination. If the people's procuratorate upholds the decision not to initiate a public prosecution, the victim may institute an action in a people's court. The victim may also institute an action directly in a people's court without undergoing the petition procedure. **d.** A case where a victim has evidence to prove that a defendant has infringed upon his/her personal or property rights and shall be subject to criminal liability in accordance with the law but a public security authority or a people's procuratorate decides not to subject the defendant to criminal liability. **e.** Against a sentence of a local people's court at any level as a court of first instance, a victim or his/her legal representative shall, within five days after receiving a written sentence, have the right to request that the people's procuratorates file a protest. The people's procuratorate shall, within five days after receiving the request of the victim or his/her legal representative, make a decision on whether to file a protest and make a reply to the requesting party, etc.[①]

4. Witnesses and Their Rights

4.1. Concept, Characteristics and Conditions of Witness

A witness is a person who has knowledge of a case and makes statements to a specialstate organ.

Witnesses have the following characteristics: **a.** A witness must be a person who has knowledge of a case. **b.** A witness must be a person who has knowledge of a case outside the proceedings. The personnel participating in the investigation, examination, prosecution and trial, defenders, litigation representatives and forensic identification or evaluation experts, etc. also learn about the case, but their understanding of the case is formed in the process of litigation after the commencement of criminal procedure, so they are not witnesses. If these people know the situation of a case before the start of the proceedings, priority shall be given to being witnesses and they generally shall

---

① Articles 46, 110, 112, 113, 180 and 229 of the Criminal Procedure Law.

not participate in the handling of the case. **c.** Witnesses must be persons other than the parties.

In China's criminal proceedings, anyone who knows the circumstances of a case has the obligation to testify. However, a person who cannot distinguish right from wrong or cannot properly express himself/herself due to any physical or mental handicap or immature shall not act as a witness. A witness can only be a natural person, and no state organ, enterprise, public institution or people's organization may be a witness.

4.2. Litigation Rights of Witnesses

Witnesses have the following rights: **a.** Citizens of all nationalities shall have the right to use their native languages in litigation. **b.** Court transcripts shall be read by the parties or read out to them. A party which finds any omissions or errors in the transcripts may request supplements or corrections. **c.** Subsidization shall be provided for the travel, board and lodging, and other expenses of a witness for performing the obligation to testify. **d.** He/she has the right to refuse to commit perjury. **e.** His/her true personal information, such as name, shall not be disclosed. **f.** Whoever intimidates, insults, beats, or retaliates against a witness or his/her close relatives shall be subject to criminal liability in accordance with the law if it constitutes a crime; or shall be subject to punishment in public security administration in accordance with the law if it is not criminally punishable.[①]

5. Other Litigation Participants

In addition to the above litigation participants, litigation participants in criminal proceedings also include private prosecutors, plaintiffs and the defendants of incidental civil actions, legal representatives, forensic identification or evaluation experts and interpreters. As the private prosecutors and the plaintiffs of incidental civil action are victims in a broad sense, and the defendants of incidental civil action are usually the accused of the criminal

---

① Articles 63 to 65, and 207 of the Criminal Procedure Law.

actions, no further detail will be discussed. The following is a brief introduction to legal representatives, forensic identification or evaluation experts and interpreters.

5.1. Legal Representatives

Article 108 of the Criminal Procedure Law provides that, "legal representative" means a parent, a foster parent, or a guardian of the represented person or a representative from a government authority or social organization with a duty to protect the person represented. A legal representative has an independent legal status in the litigation process, is not be bound by the will of the represented person and does not need the consent or authorization of the represented person to enter into the litigation and exercise the representative rights. Where the legal representative and the represented person disagree with each other on whether to exercise a joint right of litigation, the acts of the legal representative are valid independently. Moreover, acts of the legal representative are deemed to be those of the represented person and have the same legal effect as acts of the represented person.

The main duties of legal representatives participating in criminal proceedings are to protect the personal rights, property rights, litigation rights and all other legitimate rights and interests of juveniles, persons without capacity for conduct or persons with limited capacity for conduct in accordance with the law. Therefore, legal representatives enjoy the same extensive litigation rights as represented persons. Certainly, from the theoretical perspective, legal representatives cannot perform specific acts on behalf of the represented persons. For example, legal representatives cannot make confessions, arguments or statements on behalf of the represented persons, nor can he/she undertake obligations on behalf of the represented persons that are related to personal freedom.

5.2. Forensic Identification or Evaluation Experts

In criminal proceedings, a forensic identification or evaluation expert refers to a person who is designated or engaged by a public security or judicial organ to make analysis and judgment on the special issues involved in a criminal case with his/her own special knowledge or skills, and to put forward written identification or evaluation opinions. The written analysis, judgment and opinions of the forensic identification or evaluation expert is called identification or evaluation opinion, which is one of the statutory types of evidence.

In general, a forensic identification or evaluation expert shall meet the following conditions: **a.** The expert shall be a natural person. An entity may not be the expert. **b.** The expert must possess certain special knowledge or skills. In the identification or evaluation activities, the expert shall give analytical opinions on special issues mainly according to his/her special knowledge or skills. **c.** The expert is appointed or engaged by a special organ. No party or his/her agent may engage an expert to conduct the identification or evaluation. **d.** The expert must have no interest in any party to the case; otherwise, the person concerned shall have the right to apply for his/her disqualification.

An expert is entitled to the following litigation rights according to law: **a.** the right to learn about the case related to the identification or evaluation; **b.** the right to request the appointing or engaging authority to provide sufficient materials for identification or evaluation, the right to request the relevant authority to provide supplementary if the materials provided for identification or evaluation are insufficient or do not meet the conditions for making identification or evaluation opinions, an expert has the right to request the relevant authority to provide supplementary materials, and the right to refuse the request if the supplemntary materials are not provided; **c.** the right to ask for conditions necessary for identification or evaluation; **d.** charging identification or evaluation fees. In addition, if an expert testifies in litigation, the personal safety of the expert and his/her close relatives shall be protected according to the law.

Meanwhile, an expert shall assume the following litigation obligations: **a.** making evaluation in an honest manner, and refraining from making false evaluation opinions on purpose; **b.** keeping confidential the information about the case and the privacy of relevant persons obtained from the evaluation; **c.** appearing in court to answer inquiries and questions of judges, public prosecutors, defenders, the defendant and other persons. If an expert refuses to appear and testify as a witness in court after being notified by the people's court, his/her opinion shall not be used as a basis for deciding the case.

5.3. Interpreters

Interpreters mainly translate foreign languages, minority languages, deaf-mute gestures, braille, etc. Interpreters shall not have an interest in the case or the parties, otherwise they shall withdraw.

An Interpreters is entitled to the following rights during the litigation proceedings: **a.** to be informed of case information related to the contents of the translation; **b.** to consult and record the transcripts containing the contents of the translation, and to ask for amendments or supplements if it does not conform to the actual contents of the translation; and **c.** to receive appropriate remuneration and financial compensation. At the same time, an interpreters shall have the obligation to translate according to the original meaning of the language, and shall not conceal, distort or forge any false information, he/she shall bear the legal responsibility in case of falsification. Any case information and the privacy of others learned in the translation activities shall be kept confidential by the interpreters.

CHAPTER FOUR

Restriction on and Deprivation of Freedom of Criminal Suspect and Defendant

In criminal proceedings, means of restricting or depriving the personal freedom of criminal suspects or defendants are called compulsory measures, and include five types: forced appearance, bail, residential confinement, detention and arrest.

1. Forced Appearance

1.1. Concept and Characteristics of Forced Appearance

Forced appearance refers to a compulsory measure adopted by public security authorities, people's procuratorates and people's courts to compel a criminal suspect or defendant who is not held in custody to appear for interrogation according to law. It is the lightest compulsory measure in criminal proceedings in China.

Forced appearance has the following characteristics: **a.** The object of forced appearance is the criminal suspect or defendant who is not held in custody. A criminal suspect who has been detained or arrested may be interrogated directly, without using forced appearance. **b.** The purpose of forced appearance is to force a criminal suspect or defendant to appear for interrogation, with no effect of detention. The duration of forced appearance shall not exceed the statutory time limit, and the person compelled to appear for interrogation shall be immediately released after interrogation.

1.2. Object and Applicable Subject of Forced Appearance

(1) Objects to Which Forced Appearance Apply

Forced appearance, as a compulsory measure in criminal proceedings, can only be applied to criminal suspects and defendants, and is not applicable to private prosecutors, victims, plaintiffs and defendants of incidental civil action, witnesses, experts, interpreters and other litigation participants.

(2) Applicable Subject of Forced Appearance

The authorities that have the power to decide to apply forced appearance include public security authorities, people's procuratorates and people's courts.

Other authorities that exercise the power of investigation are also entitled to take the measure of forced appearance, for example, state security authorities and military security authorities.

1.3. Procedure for Forced Appearance

In accordance with the provisions of the Criminal Procedure Law and general judicial practice, the following procedure shall apply to forced appearance:

First, the case handler shall make an application and fill in a Report on Application of Forced Appearance. Upon examination by the person-in-charge of the department, a summon of forced appearance shall be issued upon approval of the director of the public security bureau, the chief procurator of the people's procuratorate and the president of the people's court. The summon shall specify the name, gender, age, native place, residential address, work place of the person compelled to appear for interrogation, cause of action, time and place for interrogation, and reasons for forced appearance.

Second, forced appearance shall be conducted within the city or county where the person compelled to appear is located. Where a public security authority, people's procuratorate, or people's court compels appearance of a criminal suspect or defendant outside its jurisdiction, it shall notify the local public security authority, people's procuratorate, or people's court, and the latter shall provide assistance.

Third, when compelling a criminal suspect or defendant to appear for interrogation, the "Summon of Forced Appearance" shall be presented to the criminal suspect or defendant. There shall be at least two investigators or judicial officers to enforce the forced appearance. If the criminal suspect or defendant refuses to follow the forced appearance, restraint tools such as batons, police ropes or handcuffs may be used to force him/her to appear.

Fourth, after the criminal suspect or defendant arrives, he/she shall be ordered to fill in the time of arrival in the "Summon of Forced Appearance". Then he/she shall be interrogated immediately. After the interrogation, he/she shall fill in the end time of the interrogation on the "Summon of Forced Appearance". If the criminal suspect refuses to do so, investigators shall note such on the "Summon of Forced Appearance".

Fifth, after the interrogation, if the person compelled to appear meets conditions of taking other compulsory measures, such as detention or arrest, other compulsory measures shall be taken according to the law. If it is not necessary to take other mandatory measures, he/she shall be released to restore personal freedom.

Sixth, the duration of interrogation by summons or forced appearance may not exceed 12 hours; or, if it is necessary to detain or arrest a criminal suspect in an extraordinarily significant or complicated case, the duration of interrogation by summons or forced appearance may not exceed 24 hours. A criminal suspect shall not be actually held in custody by successive summons or forced appearance.[①]

Seventh, during the period of forced appearance, the meals and necessary rest time of the criminal suspect shall be ensured. As needed for handling a case, the criminal suspect may be compelled to appear for interrogation for several times, but there are no explicit provisions on the time limit between two forced appearance. In order to prevent de facto detention disguised as successive forced appearance and ensure that the person compelled to appear has a certain period of normal living and rest, it is better to ensure the time between two forced appearance is no less than 24 hours.

2. Bail

The term "bail" refers to a compulsory measure adopted in the course of criminal proceedings in which a public security authority, a people's procuratorate, or a people's court order a criminal suspect or defendantto provide a surety or pay a bond so as to ensure that the criminal suspect or defendant will not evade or obstruct investigation, prosecution and trial, and that the criminal suspect or defendant will appear once being summoned.

2.1. Scope of Application on Bail

Pursuant to Article 67 of the Criminal Procedure Law, a people's court, a

---

① Article 119 of the Criminal Procedure Law.

people's procuratorate, and a public security authority may grant bail to a criminal suspect or defendant under any of the following circumstances: **a.** The criminal suspect or defendant may be sentenced to supervision without incarceration, limited incarceration, or an accessory penalty only. **b.** The criminal suspect or defendant may be sentenced to fixed-term imprisonment or a heavier penalty but will not cause danger to the society if granted bail. **c.** The criminal suspect or defendant suffers a serious illness, cannot take care of himself/herself or is a pregnant woman or a woman who is breastfeeding her own baby, and will not cause danger to the society if granted bail. **d.** The term of custody of the criminal suspect or defendant has expired but the case has not been closed, and a bail is necessary.

2.2. Methods of Guarantee for Bail

Article 68 of the Criminal Procedure Law provides that: "Where a people's court, a people's procuratorate, and a public security authority decide to grant bail to a criminal suspect or defendant, it shall order the criminal suspect or defendant to provide a surety or pay a bond."

Therefore, there are two methods of guarantee for bail: a surety and a bond. Only one of them can be chosen. A given criminal suspect or defendant who has been granted bail cannot be required to simultaneously provide a surety and a bond.

(1) Guarantee by a Surety

Guarantee by a surety, also known as guarantee by people, refers to a form of guarantee in which a public security authority, a people's procuratorate or a people's court orders the criminal suspect or defendant to provide a surety and issue letters of guarantee, promising that the guaranteed individual will perform his/her legal and discretionary obligations during the period of bail, and will not evade or obstruct investigation, prosecution and trial, and will appear once being summoned. When a public security or a judicial organ is deciding to grant bail for a criminal suspect or defendant who meets the conditions for bail and have one of the following circumstances, it may instruct him/her to provide a surety or sureties: **a.** He/she is incapable of paying a bond. **b.** He/she is a juvenile or he or she reaches the age of 75. **c.** Other circumstances under which it is inappropriate to collect a bond.

Pursuant to Article 69 of the Criminal Procedure Law, a surety must meet the following conditions: **a.** not involved in the case; **b.** able to perform a surety's obligations; **c.** enjoying political rights and not restricted in personal freedom; and **d.** having a fixed residence and steady income. When it is decided to grant bail for the criminal suspect or defendant, he/she may be ordered to provide one or two sureties.

A surety shall perform the following obligations: **a.** supervising the bailed person in complying with the provisions of Article 71 of Criminal Procedure Law; and **b.** after discovering that the bailed person may commit or has committed a violation of Article 71 of Criminal Procedure Law, reporting it to the executing authority in a timely manner. Where the bailed person has committed a violation of Article 71 of Criminal Procedure Law and the surety fails to perform surety obligations, the surety shall be fined, and if any crime is committed, criminal liability shall be investigated in accordance with the law.[①]

(2) Guarantee by a Bond

Guarantee by a bond refers to a form of guarantee in which a public security authority, a people's procuratorate or a people's court orders the criminal suspect or defendant to provide a bond and issue a letter of guarantee, promising that the guaranteed individual will perform his/her legal and discretionary obligations during the period of bail, and will not evade or obstruct investigations, prosecutions and trials, and will appear once being summoned.

The authority deciding on a bail shall decide the amount of a bond after fully considering the need to ensure normal legal proceedings, the danger of the person to be bailed to the society, the nature and circumstances of the case, the gravity of the possible punishment, the financial condition of the person to be bailed, and other factors.[②] The bond for adults shall be no less than 1,000 yuan, and for juveniles shall not be less than 500 yuan. The person providing the bond shall deposit the bond into a special account at a bank designated by the executing authority. Pursuant to Article 73 of the Criminal Procedure Law, where a criminal suspect or defendant has not violated the provisions of Article 71 of Criminal Procedure Law during the period of waiting for trial on bail, he/she

---

① Article 70 of the Criminal Procedure Law.
② Article 72 of the Criminal Procedure Law.

may receive a refund of the bond at the bank on the basis of a notice of termination of waiting for trial on bail or relevant legal instrument, at the end of the period of waiting for trial on bail.

2.3. Procedures of Bail

The procedures of bail can be divided into two kinds: first, a public security authority, a procuratorate or a court directly and proactively decides to grant bail according to the specific circumstances of a case; second, upon the application of the criminal suspect or defendant or his/her legal representative, close relative or the lawyer appointed, a decision is made to grant bail.

(1) Application for Bail

Persons entitled to apply for bail include: the criminal suspect, the defendant and his/her legal representative, close relative and defender. Generally, an application for bail shall be made in writing. Oral form may be used only in special circumstances.

(2) Decision of Granting Bail

In the process of handling cases, people's courts, people's procuratorates or public security authorities all have the power to grant bail to the criminal suspects or defendants. Specifically, officers handling the case shall prepare an Opinion Letter on Granting Bail. Upon examination by the person-in-charge of the case-handling department, it shall be submitted to the director of the public security bureau, the chief procurator of the people's procuratorate or the president of the people's court above the county level for review and approval.

The procedures for granting bail are as follows: the officer handling the case shall fill in a Bail Decision Letter and a Notice on Enforcement of Bail. Upon examination by the person-in-charge of the case-handling department, it shall be signed and issued by the director of the public security bureau, the chief procurator of the people's procuratorate or the president of the people's court above the county level.

(3) Execution of Bail

Pursuant to Article 67 of the Criminal Procedure Law, bail shall be executed by a public security authority. In the event that a people's procuratorate or a people's court decides to grant bail, a Bail Decision Letter and a Notice on

Enforcement of Bail shall be served upon a public security authority, and the public security authority shall execute bail. According to the Interpretation of Criminal Procedure Law by the Supreme People's Court, the public security authority therein generally refers to the local public security authority at the same level. If the accused does not reside locally, the execution shall be handed over to the public security authority at the place where he/she resides. If guarantee is made by a surety, the Letter of Guarantee shall be served upon the public security authority at the same time. However, pursuant to Article 2 of the Regulations on Several Issues concerning Bail, where a state security authority decides to grant bail, or a people's procuratorate or a people's court decides to grant bail when handling a criminal case transferred from a state security authority, such a decision shall be executed by the state security authority.

When the public security authority executes the decision on bail, the Bail Decision Letter shall be read out to the criminal suspect or defendant granted bail, ask the criminal suspect or defendant to sign or press fingerprints, and at the same time, inform him/her of the legal provisions that he/she shall abide by and legal liability for violation of the relevant provisions.

(4) Rules to Be Observed by the Person Granted Bail During the Period of Bail and Handling of Violations

With regard to the rules to be observed by the person granted bail during the period of bail, Article 71 of the Criminal Procedure Law sets forth the rules in two categories:

The first category contains regulations that all persons granted bail should abide by, including: **a.** not leaving the city or county where he/she resides without the approval of the executing authority; **b.** reporting any change of his/her residence address, employer, or contact information to the executing authority within 24 hours of such change; **c.** appearing before court in a timely manner when summoned; **d.** not interfering in any way with the testimony of witnesses; and **e.** not destroying or forging evidence or making a false confession in collusion.

The other category contains selective provisions according to the situation of the cases. Based on the circumstances of a case, a people's court, a people's procuratorate, and a public security authority may order a bailed criminal suspect or defendant to comply with one or more of the following provisions:

a. not entering particular places; b. not meeting or communicating with particular persons; c. not engaging in particular activities; and d. delivering his/her passport and other international travel credentials and driver's license to the executing authority for preservation.

Where the bailed person has committed a violation of Article 71 of Criminal Procedure Law and the surety fails to perform surety obligations, the surety shall be fined, and if any crime is committed, criminal liability shall be pursued in accordance with the law. Where a bailed criminal suspect or defendant violates any provision, if a bond has been paid, part or all of the bond shall be forfeited, and, based on the actual circumstances, the criminal suspect or defendant shall be ordered to make a statement of repentance, pay a bond or provide a surety again, or be placed under residential confinement or arrested. Where any violation of the bail provisions entails an arrest, the criminal suspect or defendant may be detained first.[①]

(5) Bail Period and Bail Termination

Pursuant to Article 79 of the Criminal Procedure Law, the period of bail granted by a people's court, a people's procuratorate, or a public security authority to a criminal suspect or defendant shall not exceed 12 months. During the period of bail, the investigation, prosecution, and trial of a case shall not be suspended. Bail shall be terminated under two circumstances: first, if it is discovered during the period of bail that the bailed person is a person whose criminal liability should not be investigated; second, the term for bail has expired. In either case, the bail shall be terminated in a timely manner and the bailed person and the entities concerned shall be notified in a timely manner.

3. Residential Confinement

Residential confinement refers to a compulsory measure adopted by a people's court, a people's procuratorate, or a public security authority during criminal proceedings against a criminal suspect or defendant to order him/her not to leave his/her domicile, or if he/she has no fixed domicile, not to leave

---

① Articles 70 and 71 of the Criminal Procedure Law.

the designated domicile without authorization, and to monitor and control the activities of the criminal suspect or defendant.

Residential confinement is mainly adopted under certain specific circumstances where the conditions for arrest are met. It may also be adopted under certain circumstances where the conditions for bail are met. In terms of spiritual substance, residential confinement is an alternative measure to arrest, the main purpose of which is to reduce the rate of detention and is an important manifestation of implementing principle of proportionality in the issue of compulsory measures.

3.1. Application Scope of Residential Supervision

Pursuant to Article 74 of the Criminal Procedure Law, under any of the following circumstances, a people's court, a people's procuratorate, and a public security authority may place a criminal suspect or defendant who meets the conditions for arrest under residential confinement: **a.** The criminal suspect ordefendant suffers a serious illness or cannot take care of himself/herself. **b.** The criminal suspect or defendant is a pregnant woman or a woman who is breastfeeding her own baby. **c.** The criminal suspect or defendant is the sole supporter of a person who cannot take care of himself/herself. **d.** Considering the special circumstances of the case or as needed for handling the case, residential confinement is more appropriate. **e.** The term of custody has expired but the case has not been closed, and residential confinement is necessary. Where a criminal suspect or defendant meets the conditions for bail but is neither able to provide a surety nor able to pay a bond, he/she may be placed under residential confinement.

(1) Decision of Residential Confinement

Where a people's court, a people's procuratorate or a public security authority decides upon residential confinement of a criminal suspect or defendant, the officer handling the case shall prepare an Opinion Letter on Residential Confinement. Upon examination by the person-in-charge of the case-handling department, it shall be submitted to the director of the public security bureau, the chief procurator of the people's procuratorate or the president of the people's court for review and approval. A Residential Confinement Decision Letter and a Notice on Enforcement of Residential Confinement shall be prepared then.

(2) Execution of Residential Confinement

Residential confinement shall be executed by a public security authority. With regard to the residential confinement decided by a people's court and a people's procuratorate, the people's court or the people's procuratorate shall serve the Residential Confinement Decision Letter and a Notice on Enforcement of Residential Confinement upon the public security authority in time, and the public security authority shall execute residential confinement.

When the public security authority executes the decision on residential confinement, the Residential Confinement Decision Letter shall be read out to the criminal suspect or defendant under residential confinement, the criminal suspect or defendant shall be asked to sign or press finger prints thereon, and be informed of the legal provisions that he/she shall abide by and legal liability for violation of the relevant provisions.

3.2. Premise of Residential Confinement

Pursuant to Article 75 of the Criminal Procedure Law, residential confinement shall be executed at the residence of a criminal suspect or defendant; or may be executed at a designated residence if the criminal suspect or defendant has no fixed residence. Where the execution of residential confinement at the residence of a criminal suspect or defendant suspected of compromising state security or terrorist activities may obstruct the criminal investigation, it may be executed at a designated residence with the approval of the public security authority at the next higher level. However, residential confinement may not be executed at a place of custody or a place specially used for handling cases.

As can be seen from the above provisions, the Criminal Procedure Law has very clear and strict provisions on the premise of residential confinement. In general, residential confinement can only be carried out in his/her residence. The only reason for not carrying out residential confinement at his/her residence is that he/she has no fixed residence, and obstruction of investigation cannot be used as a ground for changing the location of residential confinement. For two specific types of cases, during the investigation stage, only with the approval of the public security authority at the next higher level, may residential confinement be conducted at the designated residence on the ground of obstructing the investigation.

In order to prevent the abuse of residential confinement at the designated residence in judicial practice and prevent it from evolving into disguised detention, Article 75 of the Criminal Procedure Law specifically stipulates the restriction mechanism, the main contents of which are as follows: **a.** Where a criminal suspect or defendant under residential confinement has a defender, the provisions of Article 34 of this Law shall apply. **b.** If residential confinement is executed at a designated residence, the family of the person under residential confinement shall be notified within 24 hours after residential confinement is executed, unless such notification is impossible. **c.** People's procuratorates shall oversee the legality of decisions and execution of residential confinement at a designated residence. In addition, relevant judicial interpretations also stipulate that a person under residential confinement shall not be required to pay expenses if residential confinement is executed at a designated residence.

Considering greater restrictions are imposed on the personal freedom of a person under residential confinement at a designated residence, Article 76 of the Criminal Procedure Law specifically stipulates that: The term of residential confinement at a designated residence shall decrease the term of punishment. For a sentence of supervision without incarceration, one day of residential confinement equals one day of the term of punishment; for a sentence of limited incarceration or fixed-term imprisonment, two days of residential confinement equals one day of the term of punishment.

3.3. Rules to Be Observed by the Person Under Residential Confinement and Handling of Violations

Pursuant to Article 77 of the Criminal Procedure Law, a criminal suspect or defendant under residential confinement shall comply with the following provisions: **a.** not leaving the residence where residential confinement is executed without the approval of the executing authority; **b.** not meeting or communicating with others without the approval of the executing authority; **c.** appearing before court in a timely manner when summoned; **d.** not interfering in any way with the testimony of witnesses; **e.** not destroying or forging evidence or making a false confession in collusion; and **f.** delivering his or her passport and other international travel credentials and driver's license to the executing authority for preservation.

In order to strictly supervise the persons under residential confinement in complying with the above provisions, in addition to methods for regular monitoring, Article 78 of the Criminal Procedure Law specifically stipulates that: "Executing authorities may oversee criminal suspects or defendants under residential confinement regarding their compliance with residential confinement provisions by electronic monitoring, random inspection, and other surveillance means; and during the period of criminal investigation, may monitor the communications of criminal suspects under residential confinement."

Pursuant to Article 77 of the Criminal Procedure Law, a criminal suspect or defendant under residential confinement who seriously violates any provision of the preceding paragraph may be arrested; and if arrest is necessary, the criminal suspect or defendant may be detained first.

3.4. Period of Residential Confinement and Termination

Pursuant to Article 79 of the Criminal Procedure Law, the period of residential confinement shall not exceed 6 months. During the period of bail or residential confinement, the investigation, prosecution, and trial of a case shall not be suspended. Residential confinement shall be terminated under two circumstances: first, if it is discovered during the period of residential confinement that the person under residential confinement is a person whose criminal liability should not be investigated; second, the term for residential confinement has expired. In either case, the residential confinement shall be terminated in a timely manner and the person under residential confinement and the entities concerned shall be notified in a timely manner.

4. Detention

Detention means a compulsory measure whereby, in the process of investigation, the public security authorities or people's procuratorates temporarily deprive the personal freedom of persons caught in acts of committing crimes or major criminal suspects according to law under emergency circumstances. The term "detention" as used herein specially refers to criminal detention.

In China's legal system, in addition to criminal detention, there are administrative detention and judicial detention. Administrative detention is an administrative penalty imposed on specific offenders in accordance with the Public Security Administration Punishments Law. Judicial detention is a disciplinary measure granted against a participant in the course of action, including both civil and criminal, for serious violations of order of the court. The three types of detention are different in legal nature, the authorities using the detention, the object and the conditions of application and the term of application, therefore cannot be mixed up.

4.1. Characteristics of Detention

First, the authorities which have the power to decide on detention are generally public security authorities. In cases investigated by a people's procuratorate, the people's procuratorate shall also have the power to decide to detain a criminal suspect who attempts to commit suicide or escape or is at large after committing a crime, or a criminal suspect who may possibly destroy or forge evidence or make a false confession in collusion; and a people's court has no power to decide on detention. All the detentions, whether decided by the public security authorities or the people's procuratorates, shall be executed by the public security authorities.

Second, detention is a compulsory measure used in emergency situations. Detention may be taken only in emergency situations where immediate deprivation of the personal freedom of persons caught in acts of committing crimes or major criminal suspects is necessary in the absence of sufficient time to complete the formalities for arrest; If there is no emergency and the public security authorities or the people's procuratorates have time to handle the formalities for arrest, there is no need to detain them first.

Third, detention is a temporary measure. As a result, the duration of detention is comparatively short, and as the litigation proceedings progress, detention must be changed, either to arrest, or to bail or residential confinement, or to the release of the detainee.

4.2. Conditions of Detention

Criminal detention must meet two conditions. First, the detainee is a person who is committing a crime or a major criminal suspect. Second, it falls within one of the statutory emergency situations. Pursuant to Article 82 of the Criminal Procedure Law: Under any of the following circumstances, a public security authority may first detain a person who is committing a crime or is a major criminal suspect: **a.** The person is preparing to commit a crime, is committing a crime, or is discovered immediately after committing a crime. **b.** A victim or an eyewitness identifies the person as the one committing the crime. **c.** Criminal evidence is discovered from the person's body or residence. **d.** The person attempts to commit suicide or escape after committing a crime or is fugitive. **e.** The person may destroy or forge evidence or make a false confession in collusion. **f.** The identity of the person is unknown because the person refuses to disclose his/her true name and residence address. **g.** The person is strongly suspected of committing crimes from place to place, repeatedly, or in a gang. During the investigation of the cases directly accepted by the people's procuratorates, the people's procuratorates shall have the power to decide to detain the criminal suspects under the circumstances as mentioned in the preceding Items d. and e.

4.3. Procedures in Detention

(1) Decision of Detention

If a public security authority needs to detain a person who is committing a crime or a major criminal suspect, the handling entity shall fill out a Report on Application for Detention, which shall be approved by the chief of a public security authority above the county level. A Detention Order shall be issued if approved, and the entity that requested for approval of the detention shall take charge of the implementation thereof. With respect to a case which a people's procuratorate decides to detain, the case handlers shall put forward their opinions and the chief procurator shall make a decision after examination by the person-in-charge of the case-handling department. For any case for which a detention decision is made, the people's procuratorate shall deliver the written detention decision to the relevant public security authority, and that public security authority shall be responsible for executing the detention decision.

It should be noted that, when a public security authority or a people's procuratorate decides to detain the following persons with special status, it needs to report to the relevant departments for approval or filing: **a.** If a person decided to be detained is a representative to a people's congress at or above the county level, the organ which has decided to detain shall immediately report the matter to the presidium or the standing committee of the people's congress that he/she belongs to. Detention can only be carried out after approval by the presidium or the standing committee of that people's congress. **b.** When deciding to apply criminal detention to foreigners or stateless persons who do not enjoy diplomatic privileges and immunities, the application shall be reported to the relevant department for examination and approval and, at the same time, the opinions of the foreign affairs office of the province, municipality directly under the Central Government or autonomous region and the competent department of foreigners shall be solicited. **c.** In the case of criminal detention of a foreign student, the case shall be reported to the Ministry of Public Security or the Ministry of State Security for examination and approval after the opinions of the local foreign affairs offices and higher education administrative departments (bureaus) have been solicited.

(2) Execution of Detention

Public security authorities shall be responsible for the execution of detention. The following procedures shall be complied with during the execution of detention:

First, when a detention is executed, the Detention Order shall be shown to the detainee. Detention shall be announced and the detainee shall be ordered to sign or press his/her fingerprint on the Detention Order. In case of resistance during the execution of detention, coercive measures such as weapons and restraint implements may be used, but such measures shall be appropriately utilized to the necessary extent to constrain him/her only.

Second, where a public security authority executes the detention or arrest of a person in a different place, it shall notify the public security authority at the place of residence of the detainee or arrestee, and the public security authority at the place of residence of the detainee or arrestee shall provide assistance.[①]

Third, after a person is detained, the detainee shall be immediately transferred to a jail for custody, no later than 24 hours thereafter.

[①] Article 83 of the Criminal Procedure Law.

Fourth, the family of a detainee shall be notified within 24 hours after detention, unless such notification is impossible or such notification may obstruct the criminal investigation in a case regarding compromising state security or terrorist activities. However, once such a situation disappears, the family of the detainee shall be immediately notified.① In addition, in accordance with Article 37 of the Lawyers Law, where a lawyer is suspected of a crime during participation in a legal proceeding, the criminal investigation authority shall notify the law firm employing the lawyer or the bar association to which the lawyer belongs in a timely manner; and where a lawyer is legally detained or arrested, the criminal investigation authority shall notify the lawyer's family in accordance with the provisions of the Criminal Procedure Law.

Fifth, a public security authority shall interrogate a detainee within 24 hours after detention. If it is discovered that the person should not have been detained, the person must be immediately released, and a certificate of release shall be issued to the person.②

Sixth, deeming that a detainee needs to be arrested, a public security authority shall, within three days after detention, file request for approval of arrest with the people's procuratorate for examination and approval. Under special circumstances, the time limit for filing such a request may be extended for one to four days. For a person strongly suspected of committing crimes from place to place, repeatedly, or in a gang, the time limit for filing request for approval of arrest for examination and approval may be extended to 30 days.③

Seventh, if a people's procuratorate deems it necessary to arrest a detainee in a case directly accepted by the people's procuratorate, it shall make a decision within 14 days after detention. Under special circumstances, the time limit for deciding an arrest may be extended for one to three days. If arrest is not necessary, the detainee shall be released immediately; or if further investigation is necessary and the detainee meets the conditions for bail or residential confinement, the detainee shall be bailed or placed under residential confinement in accordance with the law.④

---

① Article 85 of the Criminal Procedure Law.
② Article 86 of the Criminal Procedure Law.
③ Article 91 of the Criminal Procedure Law.
④ Article 167 of the Criminal Procedure Law.

5. Arrest

Arrest refers to a compulsory measure taken by a public security authority, a people's procuratorate, or a people's court to deprive personal freedom of the criminal suspect or defendant, and take him/her into custody in accordance with the law in order to prevent him/her from escaping investigation, prosecution, or trial, obstructing criminal proceedings or posing danger to society.

Arrest is the most severe compulsory measures in criminal proceedings. It not only deprives the criminal suspects and defendants of their personal freedom, but also keeps them in custody until the people's court's verdict comes into effect, unless it is found that they should not be investigated for criminal liability or the conditions for changing compulsory measures are met. The correct and timely use of arrest measures may play an important role in cracking down on crimes and maintaining social order, effectively prevent criminal suspects or defendants from false confession in collusion, destroying or forging evidence, committing suicide, escaping or continuing to commit a crime, and is conducive to comprehensively collecting evidence, ascertaining the facts of the case, confirming crimes, and ensuring the smooth progress of investigation, prosecutions and trials. So arrest is an important tool in the fight against crimes. But if arrest is used improperly, wrongly or abusively, the innocent will be harmed, the personal rights and the democratic rights of citizens will be infringed upon, the dignity and authority of the socialist legal system will be undermined, and the prestige of the public security and judicial organs will be harmed. Therefore, we must ensure that there be no unjustness and connivance. Those who are innocent and wrongly arrested should be compensated as victims in accordance with the provisions of the State Compensation Law.

5.1. Authority of Arrest

In accordance with Article 37 of the Constitution and Article 80 of the Criminal Procedure Law, the arrest of a criminal suspect or defendant must be subject to the approval of a people's procuratorate or a decision of a people's court and be executed by a public security authority. In China's criminal proceedings, the power to approve or decide on arrest is separated from the power to execute arrest.

5.2. Conditions of Arrest

There are three conditions for arrest: first, the condition of evidence; second, the condition of criminal liability; and third, the condition of social danger. The three conditions for arrest of criminal suspects and defendants are interrelated and indispensable. Only when the criminal suspects and defendants meet these three conditions can they be arrested.

(1) Condition of Evidence

The condition of evidence for arrest is that there is evidence demonstrating the facts of a crime, which should meet all of the following circumstances: **a.** there is evidence that proves facts of a crime exist; **b.** there is evidence that proves facts of a crime are committed by the suspect; **c.** the evidence demonstrating the suspect has committed a crime that has been verified.

(2) Condition of Criminal Liability

The condition of criminal liability for arrest is that punishment of fixed-term imprisonment or above may be imposed. That is, according to the facts of the case proved by evidence, with reference to the relevant provisions of the Criminal Law, the crime committed shall subject him/her to a punishment of at least fixed-term imprisonment or above. If it is only possible to impose supervision without incarceration, limited incarceration, or an accessory penalty only, and it is impossible to impose a punishment of fixed-term imprisonment or above, arrest shall not be adopted. In judicial practice, for those who may be sentenced to probation for fixed-term imprisonment, arrest is generally also not adopted.

(3) Condition of Social Danger

The condition of social danger of arrest is methods such as bail or residential confinement are not enough to prevent the occurrence of social danger, and there is a need to arrest. Based on the determination of social danger of criminal suspects and defendants, Article 81 of the Criminal

Procedure Law prescribes several circumstances under which arrest shall be executed:

First, where there is evidence to prove the facts of a crime and a criminal suspect or defendant may be sentenced to fixed-term imprisonment of 10 years or a heavier punishment, the criminal suspect or defendant shall be arrested.

Second, where there is evidence to prove the facts of a crime and a criminal suspect or defendant who once committed an intentional crime or has not been identified may be sentenced to imprisonment or a heavier punishment, the criminal suspect or defendant shall be arrested.

Third, where there is evidence to prove the facts of a crime and a criminal suspect or defendant may be sentenced to imprisonment or a heavier punishment, if residential confinement is insufficient to prevent any of the following dangers to society, the criminal suspect or defendant shall be arrested: **a.** the criminal suspect or defendant may commit a new crime; **b.** there is an actual danger to state security, public security, or social order; **c.** the criminal suspect or defendant may destroy or forge evidence, interfere with the testimony of a witness, or make a false confession in collusion; **d.** the criminal suspect or defendant may retaliate against a victim, informant, or accuser; or **e.** the criminal suspect or defendant attempts to commit suicide or escape. Where a criminal suspect or defendant waiting for trial on bail or under residential confinement seriously violates the provisions on bail or residential confinement, the criminal suspect or defendant may be arrested.

5.3. Procedures of Arrest

(1) Approval and Decision Procedures of Arrest

The procedures for the people's procuratorate to approve a public security authority's request for arresting the criminal suspect are as follows: when the public security authority deems it necessary to arrest the criminal suspect, the organ that files the case for investigation shall prepare a Letter of Request for Approval of Arrest, which shall, after being signed by the person-in-charge of the public security authority at or above the county level, be transferred along with the case file and evidence to the people's procuratorate at the same level for approval. After the people's procuratorates receive the materials of application for arrest from the public security authority, as a general rule, the case handlers shall read the case files first, then the person-in-charge of the department in charge of the examination and approval of arrest shall examine them and finally the chief procurator shall make the decision. Significant cases shall be submitted to the procuratorial committee for discussion and decision. The procuratorial organ shall, within 7 days after receiving the Letter of Request for Approval of Arrest submitted by the public security authority, make a decision to approve or disapprove the arrest: **a.** It shall approve the arrest and prepare a written decision for approval if the conditions for arrest are met. **b.** It shall disapprove the arrest and prepare a written decision to disapprove the arrest if the conditions for arrest are not met, and state the reasons for disapproval of arrest. If the arrest is not approved, the public security organ shall, upon receiving the people's procuratorate's notice disapproving the arrest, immediately release the criminal suspect in detention. If further investigation is necessary, and if the person meets the conditions for bail or residential confinement, bail or residential confinement shall be executed according to the law. If the public security authority disagrees with the people's procuratorate's decision to disapprove the arrest, it may request a reconsideration by the people's procuratorate. If the public security authority's opinion is rejected, it may request a review by the people's procuratorate at the next higher level. The people's procuratorate at the next higher level shall immediately review the matter, decide whether to modify the original disapproval decision or not, and notify the people's procuratorate at the lower level and the public security authority to execute its decision.

The procedures for a people's procuratorate to decide an arrest are as follows: when the people's procuratorate finds it necessary to take the measure of arrest for a case filed by it for investigation, the investigation department shall first fill in a Form of Examination and Approval of Arrest of Criminal Suspect, which shall be transferred together with the case file and evidence to the department in charge of examination and approval of arrest for examination, and the chief procurator shall make the decision. The arrest of a criminal suspect in a significant, difficult or complicated case shall be submitted to the procuratorial committee for discussion and decision.

The procedures for a people's court to decide an arrest are as follows: when it deems it necessary to arrest the defendant in a case of private prosecution directly accepted by it, the personnel handling the case shall submit the case to the president of the court for decision; the arrest of the defendant in a significant, difficult or complicated case shall be submitted to the judicial committee for discussion and decision. For the defendant who is not arrested when the procuratorial organ initiates a public prosecution case, the people's court may also decide to arrest him/her if it considers that he/she meets the conditions for arrest and therefore should be arrested.

In addition, the arrest of several special types of criminal suspects or defendants shall be subject to the approval of relevant department or be reported to the relevant department for record filing, and the main contents are as follows: **a.** Before the people's procuratorate approves or decides on the arrest of a criminal suspect who is a representative to a people's congress, it shall report the case to the presidium or the standing committee of the relevant people's congress for approval. **b.** For a foreigner or stateless person who is suspected of the crime of compromising state security, or is involved in a case related to political and diplomatic relations between countries, or a case difficult in the application of law, if the criminal suspect is required to be arrested, people's procuratorates at the prefecture or city level or sub-procuratorates shall conduct examination, give an opinion and report to the Supreme People's Procuratorate for examination. After consulting the Ministry of Foreign Affairs, the Supreme People's Procuratorate shall make a decision to approve the arrest. If a foreigner or stateless person is suspected of any other crime, people's procuratorates at the prefecture or city level or sub-procuratorates shall conduct examination, give an opinion and report to the people's procuratorate at the provincial level for examination. The people's procuratorate at the provincial level shall, after consulting the foreign affairs department of the government at the same level, make a decision to approve the arrest and submit the decision to the Supreme People's Procuratorate for record filing. **c.** After a people's procuratorate examines arrest requests in a case of a crime of compromising state security, or a foreign-related case or a case directly accepted by the procuratorial organ for investigation, it shall report the case to the people's procuratorate at the next higher level for record filing after approving the arrest.

(2) Execution Procedures of Arrest

The arrest of criminal suspects or defendants shall all be executed by the public security authorities. Public security authorities shall follow the procedures listed below when executing arrest:

First, there shall be no less than two officers present when enforcing an arrest. When enforcing an arrest, Arrest Order must be presented to the arrestee and arrest shall be announced. The arrestee shall be ordered to sign or press fingerprint, and the time shall be noted thereon. If the arrestee refuses to sign or press fingerprint, such a situation shall be noted on the Arrest Order.

Second, after a person is arrested, the arrestee shall be immediately transferred to a jail for custody.

Third, the family of the arrestee shall be notified within 24 hours after arrest, unless such notification is impossible.①

Fourth, a people's court or a people's procuratorate must interrogate a person arrested on its decision or a public security authority must interrogate a person arrested with the approval of a people's procuratorate within 24 hours after the arrest. If it is discovered that the person should not have been arrested, the person must be immediately released, and a certificate of release shall be issued to the person.②

Fifth, where a public security authority executes detention or arrest of a person in a different place, it shall notify the public security authority at the place of residence of the detainee or arrestee, and the public security authority at the place of residence of the detainee or arrestee shall provide assistance.③

(3) The People's Procuratorate's Supervision on Arrest

Where, during the examination and approval of an arrest, a people's procuratorate discovers any illegal investigation of a public security authority, it shall notify the public security authority to make correction, and the public security authority shall notify the people's procuratorate regarding correction.

After arresting a criminal suspect or defendant, a people's procuratorate shall continue to examine the necessity of custody. If custody is no longer

---

① Article 93 of the Criminal Procedure Law.
② Article 94 of the Criminal Procedure Law.
③ Article 83 of the Criminal Procedure Law.

necessary, it shall suggest a release of the arrestee or modification of the compulsory measure for the arrestee. The relevant authority shall notify the people's procuratorate of the handling result within 10 days.

A public security authority which releases an arrestee or replaces arrest with another compulsory measure shall notify the people's procuratorate originally approving the arrest.[1]

---

[1] Articles 95, 96 and 100 of the Criminal Procedure Law.

CHAPTER FIVE

PRE-TRIAL PHASE

Before the final judgment is made, criminal proceedings can be roughly divided into two stages: pre-trial and trial. The pre-trial stage includes specific stages such as case filing, investigation, and prosecution.

1. Case Filing

1.1. Concept and Characteristics of Case Filing

Filing cases in criminal proceedings refers to a kind of litigation activity in which public security and judicial organs decide to conduct investigation or trial as criminal cases after examining the materials of reports, accusations, voluntary surrender and private prosecutors prosecuting according to their respective scope of function and jurisdiction and when they believe there are facts of crime and criminal liabilities shall be charged.

As a symbol of the beginning of criminal proceedings, filing a case is a statutory stage that most criminal cases must go through. At the same time, this stage of litigation has relative independence and specific litigation tasks, in short, to decide whether to initiate criminal proceedings. As an independent stage of litigation, filing a case has the following characteristics:

(1) Filing a Case Is the Commencement of a Criminal Proceeding

Filing a case, investigation, prosecution, trial and enforcement are the five litigation stages established by the Criminal Procedure Law. Only after the completion of the tasks of the previous litigation stage can the next litigation stage proceed. Filing a case is the beginning of the whole criminal litigation activity.

(2) Filing a Case Is a Necessary Procedure in Criminal Proceedings

Because the specific circumstances of criminal cases are different, not every criminal case must go through the above five litigation stages. For example, a case of private prosecution does not need to have the investigation stage, and the victim shall bring a prosecution directly to the people's court; in some other cases, procedures are terminated immediately after the people's procuratorates decide not to initiate prosecution, so there is no need to go through the trial and enforcement stages. However, most criminal cases must go through the stage of filing a case before entering the criminal procedure. Only after filing a case can other stages of litigation be carried out in turn, and can the investigation, prosecution and trial activities of public security and judicial organs have the legal basis and the legal effect. Therefore, filing a case is a necessary procedure in criminal procedure.

(3) Filing a Case Is a Special Activity of a Statutory Organ

Filing criminal cases is a kind of power endowed by the law to the public security and judicial organs, and no other entity or individual has the right to file a case. Moreover, the public security and judicial organs must exercise the right to file a case according to jurisdictional scope under the law.

1.2. Sources of Materials for Filing a Case

Materials for filing a case refer to the materials relating to criminal facts and criminal suspects found by public security and judicial organs or provided by relevant entities, organizations or individuals to public security and judicial organs. They are the factual basis for the public security and judicial organs to review and decide whether to file the case. According to the provisions of China's Criminal Procedure Law and the judicial practice, sources of materials for filing cases mainly include the following:

(1) Facts of a Crime Discovered or Clues to a Crime Obtained by a Public Security Authority or a People's Procuratorate on Its Own

Article 109 of the Criminal Procedure Law stipulates that: A public security authority or a people's procuratorate which discovers any facts of a crime or a criminal suspect shall file a case for criminal investigation according to its jurisdiction.

The public security authority is on the front line of fighting against crimes. It is possible to detect crimes in the course of daily duty and task performance, and to find crime facts and clues in the course of investigation and preliminary examination. These are the sources of materials for the public security authority to file a case. The people's procuratorates, as the public prosecution organs, also undertake the function of investigation. If the existence of crime facts is found during the examination and approval of arrest and examination before prosecution and other activities and it is necessary to investigate criminal liabilities, the people's procuratorates shall also promptly file the cases for investigation within their jurisdiction. Where state security organs, military security departments, prisons, etc. discover crime facts or crime clues in the course of performing their duties, if such facts or clues meet the conditions for filing a case, the case shall also be filed.

(2) Report by Entities and Individuals

Article 110 of the Criminal Procedure Law provides that, any entity or individual which discovers any facts of a crime or a criminal suspect shall have the right and the obligation to report the crime or criminal suspect to a public security authority, a people's procuratorate, or a people's court. Report of a case refers to the act of informing a public security authority, a people's procuratorate or a people's court by an entity or individual or by a victim when discovering the facts of a crime but yet not knowing who the criminal suspect is. Report of a case to the public security and judicial organs is not only a right but also an obligation of all entities and individuals according to laws.

(3) Case Report and Accusation by a Victim

Article 110 of the Criminal Procedure Law provides that, a victim shall have the right to report a crime which infringes upon his/her personal or property rights or accuse a criminal suspect of such a crime to a public security authority, a people's procuratorate, or a people's court. Accusation means that the victims (including private prosecutors and the victims as entities) expose and inform the public security and judicial organs about the facts of the illegal infringement upon their personal and property rights and the relevant information about the criminal suspects, and request the public security and judicial organs to investigate their criminal liabilities according to law. On the one hand, the victim has a strong desire and initiative to expose the crime and punish the crime; on the other hand, in many cases, because the victim has contact with the criminal suspect and can provide more detailed and specific facts about the crime and the criminal suspect, his/her accusation is of great value for the investigation of a crime. Therefore, a victim's case report or accusation is also an important source of materials for filing a case.

Making reports and accusations are the democratic rights of citizens and shall be protected by laws of the State. No entity or individual may, under any pretext, stop, suppress or retaliate against the reporters, accusers or informants. Whoever retaliates against or frames up the reporters, accusers or informants, if the case constitutes a crime, shall be investigated for criminal liabilities according to law.

(4) Voluntary Surrender of Criminals

Voluntary surrender means that after committing a crime, a criminal voluntarily surrenders himself/herself to justice, truthfully confesses his/her crime and accepts the examination and judgment of the public security and judicial organs. The criminal's voluntary surrender is also one of the sources of materials used to file a case. A public security authority, a people's procuratorate or a people's court shall all accept a voluntary surrender made by a criminal. If a case does not fall under its jurisdiction, it shall transfer the case to the competent authority. If the case does not fall under its jurisdiction but calls for emergency measures, it shall take emergency measures before transferring the case to the competent authority. The Criminal Procedure Law takes voluntary surrender as one of the important sources of materials for filing a case, with the intention of encouraging criminals to surrender voluntarily and strive for leniency.

1.3. Conditions for Filing a Case

Conditions for filing a case refer to the basic elements that must be met for filing a case, that is, the statutory conditions that must be met for deciding the establishment of a criminal case and starting criminal prosecution. A case filing must be based on a certain amount of factual materials, but it does not mean that a case must be filed with a certain amount of factual materials. Only when the facts reflected in these materials meet the conditions for case filing can the case be filed in a correct, timely and legal manner.

Article 112 of the Criminal Procedure Law provides that, a people's court, a people's procuratorate, or a public security authority shall, according to its jurisdiction, promptly examine the materials regarding a reported crime or criminal suspect, an accusation, or a voluntary surrender. If it believes that there are any facts of a crime which require criminal investigation, it shall file a case; or, if it believes that there are no facts of a crime or the facts of a crime are obviously minor and require no criminal investigation, it shall not file a case but shall notify the accuser of the reasons for not filing a case. Against such a decision, the accuser may apply for reconsideration. In accordance with this provision, filing a case shall need to meet two conditions simultaneously: first, there are facts of a crime and it is called the factual condition; second, criminal liabilities shall be investigated, and it is called the legal condition.

(1) There Are Facts of a Crime

"There are facts of a crime" means that there are certain criminal acts that endanger the society, containing two aspects: **a.** If a case is filed for investigation into certain act, it must be an act that constitutes a crime in accordance with the Criminal Law. The filing of a case shall only be conducted for criminal acts. If the act is not a criminal act, the case shall not be filed. **b.** There shall be certain factual materials to prove that the criminal facts have actually occurred. Of course, to file a case is only the initial stage of criminal procedure. At this stage, the evidence cannot be required to prove who the suspect is and the aim, motive, means, method, etc. of the crime. However, at this stage, there must be some evidence to prove that the crime has actually happened.

(2) It Is Necessary to Pursue Criminal Liability

This is another condition that must be met for the filing of a case. Only when a crime occurs and it is necessary to pursue the criminal liability of the perpetrator in accordance with the law may it be necessary to file the case.

In accordance with Article 16 of the Criminal Procedure Law, under any of the following circumstances, a person shall not be subject to criminal liability, and if any criminal procedure has been initiated against such a person, the case shall be dismissed, a non-prosecution decision shall be made, the trial shall be terminated, or the person shall be acquitted: **a.** The circumstances of the alleged conduct are obviously minor, causing no serious harm, and the alleged conduct is therefore not deemed a crime. **b.** The time limitation for criminal prosecution has expired. **c.** Exemption of criminal punishment has been granted in a special amnesty decree. **d.** The alleged crime is handled only upon a complaint in accordance with the Criminal Law, but there is no such a complaint or the complaint has been withdrawn. **e.** The criminal suspect or defendant dies. **f.** The person is otherwise exempted by law from criminal liability. Therefore, the case shall not be filed if the criminal offender is under any of the above statutory circumstances in which the criminal liability shall not be pursued for.

Since the cases of private prosecution do not have the investigation stage, if the private prosecutors have brought the cases to the people's courts and the conditions for case filing are met, the people's courts shall accept them and directly initiate the trial procedures. Therefore, the conditions for filing a case of private prosecution shall include the following in addition to the two conditions for filing a case of public prosecution: **a.** The case is within the scope of criminal cases of private prosecution. **b.** The case is under the jurisdiction of that people's court. **c.** The victim of the criminal case files a complaint. **d.** The accused is a definite person, there is specific litigation request and the evidence can prove the criminal facts of the accused.

1.4. Standards for Filling a Case

Article 112 of the Criminal Procedure Law only provides a general condition for case filing. However, in judicial practice, investigation departments often formulate the standards for filling a case for specific crimes to refine and quantify the conditions for filling a case in order to handle specific cases which vary in many ways, for example, the Circular of the Ministry of Public Security on the Standards for Filing Drug Cases, the Provisions of the Supreme People's Procuratorate on the Standards for Filing Cases for Direct Acceptance, Filing and Investigation by the People's Procuratorates (for Trial Implementation), and the Standards for Filing Bribery Cases. As the detailed operation rules for filing cases, the case-filing standard improves the operability and facilitates the case-filing work.

1.5. Procedures for Filling a Case

The procedures for filling a case refer to steps and forms of various litigation activities at the stage of case filing. Pursuant to the provisions of the Criminal

Procedure Law, the case filing procedures include three parts: acceptance, examination and disposal of case filing materials.

(1) Acceptance of Case Filing Materials

Acceptance of case filing materials refers to acceptance by public security authorities, people's procuratorates and people's courts of materials relating to reports, accusation and voluntary surrenders. It is the commencement of the case filing process. When accepting case filing materials, the following points should be noted:

A. Public security authorities, people's procuratorates and people's courts shall all accept reports, accusations and voluntary surrender and shall not refuse or shirk them for any reason. Article 110 of the Criminal Procedure Law provides that, a public security authority, a people's procuratorate, or a people's court shall accept all reports on crimes and criminal suspects and accusations. If a case is not under its jurisdiction, it shall transfer the case to the competent authority and notify the person reporting the crime or criminal suspect or accuser; and, if the case is not under its jurisdiction but emergency measures must be taken, it shall take emergency measures before transferring the case to the competent authority.

B. Reports and accusations may be made orally or in writing for the convenience of the masses. Paragraph 1 of Article 111 of the Criminal Procedure Law provides that, reports on crimes and criminal suspects and accusations may be filed in writing or verbally. The personnel receiving verbal reports and accusations shall prepare transcripts, which shall be signed or sealed by the persons filing such reports and accusations after reading and confirmation.

C. The officer receiving the accusation or a report shall clearly explain to the accuser or the informant the legal responsibility that shall be incurred for making a false accusation or report. Paragraph 2 of Article 111 of the Criminal Procedure Law provides that, the personnel receiving accusations and reports on criminal suspects shall explain to the persons filing accusations and reports the legal liability for filing a false accusation or report. However, an accusation or report which is inconsistent with facts or even wrong shall be strictly distinguished from a false accusation or report, as long as no fabrication of facts or forgery of evidence is involved.

D. Public security and judicial organs shall keep secret for the reporters, accusers and informants, and ensure their safety and that of their close relatives. Paragraph 3 of Article 111 of the Criminal Procedure Law provides that, a public security authority, a people's procuratorate, or a people's court shall ensure the safety of persons reporting crimes and criminal suspects, accusers, and their close relatives. If a person reporting a crime or criminal suspect or an accuser is reluctant to disclose to the public his/her name and report or accusation, such information shall be kept confidential.

(2) Examination of Case Filing Materials

The examination of case filing materials means the activities whereby a public security authority, a people's procuratorate or a people's court verifies the case filing materials found by or accepted by any of them. Examination of materials for filing a case is the central link of the procedure for filing a case, and the key to filing a case correctly and timely. The process of examining materials is to confirm the existence of facts of a crime, and to analyze and assess whether such facts of a crime need to be pursued for criminal liability, according to the conditions for filing a case as prescribed by law.

Through the examination, it shall be ascertained whether or not the incident reflected in the materials is a criminal act; if it is a criminal act, whether or not there is any reliable evidential material to prove it; whether or not it is necessary to pursue for the criminal liability of the violator according to law; and whether there is any circumstance under which no criminal liability shall be pursued. When examining the materials for filing a case, the public security and judicial organs may request the entity or individual making reports and accusations to provide supplementary materials, or request them to provide supplementary explanation, and may also carry out necessary investigation.

(3) Disposal of Case Filing Materials

The disposal of case filing materials means that a public security authority, a people's procuratorate or a people's court makes a decision on whether or not to file a case according to different situations after examining the case filing materials. This is the final result of case filing proceeding.

Article 112 of the Criminal Procedure Law provides that, a people's court, a people's procuratorate, or a public security authority shall, according to its jurisdiction, promptly examine the materials regarding a reported crime or criminal suspect, an accusation, or a voluntary surrender. If it believes that there are some facts of a crime which require criminal investigation, it shall file a case; or, if it believes that there are no facts of a crime or the facts of a crime are obviously minor and require no criminal investigation, it shall not file a case but shall notify the accuser of the reasons for not filing a case. There are two ways to deal with case filing materials: decision of case-filing and decision of no case-filing.

A. Decision of Case-filing and the Legal Formalities to Be Proceeded with. After examining the materials of case filing, if the public security authority deems it necessary to file the case, the handling officer shall fill out the Case-Filing Report Form. Upon approval by the person in charge of the public security authority, such a case shall be transferred to the investigation department for the start of investigation. If a people's procuratorate considers it necessary to file a case after examining the documents on filing a case, it shall prepare a Report on Filing a Case and file the case upon approval of the chief procurator. It shall, within three days after deciding to file a case, submit the Registration Form for Filing a Case, the Report on Proposing to File a Case and the Decision on Filing a Case to the people's procuratorate at the next higher level for filing. As for the cases of private prosecution accepted by the people's court, the personnel of the division for accusation and complaint shall fill in the Form of Examination and Approval of Case Filing first, and upon the examination and approval of the person-in-charge, transfer them to the criminal tribunal for trial.

B. Decision of No Case-filing and the Legal Formalities to Be Proceeded with. If a decision of no case-filing is made, a Decision Letter on No Case-filing shall be prepared, specifying the of sources of case materials, reasons and legal basis for deciding not to file the case and the authority that decides not to file the case, etc. At the same time, the accuser shall be notified of the reasons why the case will not be filed. If the accuser disagrees with the decision, he/she may ask for reconsideration. The reconsideration application filed by the accuser shall be examined and replied in a timely manner.

1.6. Supervision Over Case Filing

If the accuser is not satisfied with the decision of no case-filing, he/she may apply for reconsideration with the authority that has made the decision not to file the case, or request the people's procuratorate to supervise without reconsideration. Article 113 of the Criminal Procedure Law provides that, where a people's procuratorate deems that a public security authority fails to file a case that shall be otherwise filed for criminal investigation, or a victim expresses to a people's procuratorate the opinion that a public security authority fails to file a case that shall be otherwise filed for criminal investigation, the people's procuratorate shall require the public security authority to state the reasons for not filing a case. If the people's procuratorate deems that the reasons for not filing a case provided by the public security authority are unfounded, it shall notify the public security authority to file a case, and, after receiving the notice, the public security authority shall file a case.

2. Investigation

2.1. Investigation Overview

(1) Concept and Characteristics of Investigation

Article 108 of the Criminal Procedure Law provides that, "criminal investigation" means the work of collecting evidence and ascertaining the facts of a case conducted, and the related compulsory measures taken, by public security authorities and people's procuratorates in accordance with the law in handling criminal cases. Investigation has the following characteristics:

First, investigation is the special function and power granted by law to the public security authorities, the people's procuratorates and other authorities or departments with the investigation function.

Second, investigation organs must exercise their power to investigate strictly in accordance with the law. Investigation organs and investigators must conduct investigations in accordance with the legally prescribed procedures and methods. Only in this way can the facts of cases be ascertained in accordance with the law, and crimes be punished accurately and promptly, so as to effectively protect the legitimate rights and interests of citizens from being infringed upon.

Third, investigation activities had statutory contents and methods, i.e. the work of collecting evidence and ascertaining case facts, and relevant compulsory measures. The former refers to the activities of interrogating the criminal suspect, interviewing the witness and the victim, conducting inquest, examining and searching, seizing material evidence and documentary evidence, conducting evaluation and issuing a wanted order as specified in the Criminal Procedure Law; relevant compulsory measures refer to various methods of restricting or depriving personal freedom such as forced appearance, bail, residential confinement, detention and arrest as prescribed in the Criminal Procedure Law.

(2) Investigation Tasks

The investigation tasks could be viewed in two ways.

First, collecting evidence, ascertaining the facts of a crime and locating the criminal suspect. With respect to a criminal case which has been filed, the investigation organ shall, through investigation activities, collect and obtain various kinds of evidence to prove the criminal suspect is guilty or innocent or to prove the crime to be minor or severe. It shall accurately ascertain the nature and time and place of the crime, the motive and purpose of the crime, the means and result of the crime, and other particulars of the crime. During the process of investigation, it may detain a person who is committing a crime or a major criminal suspect first according to law; for any criminal suspect who meets the conditions for arrest shall be arrested according to law; and if a criminal suspect who should be arrested is at large, a wanted order shall be issued and effective measures shall be taken to pursue him/her for arrest and bring him/her to justice.

Second, protecting innocent persons from being investigated for criminal liability, respecting and safeguarding human rights, and safeguarding the litigation rights of criminal suspects and other litigation participants. As tasks in criminal proceedings, "protecting innocent persons from being prosecuted criminally", "respecting and safeguarding human rights" and "safeguarding the defense right and other litigation rights legally enjoyed by criminal suspects and other litigation participants" shall also be implemented at the investigation stage. Therefore, if it is found during the course of investigation that the criminal suspect's criminal liability should not have been investigated, the investigation organ shall dismiss the case, and if the criminal suspect has been detained or arrested, he/she shall be released immediately; it shall inform the criminal suspect of the right to defend himself/herself and the right to appoint a lawyer to defend himself/herself; it shall not extort confessions by torture, or collect evidence by threat, enticement, deceit or any other illegal means, or force any person to commit self-incrimination.

(3) Principles of Investigation

Investigation principles refer to the basic principles that investigation authorities shall abide by in criminal procedures. They are a series of basic codes of conduct that investigators must abide by in criminal litigation activities. The principles of investigation are as follows:

A. The principle of promptness. Investigation work must be prompt and timely, which is decided by the characteristics of investigation work itself. Investigation work is a litigation activity with strong timeliness. Therefore, the investigation organ shall, after receiving the report of a case, immediately organize the investigation force, formulate the investigation plan, take investigation measures in time and collect all kinds of evidence related to the case.

B. The principle of objectivity and comprehensiveness. This principle requires investigators to start from the actual situation of the case, and collect evidence in a down-to-earth manner. It is necessary to collect not only the evidence which can prove that the criminal suspect is guilty or the conduct is severe, but also the evidence which can prove that the criminal suspect is innocent or the conduct is minor.

C. The principle of legality of procedures. Investigation is a serious activity of law enforcement. When conducting investigation activities, investigative organs and investigators must strictly observe the statutory procedures and collect evidence in strict accordance with the Criminal Procedure Law. It is strictly prohibited to extort confessions by torture or to collect evidence by threat, enticement, deceit or other illegal means. Compulsory measures such as arrest and detention shall also be taken in accordance with the statutory conditions and procedures.

2.2. Investigation Activities

Investigation activities shall mean various special investigation activities carried out by investigation authorities in the process of handling cases in accordance with the provisions of laws. Investigation activities in criminal proceedings mainly include the following eleven types.

(1) Interrogation of a Criminal Suspect

The term "interrogation of a criminal suspect" refers to an investigation activity whereby an investigator interrogates a criminal suspect in respect of the facts and other issues relating to the case in words under statutory procedures. The following procedures and requirements shall be followed in the interrogation of a criminal suspect:

A. Requirements on the personnel conducting interrogation. Pursuant to Article 118 of the Criminal Procedure Law, the interrogation of a criminal suspect must be conducted by the investigators of a people's procuratorate or a public security authority. In order to improve the efficiency of interrogation, ensure the quality and safety of interrogation, during interrogation, there must be two or more investigators. The interrogation of criminal suspects in the same case shall be conducted separately.

B. Time and place of interrogation. Articles 118 and 119 of the Criminal Procedure Law provide that, a criminal suspect for whom an arrest or detention is not necessary may be summoned to a designated place in the city or county where the criminal suspect resides or his/her residence for interrogation, but credentials from the people's procuratorate or public security authority shall be produced. A criminal suspect discovered on the scene may be verbally summoned after a work pass is produced, but it shall be noted in the interrogation transcript. After a criminal suspect is transferred to a jail for custody, the investigators shall conduct interrogation of the criminal suspect inside the jail. The duration of interrogation by summons or forced appearance may not exceed twelve hours; or, if it is necessary to detain or arrest a criminal suspect in an extraordinarily significant or complicated case, the duration of interrogation by summons or forced appearance may not exceed twenty-four hours. A criminal suspect who has been detained or arrested shall be interrogated within twenty-four hours after being detained or arrested. If it is found that the criminal suspect should not have been detained or arrested, he must be immediately released.

C. Steps and methods of interrogation. Article 120 of the Criminal Procedure Law provides that, when interrogating a criminal suspect, the investigators shall first ask the criminal suspect whether he/she has committed any criminal act, allow him/her to state the facts of a crime or explain his/her innocence, and then ask him/her questions. The criminal suspect shall truthfully answer the questions of the investigators, but have the right to refuse to answer questions which are irrelevant to the case. The investigators shall, when interrogating a criminal suspect, inform the criminal suspect of his/her procedural rights and the provisions of law on leniency if he/she truthfully confesses to his/her crime as well as acknowledgment of guilt and acceptance of punishment.

D. Provisions on interrogation of special criminal suspects. Article 121 of the Criminal Procedure Law provides that, when a criminal suspect who suffers hearing or speech impairment is interrogated, a person familiar with the sign language for hearing- and speech-impaired persons shall participate in the interrogation, which shall be noted in the transcripts.

E. The production of interrogation transcripts. An interrogation transcript shall be made when a criminal suspect is interrogated. The transcript shall faithfully record the questions, answers and information of other persons on the scene. According to Article 122 of the Criminal Procedure Law, the interrogation transcripts shall be confirmed by a criminal suspect, and, if the criminal suspect is unable to read, the transcripts shall be read out to him/her. If there are any omissions or errors in the transcripts, the criminal suspect may suggest supplements or corrections. After confirming that the transcripts are free from error, the criminal suspect shall sign or seal the transcripts. The investigators shall also sign the transcripts. A criminal suspect shall be permitted to personally write a confession, if he/she so requests. When necessary, the investigators may also require the criminal suspect to personally write a confession.

F. Provisions on audio and video recording of interrogation. Article 123 of the Criminal Procedure Law provides that, when interrogating a criminal suspect, the investigators may keep an audio or visual record of the interrogation process; and, in a case regarding a crime punishable by life imprisonment or the death penalty or any other significant crime, the investigators must keep an audio or visual record of the interrogation process. An audio or visual record shall cover the entire process of interrogation to ensure integrity.

(2) Interviewing a Witness or Victim

The term "interviewing a witness" refers to an investigation activity whereby investigators investigate verbally from a witness under statutory procedures to obtain information about a case. The purpose of interviewing a witness is to obtain testimony which can prove the facts of a case, to find out clues to the case through testimony, to find out the criminal suspect and to ascertain the facts of the case. Interviewing witness is of great significance in discovering and collecting evidence, solving cases and proving crimes. The following procedures and requirements shall be followed in interviewing a witness:

A. Place of interview and the number of people interviewed. Article 124 of the Criminal Procedure Law provides that, the investigators may interview a witness on the crime scene, at the place of the witness's employer or residence, or at a place proposed by the witness, and, when necessary, may notify a witness to provide testimony at the people's procuratorate or public security authority. When interviewing a witness on the crime scene, the investigators shall produce their work passes, and, when interviewing a witness at the place of the witness's employer or residence or a place proposed by the witness, the investigators shall produce the credentials from the people's procuratorate or public security authority. In order to ensure the legality of interviewing a witness, generally no less than two interviewers shall be present.

B. Witnesses shall be interviewed individually. When two or more witnesses need to be interviewed in the same case, the investigators shall interview each witness separately. When a witness is interviewed, there should be no presence of other witnesses, nor should it be allowed to hold a group meeting in which witnesses can discuss and testify in groups, in order to avoid interaction among witnesses.

C. Steps and methods of interviewing a witness. In the interview, the witness should first be asked to make a continuous and detailed account of what he/she knows and the source of the facts stated. Then the witness should be asked questions and provide answers based on his/her account, in combination with the facts to be determined in the case and the relevant circumstances. In order to ensure that the witness can truthfully provide evidence, Article 125 of the Criminal Procedure Law provides that, when a witness is interviewed, the witness shall be informed of the requirement of truthfully providing evidence and testimony and the legal liability for perjury or concealing criminal evidence. Meanwhile, investigators shall also inform the witness of the various litigation rights he/she is entitled to under the law to guarantee the safety of the witness and his/her close relatives.

D. The provisions of interviewing special witnesses. When a witness under the age of 18 is interviewed, his/her legal representative shall be notified to be present. If such notification is impossible, the legal representative is unable to be present, or the legal representative is an accomplice, other adult relatives of the juvenile or a representative from his/her school or entity, the villagers' committee or residents' committee of the place where he/she resides, or a juvenile protection organization may be notified to be present. When a witness who is deaf or mute is interviewed, an interpreter who has a good command of sign language shall be present, and the matter shall be noted in the record. When a person or foreigner who is not familiar with the local language is interviewed, an interpreter shall be hired for him/her.

E. The making of the inquiring record. According to Article 126 of the Criminal Procedure Law, a witness' statement shall be recorded in writing, which shall be presented to the witness for verification or be read out to him/her. If there are omissions or errors in the writing, the witness may make additions or corrections. If a witness acknowledges that the record is correct, he/she shall sign or affix his/her seal to it. The investigators shall also sign the record. If a witness requests to write a testimony by himself/herself, he/she shall be allowed to do so. When necessary, the investigators may also require the witness to write a written testimony.

The term "interviewing a victim" refers to investigation activities conducted by investigators over a person directly harmed by a criminal act in accordance with statutory procedures to investigate the injuries suffered by him/her and the circumstances of the criminal suspect involved in a crime. Procedures for interviewing witnesses are applicable to interviewing victims. However, a victim is a party to criminal proceedings and has different status from other witnesses, therefore, when interviewing, we should not only see that he/she is the object of direct infringement by criminal acts who knows more about facts of a crime and the criminal, but also remind him/her that he/she has an interest in the case.

To the victim's statement, we should not only listen carefully, but also pay attention to the analysis of whether it is reasonable, and whether there is something exaggerated. The privacy of the victims shall be kept confidential. Effective measures shall be taken to ensure the personal safety of a victim.

(3) Inquest and Examination

"Inquest and examination" refers to a kind of investigation which is conducted by the investigators to investigate, examine or inspect the sites, articles, persons and corpses relevant to a crime in order to discover and collect various traces and articles left by criminal activities. Inquest and examination are of the same nature except for different objects. Among them, the object of inquest is the scene, articles and corpses, and the object of examination is the body of a living person. According to the different objects and contents, inquest and examination can be divided into four types, namely, scene investigation, examination of articles, personal examination and postmortem examination.

A. Scene investigation. Scene investigation means an investigation activity which is conducted by the investigators to investigate the place where the crime is committed by the criminal and the site where criminal traces and articles are left. First of all, in such investigation, the scene should be protected. Article 129 of the Criminal Procedure Law provides that, any entity or individual shall have the duty to protect a crime scene and immediately notify a public security authority to send personnel to conduct a crime scene investigation. Second, scene investigation shall be the responsibility of the investigation department of the public security organ at or above the county level. Scene investigation shall be conducted by investigators; when necessary, experts may be assigned or retained to conduct the investigation under the direction of the investigators. Upon receipt of notification, the investigators carrying out the investigation shall immediately rush to the scene of the crime, and shall hold the crime scene inspection warrant. There shall be at least two persons conducting the inspection of the scene of a case by public security organs. Third, in the process of scene investigation, the investigators shall understand the original conditions of the scene from the discoverer, reporter and protector of the scene, and then demarcate the scope of investigation, which shall be carried out from outside to inside, from key points to general, and shall be carried out step by step in a planned way. They shall carefully observe the features, locations and states of each article and trace at the scene, analyze their mutual relations, and employ relevant technical means to find, extract and preserve evidence. Any victim at the scene of the crime shall be timely sent to a nearby medical institution for treatment; the corpse should be examined as necessary first, and if needed, then the forensic doctor should make an autopsy and examination according to law. At the scene of computer crime, computer service shall be stopped immediately, and measures should be taken to safeguard the computer and related equipment. Fourth, during investigating of the scene, it is necessary to take photos and make drawings of the scene and make written records. The written records of scene investigation shall include the following contents: time of investigation, location of the site, and relationship with its surroundings, changes and damages to articles at the site, various traces, items, their locations and features left by the criminal suspect on the site, extracted traces, physical evidence, and biological samples, etc. and shall attach photos thereto. The scene of a major case shall be videotaped. The investigators, other people participating in the investigation and eyewitnesses shall sign and give a clear indication of the time on the record of the scene investigation.

B. Inspection of articles. Inspection of articles refers to a kind of investigation activity in which investigators examine and verify the collected articles and their traces to determine whether they have any connection with the case. When inspecting the articles, investigators should carefully examine the characteristics of the articles, pay attention to the relationship between the articles and the surroundings if the articles are on the scene, and analyze the changes of the characteristics and traces of the articles. Through analysis and research, investigators should determine whether and how the articles and traces are related to the facts of the case. If the investigators are unable to judge the characteristics of the articles, they shall designate or retain persons with special knowledge to make an evaluation. When inspecting the articles, written records shall be made, in which the inspection process, features of articles and their traces shall be recorded in detail. The written records of inspection shall be signed or sealed by investigators, other personnel participating in the inspection and eyewitnesses, and the time shall be specified.

C. Physical examination. Physical examination refers to the investigation activities of examining and checking the body of a victim or criminal suspect, extracting fingerprint information, and collecting blood, urine and other biological samples in order to determine some characteristics, injury or physiological condition of the victim or criminal suspect. A physical examination is a special examination of the body of a living person. In accordance with Articles 132 and 133 of the Criminal Procedure Law, the personal examination of a victim or criminal suspect must be conducted by investigators. When necessary, forensic doctors or doctors may also be engaged under the supervision of investigators to conduct such an examination in strict accordance with law. A person may not commit any act that insults the personality or other lawful rights and interests of the victim or criminal suspect. Where a criminal suspect refuses to be examined, the investigators may conduct a compulsory examination if deeming it necessary. However, a physical examination of the victim shall be conducted with the consent of the victim, and a compulsory examination is not allowed. The examination of the body of a female shall be conducted by female personnel or doctors. Transcripts of a crime scene investigation or examination shall be prepared. It shall be signed or sealed by the investigators and the forensic doctor or doctor who conducts the examination.

D. Postmortem examination. Postmortem examination refers to an investigation activity in which examination or autopsy of the corpse of an abnormally dead person is conducted by a forensic doctor or doctor under the direction of investigators. The purpose of postmortem examination is to determine the time and cause of death, the means and methods of death, and to provide a basis for ascertaining case facts and the criminal. Pursuant to Article 131 of the Criminal Procedure Law, where the cause of death of a person is unknown, a public security authority shall have the authority to decide an autopsy but shall notify the family members of the deceased to be present. The postmortem examination shall be presided over by the investigators and conducted by a forensic doctor or doctor. The information on the postmortem examination shall be recorded in detail in written transcripts, and shall be signed or sealed by the investigators and the forensic doctors or doctors.

(4) Investigative Reenactment

The term "investigative reenactment" refers to a kind of investigation activity that is conducted to repeat or experiment a case-related event or fact under the original conditions so as to determine whether or how it can occur under suchcertain conditions. The following procedures and requirements shall be followed in conducting investigative reenactments:

First, investigative reenactments shall be subject to approval by the chief of the public security organ at or above the county level, and shall be conducted by the investigators. During investigative reenactments, witnesses shall be invited to be present, and if certain expertise is needed, relevant professionals shall be invited to participate in such experiments. When necessary, the criminal suspect, victim or witness may also be required to participate in the investigation. When conducting investigative reenactments, a public security organ may request through consultation the people's procuratorate to send procurators to participate.

Second, investigative reenactments may be conducted during scene inspections or independently. Before conducting an investigative reenactment, an investigative reenactment plan shall be prepared generally, specifying the purpose of the experiment, the time and place of the experiment, the tools and articles of the experiment, the sequence and method of the experiment, and the participants, etc.

Third, the conditions of the investigative reenactment should be the same or similar to the original conditions, and the experiment should be repeated for the same situation as much as possible to ensure the accuracy of the investigation experiment.

Fourth, article 135 of the Criminal Procedure Law provides that, in investigative reenactments, any conduct that suffices to cause any danger, insult anyone, or corrupt public morals shall be prohibited.

Fifth, transcripts shall be made for an investigative reenactment, in which the purpose, time, place, conditions, process and results of the experiment shall be clearly stated. Such transcripts shall be signed by the investigators conducting the experiment, other participants and witnesses. The photos and drawings of an investigative reenactment shall be attached to the investigative reenactment transcripts. When necessary, audio or video recording of the investigative reenactment process shall be made.

(5) Search

"Search" refers to an activity of investigation in which investigators search and inspect the body, belongings and residence of a criminal suspect or anyone who might be hiding a criminal or criminal evidence, as well as other relevant places. Search is a compulsory investigation measure and an important means by which investigation authorities fight against crimes.

Search is directly related to the freedom of citizens and the right of inviolability of their homes. The Constitution of our country clearly stipulates: unlawful search of the person of citizens or a citizen's residence is prohibited. Therefore, searches must be conducted strictly in accordance with legal procedures.

First, a search may only be conducted by the investigators of a public security organ or a people's procuratorate. No other organ, entity or individual shall have the right to search the person or residence of a citizen. The object of a search may be the criminal suspect or the other person who may conceal a criminal or criminal evidence. A search may be made against the person, or against the residence or belongings of the person searched and other relevant places. The purpose of a search is to discover and collect evidence regarding a crime and to track down a concealed criminal suspect. A search measure may not be misused for any other purpose.

Second, when conducting a search, a search warrant must be shown to the person being searched. Otherwise, the person being searched has the right to refuse to search. A search warrant of a public security organ shall be signed and issued by the chief of the public security organ at or above the county level. A search warrant of a people's procuratorate shall be signed and issued by the chief procurator. However, Article 138 of the Criminal Procedure Law provides that as to an investigator, "when an arrest or detention is conducted, a search may be conducted without a search warrant in case of emergency". In investigation practices, emergencies as mentioned herein refer to: persons carrying weapons for committing violent criminal acts or suicide; persons likely to conceal explosives, deadly poisons and other dangerous substances; persons likely to destroy or transfer criminal evidence; and persons likely to conceal other criminal suspects. In these emergencies, there was no time to process the examination and approval of searches, so searches are permitted with detention and arrest warrants.

Third, during a search, the person to be searched or his/her family members, neighbors or other eyewitnesses shall be present at the scene.

Fourth, search of body of a female shall be conducted by female personnel. During a search, the property of the person searched shall not be damaged without reason. No personal private life discovered in a search which is irrelevant to the case may be divulged.

Fifth, a transcript shall be made of the circumstances of a search, and it shall be signed or sealed by the investigators and the person searched or his/her family members, neighbors or other eyewitnesses. If the person searched or his/her family member is fugitive or refuses to sign or seal the transcript, this shall be noted in the transcript.

(6) Seizure and Impoundment

"Seizure and impoundment" refers to a type of investigation activity that investigative organs forcibly seize, detain and withhold the property and documents related to a case. In investigation practice, "seizure" is often aimed at real estate, while "impoundment" is often aimed at movables. Article 141 of the Criminal Procedure Law provides that, all objects and documents discovered during criminal investigation that may be used to prove the guilt or innocence of a criminal suspect shall be seized or impounded; and those irrelevant to a case may not be seized or impounded. Seizure and impoundment have a direct bearing on citizens' property, freedom of communication and other rights, and therefore must be carried out in strict accordance with legal procedures. The details are as follows:

Seizure and impoundment shall be subject to the approval of the responsible person of the public security organ or investigation department, and a written decision shall be made. Where it is necessary to seize land, houses and other real estate, or special movable property including ships, aircraft and other large machinery, equipment unsuitable for movement during the process of investigation, approval by the chief of the public security organ at or above the county level shall be obtained, and a written decision for seizure shall be issued; and where it is necessary to impound any property or document, the approval of the chief of the investigation department of the public security organ shall be obtained, and a written decision on impoundment shall be prepared. Where it is necessary to impound any property or document during scene investigation or search, it shall be determined by the scene commanders; however, where the value of property or documents to be impounded is relatively high or may seriously affect the normal production and operation, approval by the chief of the public security organ at or above the county level shall be obtained, and a written decision on impoundment shall be prepared.

There shall be at least two investigators involved in the implementation of seizure or impoundment, and the investigators shall present a written decision for seizure or impoundment. When seizure or impoundment is carried out, the investigators may order the holder to take the initiative to hand over the property and documents that should be seized or impounded; if the holder refuses to hand over, the investigators may compulsorily seize or impound the property and documents.

The investigators shall go through seizure and impoundment formalities in accordance with the law. The investigators shall, in conjunction with the eyewitnesses and the holder of the seized or impounded property and documents, make a detailed check of the property and documents seized or impounded, and make a list of the property and documents seized or impounded at the scene, which shall be signed by the investigators, the holder and the eyewitnesses; where it is impossible to determine the property or documents of the holder, or the holder refuses to sign, the investigators shall indicate the situation in the list. Where such valuables as cultural relics, gold and silver, jewels and precious calligraphy and paintings are impounded in accordance with the law, photos or videos shall be taken, and the forensic identification and evaluation and price assessment shall be made in a timely manner.

Impoundment of the mail and telegrams shall be performed strictly according to the law. Article 143 of the Criminal Procedure Law provides that: "Deeming it necessary to impound the mail and telegrams of a criminal suspect, with the approval of a public security authority or a people's procuratorate, the investigators may notify the post and telecommunications authority to check and deliver the relevant mail and telegrams for impoundment." When it is no longer necessary to impound the mail or telegram, upon the approval of the chief of the investigation organ at or above the county level, a notice on releasing the impoundment of the mail or telegram shall be made, and the post and telecommunications department or network service provider shall be notified immediately to implement the notice. If any property, document, mail, e-mail or telegram that has been seized or impounded is found to be irrelevant to the case upon investigation, the seizure and impoundment shall be released within three days and the property, document, mail, e-mail or telegram shall be returned to the original owner or the original post and telecommunication department or the network service provider.

Custody and disposal of physical evidence and documentary evidence after seizure and impoundment. The investigation organ shall take good care of the seized or impounded property (including the fruits of the property) and documents for examination. No entity or individual may use, replace, damage or dispose by itself.

Transcripts of seizure and impoundment shall be made. Transcripts shall be made of the circumstances of seizure and impoundment, which shall be signed by the investigators, the holder and the eyewitnesses. If it is impossible to determine the holder or the holder refuses to sign, the investigators shall indicate the situation in the transcript.

(7) Inquiry and Freezing

The term "inquiry and freezing" refers to an investigation activity whereby the investigation organ, in light of the needs of criminal investigation, make inquires on the criminal suspect's deposits, remittances, bonds, stocks, fund shares, and other property with the financial institutions, securities companies, post and telecommunications organs or enterprises according to law, and freezing the suspect's property when necessary. The procedures for inquiry and freezing are as follows:

A. Approval and execution of inquiry and freezing. Any inquiry or freezing of deposits or remittance or other property of a criminal suspect with financial institutions or other entities shall be subject to approval by the chief of the public security authority at or above the county level, a notice on assistance in inquiry or freezing of property shall be issued, and the financial institutions or other entities shall be notified to implement.

B. No repeated freezing. If the deposits, remittances or other property of a criminal suspect have been frozen, they shall not be frozen for a second time, but may be frozen in a waiting order. No matter for what reason the deposits, remittances or other property of a criminal suspect are frozen or which authority takes such measures, the investigation organ shall not take freezing measures again. Although the investigating organs shall not freeze repeatedly, they are eligible to require such entities as the financial institutions to notify the investigating organs prior to the lifting of freezing, so that the investigating organs can wait in line and take freezing measures immediately when freezing is lifted.

C. Term of freezing. A freezing of deposits, remittances and other property shall be valid for six months, and of bonds, stocks, fund shares and other securities shall be valid for two years. If the term needs to be extended due to special reasons, the investigation organ shall go through the formalities for continuing the freezing before the expiration of the term of freezing. If the approval procedure for continuing freezing has not gone through within the time limit, the freezing shall be regarded as being lifted automatically.

D. The sale of frozen property. The investigation organ shall inform the parties or their legal representatives or agents of the right to apply for the sale of the frozen bonds, stocks, fund shares and other property. If a right holder files a written application for selling the frozen bonds, stocks, fund shares and other property, which does not damage the interests of the State, the victim and other right holders, nor does it affect the normal litigation proceeding, and the validity period of the frozen bills of exchange, promissory notes or cheques is about to expire, upon approval by the chief of the investigation organ at or above the county level, they may be sold or realized according to law, and the proceeds therefrom shall continue to be frozen.

E. Termination of the freezing measure. Article 145 of the Criminal Procedure Law provides that, where the seized or impounded objects, documents, mail, or telegrams or the frozen deposits, remittances, bonds, stocks, fund shares, and other property which proved to be irrelevant to a case after investigation, the seizure, impoundment, or freezing measure shall be terminated within three days, and the above property shall be returned.

(8) Forensic Identification and Evaluation

"Forensic identification and evaluation" means an investigation activity that is conducted by the qualified persons designated or appointed by an investigation organ to make identification and evaluation over some specialized issues involved in a case and give expert opinions.

In the practice of investigation, the scope of application offorensic identification and evaluation is very wide, all the case-related articles, documents, traces, people, corpses, can be evaluated. The forensic identification and evaluation commonly used by investigation organs include medicolegal evaluation, judicial psychiatry appraisal, toxicity evaluation, criminal scientific and technological evaluation, accounting evaluation and general technology evaluation, etc. The procedures and requirements for the forensic identification and evaluation are as follows:

There are two ways to select the expert: one is to assign, that is, the investigation organ assigns a professional personnel who has the forensic identification and evaluation qualification in its internal criminal technological evaluation department to evaluate; the other is to appoint, which is to appoint a professional personnel from other departments to evaluate. An expert appointed or engaged shall be a person who has certain special knowledge, has no interest in the case or any of the parties to the case, and can ensure the objectivity and impartiality of the forensic identification and evaluation.

The investigation organ shall provide necessary conditions for the expert to conduct forensic identification and evaluation, timely deliver to original materials of the expert such as the relevant materials for forensic identification and evaluation and comparative samples, introduce the information relating to the forensic identification and evaluation and unambiguously put forward the questions to be solved through forensic identification and evaluation, but shall not imply or force the expert to give certain forensic identification and evaluation opinions.

When conducting a forensic identification and evaluation, the expert shall abide by the professional ethics and adhere to the principle of seeking truth from facts. An expert who intentionally makes a false forensic identification and evaluation shall assume legal liability.

After completion of identification or evaluation, the expert shall prepare a written expert opinion and affix his/her signature to it. An expert opinion shall provide clear answers to the questions raised by the investigators, and state the scientific or technical basis thereof. In practice, an expert opinion is generally prepared in the form of a forensic identification and evaluation report.

The investigators shall examine the expert opinions of the experts. In case of any doubt, they may require the experts to make supplementary forensic identification and evaluation. When necessary, they may designate or appoint other experts to conduct forensic identification and evaluation again. Pursuant to Article 148 of the Criminal Procedure Law, the criminal investigation authority shall inform a criminal suspect and a victim of the expert opinion to be used as evidence. Upon application of the criminal suspect or victim, a supplementary identification or evaluation or a re-identification or re-evaluation may be conducted to protect the legitimate rights and interests of criminal suspects and victims.

(9) Identification

"Identification" means the investigation activity whereby the victims, witnesses or criminal suspects, with the instruction of the investigators, identifie and confirm the articles, documents, corpses, places or the criminal suspects that are relevant to the crimes.

In accordance with the Provisions on the Procedures for Handling Criminal Cases by Public Security Authorities and the Rules of Criminal Procedure for People's Procuratorates, identification shall meet the following procedures and requirements:

Identification shall be presided over by the investigators, and there shall be at least two investigators presiding over the identification. In order to ensure the objectivity and legality of the identification, the witness shall be invited to participate in the identification activities.

Prior to the identification, the investigators shall inquire of the identifier in detail about the specific characteristics of the object identified, and prohibit the identifier from seeing the object identified. At the same time, the identifier shall be informed of the legal liability to assume for intentional false identification.

When several identifiers identify the same object, each identifier shall do the identification independently, so as to prevent the identifiers from influencing each other and making false identification.

In identification, the object to be identified shall be mixed up with other objects with similar features and no hint shall be given to the person identifying the object. When identifying the criminal suspect, the number of persons to be identified shall be no less than seven for public security organs and between five to ten for procuratorial organs. When identifying the photos of the criminal suspect, the number of photos shall be no less than ten for public security organs and between five to ten for procuratorial organs. When identifying the articles, the number of mixed articles of the same kind shall be no less than five, and the photos shall be no less than five. However, if certain objects are to be identified, such as places and corpses, or the identifiers can accurately describe the unique characteristics of the articles, the number of objects for comparison is not subject to the restriction.

With regard to the identification of criminal suspects, if the identifiers are reluctant to do so in public, they may be conducted without revealing the identifiers and confidentiality of identifiers shall be ensured.

A transcript shall be made of the circumstances for identification, which shall be signed by the investigators, the identifiers and the eyewitnesses. Photos shall be taken of the object identified, and audio or video recordings of the identification process may be made when necessary.

(10) Special Investigation Measures

Section 8, Chapter II of Part Two of the Criminal Procedure Law provides for special investigation measures, including three types of investigation acts: technical investigation, secret investigation and controlled delivery. Technical investigation refers to a special investigation measure whereby a public security authority or a people's procuratorate, based on the needs of criminal investigation and after going through a strict approval procedure, uses technical equipment to collect evidence or track down criminals. Secret investigation refers to investigative activities conducted by relevant assigned personnel hiding their identities as decided by the chief of public security organs at or above the county level, based on the necessity of investigation. Secret investigation mainly includes undercover investigation, disguised investigation and enticement investigation. Controlled delivery is an international common and effective means of investigation for solving drug and other contraband cases. It means that when investigation authorities find relevant clues of drugs and other contraband, the "deliver" process or relevant personnel will be under confidential and strict monitoring and control by the investigation authorities, and naturally "deliver" drugs and other contraband to the final consignee according to the direction, route, place and manner planned or agreed upon by a criminal in advance, in order for investigative organ to discover all the criminals involved in the case and catch them all.

(11) Wanted Order

A wanted notice means an investigation activity in which a public security authority issues a wanted order and takes effective measures to pursue a fugitive criminal suspect who should be arrested and bring him/her to justice.

During the course of investigation, if it is necessary to arrest a criminal suspect through a wanted order who should be arrested but is at large, the investigators shall report to the chief of the investigation organ at or above the county level for decision. Public security organs at or above the county level may directly issue wanted orders within areas under their jurisdiction; and they shall request a higher-level public security organ with the proper authority to issue such orders for areas beyond their jurisdiction. Where necessary, a reward notice may be released upon approval of the chief of the public security organ at or above the county level. Upon receipt of the wanted order, the relevant public security organ shall promptly arrange for a search. After the relevant public security organ has caught a criminal suspect, it shall report to the chief of the public security organ at or above the county level for approval for holding the suspect in custody with the wanted order or relevant legal documents, and notify the organ issuing the wanted order for verification and go through the handover formalities. Where it is verified that the criminal suspect has voluntarily surrendered himself/herself, or has been shot or captured, or there is any other circumstance under which it is unnecessary to issue a wanted order, the releasing organ shall revoke the wanted order within the original notice scope.

2.3. Close of Investigation

The close of investigation refers to a litigation activity in which the investigation organ, through a series of investigation activities, believes that the facts of the case have been ascertained, that the evidence is solid, sufficient, and enough to determine whether the criminal suspect has committed a crime, and whether he/she should be pursued for criminal liability, therefore the investigation organ decides to close the investigation by making case-dismiss decision or forward handling opinions according to law.

(1) Conditions for Close of Investigation

In accordance with the legal provisions and real practices, the conditions for close of investigation are: **a.** the facts of the case are clear; **b.** the evidence is solid and sufficient; and **c.** the legal procedures are complete. All of the above three conditions must be met at the same time.

(2) Process of the Close of Investigation

Pursuant to Articles 162 and 163 of the Criminal Procedure Law, to close the investigation of a case, a public security authority shall ensure that the facts of a crime are clear and the evidence is solid and sufficient, prepare a written prosecution opinion, which shall be transferred to the people's procuratorate at the same level for examination and decision along with the case file and evidence. Where it is discovered during criminal investigation that a criminal suspect shall not be subject to criminal liability, the case shall be dismissed; and, if the criminal suspect has been arrested, he/she shall be immediately released, a certificate of release shall be issued to him/her, and the people's procuratorate originally approving the arrest shall be notified.

(3) Time Limit for Custody During Investigation

The time limit for holding a criminal suspect in custody during investigation shall mean the period between the time when the criminal suspect is arrested during investigation and the time when the investigation is concluded or the time he is released. In accordance with Articles 156 to 160 of the Criminal Procedure Law, the period of custody during criminal investigation after a criminal suspect is arrested shall not exceed two months. If the investigation of a complicated case cannot be closed within the period, the period may be extended for one month with the approval of the people's procuratorate at the next higher level. Where the investigation of the following cases cannot be closed within the period as set forth in Article 156 of this Law, the period may be extended for two months with the approval or decision of the people's procuratorate of a province, autonomous region, or municipality directly under the Central Government: **a.** significant and complicated cases in outlying areas where traffic is very difficult; **b.** significant cases regarding criminal gangs; **c.** significant and complicated cases regarding crimes committed from place to place; and **d.** significant and complicated cases with a wide involvement and difficulty in gathering evidence. Where a criminal suspect may be sentenced to fixed-term imprisonment of ten years or more and the investigation of the case cannot be closed even upon expiration of the period as extended under Article 158 of this Law, the period may be extended for another two months with the approval or decision of the people's procuratorate of a province, autonomous region, or municipality directly under the Central Government. Where, during a relatively long period of time, it is inappropriate to transfer an extraordinarily significant and complicated case for trial for special reasons, the Supreme People's Procuratorate shall file a request with the Standing Committee of the National People's Congress for approval of a postponed trial of the case. Where, during the period of criminal investigation, a criminal suspect is discovered to have committed another major crime, the period of custody during criminal investigation shall be recounted from the date of discovery according to the provisions of Article 156 of this Law. Where the identity of a criminal suspect is unknown because the criminal suspect refuses to disclose his/her true name and residence address, an identity investigation shall be conducted, and the period of custody during criminal investigation shall be counted from the day when his/her identity is established, before which, however, criminal investigation and collection of evidence shall not be suspended. Where the facts of a crime are clear and the evidence is solid and sufficient, even if the identity of the criminal suspect cannot be established, the criminal suspect may be prosecuted and tried by the name claimed by the criminal suspect.

2.4. Supplementary Investigation

Supplementary investigation refers to the litigation activities in which the public security authorities or the people's procuratorates continue to conduct investigations in accordance with the legal procedures and on the basis of the original investigation work in respect of part of the facts and circumstances of cases. Supplementary investigation is not a necessary procedure in every criminal case. It is a kind of investigation activity in respect of part of the facts and circumstances of the case when the investigation task has not been completed in the original investigation.

In accordance with the provisions of the Criminal Procedure Law, supplementary investigation is divided into the following three types in procedures:

A. Supplementary investigation at the stage of reviewing the request

for arrest. Article 90 of the Criminal Procedure Law provides that, after examining a case where a public security authority has filed a request for approval of arrest, if the people's procuratorate decides to disapprove the arrest, it shall explain the reasons for disapproval and, when necessary, notify at the same time the public security authority to conduct a supplementary investigation. In order to ensure a smooth investigation, a public security organ may, during the period of supplementary investigation, take measures of bail or residential confinement over the criminal suspect.

B. Supplementary investigation at the stage of prosecution conditions review. Article 175 of the Criminal Procedure Law provides that, where a supplementary investigation is necessary, the people's procuratorate examining a case may return the case to a public security authority for supplementary investigation or conduct supplementary investigation itself instead. The supplementary investigation of a case shall be completed within one month. Supplementary investigation may only be conducted twice. Where, after supplementary investigation has been conducted twice for a case, a people's procuratorate still deems that evidence is insufficient and the case does not meet the conditions for a public prosecution, the people's procuratorate may decide not to initiate a public prosecution.

C. Supplementary investigation at the stage of court trial. Articles 204 and 205 of the Criminal Procedure Law provide that, during the trial of a case, the procurators discover that a case in public prosecution requires supplementary investigation and suggest such investigation to the court, the trial may be postponed, a people's procuratorate shall complete supplementary investigation within one month.

In accordance with the provisions of law, supplementary investigation may be conducted by two methods: returning for supplementary investigation and self-supplementary investigation. The cases returned for supplementary investigation shall be cases filed for investigation by the public security authority, and the people's procuratorate may not return the cases directly accepted by itself to the public security authority for supplementary investigation. Where the people's procuratorate deems that the facts of a crime are unclear, the evidence is insufficient, or any crime or criminal suspect in the same case is omitted, and other circumstances require further investigation, it shall give specific written opinions, and return them together with the case materials to the public security organ for further investigation. The cases to be investigated additionally by themselves may be the cases originally filed by the public security organs for investigation or the cases directly accepted by the people's procuratorates for investigation.

If a case is at the stage of prosecution conditions review and supplementary investigation is needed, the people's procuratorate may return the case to the public security organ for supplementary investigation or conduct the investigation itself; or if a case is under trial and requires supplementary investigation, the procuratorate may only conduct supplementary investigation by itself and may not return the case to a public security organ. However, when necessary, it may request the public security organ to provide assistance.

2.5. Investigation Supervision and Remedies

(1) Investigation Supervision

Investigation supervision refers to supervision carried out by the people's procuratorates over the legality of the investigation activities of the public security organs and other investigation organs. Investigation supervision is mainly over: **a.** collecting confessions of criminal suspects by torture or other illegal means; **b.** collecting testimony of witnesses and statements of victims by violence, threat or other illegal means, or preventing witnesses from giving testimony or instigating others to give false testimony; **c.** forging, concealing, destroying, exchanging or privately altering evidence, or helping any party to destroy or forge evidence; **d.** engaging in conducts of playing favoritism and making falsehood, indulging and harboring criminals; **e.** intentionally creating an unjust, false or misjudged case; **f.** seeking illegal interests by taking advantage of his position in investigation activities; **g.** illegally detaining others or depriving others of their personal freedom by any other means; **h.** illegally searching others' bodies or residences, or illegally breaking into others' residences; **i.** illegally taking technical investigation measures; **j.** withdrawing a case when the case shall not be withdrawn during investigation, etc.

A people's procuratorate may discover illegal acts of an investigation organ and its staff by way of examination before arrest, examination before prosecution, acceptance of a complaint and accusation, etc. If the circumstances of illegal acts are minor, correction opinions may be orally proposed. If the circumstances of illegal acts are relatively serious, a written notice on correcting the illegal acts shall be issued and notified. If the investigation and supervision department or the public prosecution department of a people's procuratorate discovers that an investigator has committed illegal acts in the course of investigation and the circumstances are serious to constitute a crime, the case shall be transferred to the relevant department to be investigated for criminal liability in accordance with the law.

(2) Investigation Remedy

Investigation remedy refers to a type of consequential remedial measures adopted by the parties concerned and their defenders or their litigation representatives thereof or interested parties request relevant authorities to rectify or deal with during the investigation stage when their lawful rights and interests are infringed upon.

Article 117 of the Criminal Procedure Law stipulates the remedial measures for investigation: A party or a defender or a litigation representative thereof or an interested party shall have the right to file a petition or accusation with a judicial authority regarding any of the following conduct of the judicial authority or any of its personnel: **a.** refusing to release a criminal suspect or defendant or terminate or modify a compulsory measure taken, when the statutory term of the compulsory measure expires; **b.** refusing to refund a bail bond that shall be refunded; **c.** seizing, impounding, or freezing any property irrelevant to a case; **d.** refusing to terminate a measure of seizing, impounding, or freezing property that shall be terminated; or **e.** embezzling, misappropriating, distributing in private, replacing, or illegally using any seized, impounded, or frozen property. The authority accepting the petition or accusation shall handle it in a timely manner. Against the handling result, the party, the defender or the litigation representative thereof or the interested party may file a petition with the people's procuratorate at the same level; or, if the case is directly accepted by the people's procuratorate, may file a petition with the people's procuratorate at the next higher level. The people's procuratorate shall examine the petition in a timely manner and, if it is true, notify the relevant authority to make corrections.

3. Prosecution

3.1. General Overview

(1) Concept and Classification of Prosecution

Criminal prosecution refers to the litigation activity whereby the State organs and citizens with the right to prosecute bring a lawsuit before the court according to law and request the court to try the accusation so as to determine the criminal liabilities of the accused and give him/her criminal sanctions according to law. Based on the subject of prosecution, there are two kinds of prosecution: public prosecution and private prosecution. The term "public prosecution" refers to a kind of litigation activity in which the special organs and officials established by the State file claims to courts requesting the courts to determine the criminal liabilities of the accused through trial and to give corresponding sanctions. Private prosecution means the litigation activities that the victims or their legal representatives and other individuals or groups having the right to prosecute in accordance with law directly initiate a lawsuit in court with competent jurisdiction to pursue the criminal liability of the accused.

(2) Task and Significance of Prosecution

The task of the prosecution is to have an organ or individual with the right to prosecute to file a claim to court with competent jurisdiction on the basis of facts and law, and to provide relevant evidence in support of the claim, so as to determine the criminal liability of the accused. The significance of the prosecution is as follows: **a.** Start the trial procedure. One of the basic principles of modern criminal procedure is "no prosecution, no trial", that is, prosecution is the precondition and foundation of trial, and without the prosecution, the court cannot proactively investigate the crime. **b.** From the point of view of litigation function, prosecution is the implementation method of criminal complaint function, one of the three main functions of modern criminal procedure. **c.** From the perspective of validity, the prosecution limits the trial scope of the case. The principle of separating trial from prosecution requires that the trial scope of the court is limited by the prosecution scope, that is, the court can only try parties prosecuted crimes, and must keep the identity of the target of trial and the prosecution.

3.2. Examination for Prosecution

(1) Concept and Significance of Examination for Prosecution

The term "examination for prosecution" refers to a litigation activity in which the people's procuratorate, after accepting the case transferred by the investigation organ or department after the investigation organ or department closes the investigation, examines and verifies the facts and evidence of the crime, the nature of the crime and the applicable laws, etc. determined by the investigation organ or department, and makes a decision on the handling of the case. Article 169 of the Criminal Procedure Law provides that, any case requiring initiation of a public prosecution shall be subject to the examination and decision of a people's procuratorate. This provision indicates that, in cases of public prosecution, the people's procuratorate, as the public prosecution organ, is the only organ that represents the State to prosecute crimes. Examination of prosecution is an inevitable procedure for cases of public prosecution, a link connecting investigation and trial procedures, and is of great significance for the correct handling of criminal cases and realization of the tasks of criminal proceedings.

(2) Acceptance of Cases Transferred for Examination for Prosecution

Acceptance refers to the acceptance of a case transferred for examination for prosecution by the examination department of the people's procuratorate after the preliminary procedural examination. The contents of the preliminary examination shall include: whether the prosecution opinion from investigation organs and the case materials are complete, whether the binding and transfer of the case files comply with the relevant requirements and regulations, whether the litigation documents and technical evaluation materials have been bound into files; whether the objects transferred are consistent with the list of objects, and whether objects used as evidence have been transferred with the case; whether the criminal suspect is available and whether compulsory measures are taken; whether the case is under the jurisdiction of the court, etc.

The case management department of a procuratorate shall, through the preliminary review, handle the cases as follows in the light of different circumstances:

If it believes that the conditions for acceptance are met, it shall make a registration in a timely manner, and immediately transfer the case files and the case acceptance registration form to the relevant case handling department for handling.

Where it deems that the materials of the case are not complete, it shall timely require the department transferring the case to supplement the relevant materials.

If the criminal suspect is at large, the public security organ shall be required to take measures to ensure the presence of the criminal suspect before transferring the case for examination for prosecution. If some of the criminal suspects in a joint crime case are at large, the examination for prosecution of available criminal suspects shall be conducted in accordance with the law.

(3) Content of Examination for Prosecution

Pursuant to Article 171 of the Criminal Procedure Law, during the examination of a case, a people's procuratorate must ascertain: **a.** whether the facts and circumstances of a crime are clear, whether evidence is solid and sufficient, and whether the nature of a crime and the charges are correctly determined; **b.** whether there are any omitted crimes or other persons subject to criminal liability; **c.** whether a criminal suspect shall not be subject to criminal liability; **d.** whether there is an incidental civil action; and **e.** whether the criminal investigation of the case is legally conducted.

(4) Procedure and Method of Examination for Prosecution

To ensure smooth proceeding of the examination for prosecution, the detailed method and procedure of examination for prosecution shall conform to the following requirements:

A. Cases under examination for prosecution by the people's procuratorates at all levels shall be compatible with the trial jurisdiction of the people's courts.

B. Review of file materials. After receiving a case, the personnel handling the case shall promptly examine whether the materials of the case transferred by public security organs or other criminal investigation departments are complete, whether there are "Prosecution Opinion", evidential materials and other legal documents. When examining a case, the people's procuratorate may require the public security organ to provide evidential materials necessary for the court trial; if it has any doubt, it may inquire investigators; if it believes that any evidence has been collected by illegal means, it may require the public security organ to explain the legality of evidence collection. Case files shall be reviewed carefully and a written record shall be made for reviewing case files.

C. Interrogation of criminal suspects. Interrogation of criminal suspects is a necessary procedure of people's procuratorates in examination for prosecution. Interrogation of criminal suspects can only be conducted by prosecutors, who shall be informed of the right to apply for disqualification. There shall be at least two prosecutors present at the time of interrogation. They shall first ask the criminal suspect whether or not he/she has committed any crime, and let him/her state the circumstances of his/her guilt or explain his/her innocence. Then they shall determine the key points of the evidence to be reviewed according to the statement of the criminal suspect and review of the case file, and ask the criminal suspect for answers. The interrogation of criminal suspects shall be conducted separately, and the transcripts thereof shall be made.

D. Listen to the opinions of the defender, the victim and his/her litigation representative. This is a necessary procedure in examination for prosecution by the people's procuratorate. The written opinions of the defender, the victim, and his/her litigation representative shall be attached to the case file by the people's procuratorate.

E. Supplementary investigation. Supplementary investigation has two forms: one is that the case is returned by the people's procuratorate to the public security organ for supplementary investigation. This form is generally applicable to cases in which the main criminal facts are unclear or insufficient in evidence, or important criminal facts and the accomplices who should be held criminally liable are omitted. For a case that needs to be returned for further investigation, the people's procuratorate shall prepare a Decision on Returning for Further Investigation, in which the reasons for returning for further investigation and the specific matters and requirements for further investigation shall be clearly stated. The other is that the people's procuratorate conducts the investigation on its own. This method generally applies to a case that only some minor facts of crime or circumstances are unclear or insufficient in evidence, or involve illegal acts committed by the public security organ during its investigation activities, or the people's procuratorate has disagreements to a comparatively great extent with the public security organ over ascertaining facts and evidence, or the case has been returned to the public security organ but has not yet been clarified. Where a self-investigated case requires supplementary investigation, the department of examination of the people's procuratorate shall return the case to the investigation department of this people's procuratorate. In cases where supplementary investigation is to be conducted, it shall be completed within one month. Supplementary investigation may be conducted twice at most.

F. Make a decision. After a series of examination activities have been carried out and all the facts of a case have been found out, the procurator shall prepare a Letter of Opinion on Case Examination. The procurator shall, in light of the specific circumstances of the examination, put forward his/her opinions on whether to prosecute or not, and whether to initiate an incidental civil action or not, and submit such opinions to the chief of the examination department for examination. The chief of the examination department shall, after examining the case, give examination opinions and submit such opinions to the chief procurator or the procuratorial committee for decision on whether to initiate a prosecution or not.

(5) Time Limit for Examination for Prosecution

Article 172 of the Criminal Procedure Law provides that, a people's procuratorate shall, within one month, make a decision on a case transferred by a supervisory authority or public security authority for prosecution, and in a significant or complicated case, the period may be extended by fifteen days; or if the criminal suspect admits guilt and accepts punishment, and the conditions for the application of the expedited procedure are met, the decision shall be made within ten days, and the period may be extended to fifteen days if the criminal suspect may be sentenced to fixed-term imprisonment of more than one year. Where the jurisdiction of a people's procuratorate over a case being examined for prosecution is changed, the period of examination and prosecution shall be counted from the day when the people's procuratorate having jurisdiction receives the case after the change.

(6) Handling after Examination

After examining a case, when the people's procuratorate considers that the facts of crime have been verified, that the evidence is solid and sufficient and that criminal liability shall be pursued in accordance with the law, it shall make a decision to initiate a prosecution; and, according to the provisions on trial jurisdiction, initiate a public prosecution with the people's court and transfer the case file and evidence to the people's court. If it believes that a criminal suspect has no criminal facts or is under any of the circumstances as prescribed in Article 16 of the Criminal Procedure Law, it shall make a decision not to initiate a prosecution. With respect to a case that is minor in criminal circumstances and the violator needs not be given criminal punishment or needs to be exempted from it according to the Criminal Law, it may make a decision not to initiate a prosecution.

3.3. Initiating a Public Prosecution

Initiating a public prosecution is a litigation activity whereby a people's procuratorate, on behalf of the State, transfers a criminal suspect to a people's court and requests the people's court to pursue the criminal liability of the accused through trial. After the people's procuratorate makes a decision to initiate a public prosecution, the litigation status of the criminal suspect is changed to a criminal defendant.

(1) Conditions for Initiating a Public Prosecution

First, the criminal suspect's facts of a crime have been ascertained, and the evidence is solid and sufficient. According to the relevant provisions, the facts of a crime may be confirmed to have been ascertained under any of the following circumstances: **a.** For a case of single crime, the facts ascertained are sufficient for conviction and sentencing, or the facts relevant to the conviction and sentencing have been ascertained while the facts which do not affect the conviction and sentencing cannot be ascertained. **b.** If a case involves several crimes, some of the crimes has been ascertained and the conditions for prosecution are met while other crimes cannot be ascertained, the accused shall be prosecuted for the ascertained crimes. **c.** Whereabouts of crime tools and illegally obtained property cannot be ascertained, but there is other evidence sufficient to convict and impose punishment on the accused. **d.** Main contents of the testimony of the witness, the confession and defense of the criminal suspect and the statements of the victim are consistent while only a few are inconsistent, which do not affect the conviction of crime. In joint crime cases, where some criminal suspects are at large, in order to punish the criminals who have been brought to justice and whose criminal facts have been found out in time, they shall be prosecuted and tried first. After the criminal suspects at large have been brought to justice and whose criminal facts have been found out, they shall be prosecuted in another prosecution.

Second, the criminal suspect shall be pursued for criminal liability according to law. If the act of a criminal suspect falls under any of the circumstances as prescribed in Article 16 of the Criminal Procedure Law, he/she shall not be pursued for criminal liability and the decision of initiating a public prosecution shall not be made.

Third, the initiation of public prosecution by the people's procuratorate shall conform to the provisions on trial jurisdiction. After making a decision of prosecution, the people's procuratorate shall initiate a public prosecution at the people's court with jurisdiction. The public prosecution must conform to the provisions on hierarchical jurisdiction, special jurisdiction and territorial jurisdiction, and the public prosecution will not be accepted and trial procedure will not be commenced if the public prosecution is made to a court without jurisdiction.

To initiate a public prosecution against the criminal suspect, the above three conditions shall be met at the same time, the lack of any of the conditions is a violation of the law. The requirement in the Criminal Procedure Law for a case for which the people's procuratorate decides to initiate a public prosecution in terms of facts and evidence is that "the people's procuratorate considers that the criminal suspect's crime facts have been ascertained and the evidence is solid and sufficient". Here, for the requirements of facts and evidence in the Criminal Procedure Law, a subjective restrictive word such as "the people's procuratorate believes" is added in front of the condition, which is different from the provisions on the judgment conditions for guilty judgments. Such provision is made on the grounds that the evidential materials acquired at the prosecution stage may be less than those acquired by the people's court at the time of making a judgment. Meanwhile, it also fits in with the principle of "No person shall be found guilty without being judged so by a people's court in accordance with the law" as established in Article 12 of the Criminal Procedure Law.

(2) Preparation and Transfer of an Indictment

After making a decision on prosecution, the people's procuratorate shall prepare an indictment. Indictments are important judicial documents that the people's procuratorates, on behalf of the State, formally submit to the people's courts to pursue for the criminal liability of the accused. They are the written basis for the people's procuratorates to initiate public prosecution on behalf of the State, the precondition for the people's courts to exercise judicial power over the accused, and the basis for court investigation and debate as well. The basic requirements are as follows: the facts of the case shall be clear, the words shall be concise, the statement shall be accurate and precise, the format shall be standardized, and the citation of laws shall be comprehensive, accurate and appropriate.

In accordance with the relevant provisions, the indictment consists of the following parts:

A. Head. It mainly includes the name of the people's procuratorate which makes the document, the number of the document, etc.

B. Basic information of the accused. Mainly, the name, gender, age, native place, identity card number, nationality, education background, occupation, domicile, main resume (including whether there is any former criminal record) of the accused, when he/she is detained, arrested and the place of custody of the accused, etc. For cases of joint crime, the situations above of the accused shall be stated one by one.

C. Cause of action and source of the case. The cause of action is generally the summary of the content of the case, in which normally only the subject of the offence and the name of the offence shall be stated. The source of the case mainly refers to whether the case is transferred after the close of investigation by the public security organ or the investigation department of the people's procuratorate.

D. Facts and evidence of the crime. The facts and evidence of the crime are main parts of the indictment. The indictment shall clearly state the accused's charge, details of charge, evidence of the crime and the attitude of admission of guilt. When narrating the facts of crime of the accused, the time, place, process, means, motive, purpose, harmful consequences of the crime shall be stated.

E. Conclusion. That is, the grounds and legal basis for prosecution, which directly reflect the people's procuratorate's specific opinion on the legal liabilities for the crimes committed by the accused after analysis and determination of the criminal facts of the accused. The specific contents mainly include: the articles of the criminal law violated by the accused, the nature of the crime and the extent of harm to the society; whether there is a circumstance for giving a heavier or lighter punishment, and the reasons for giving a lighter or heavier punishment shall be explained in addition; the liabilities of each accused person in a joint crime; in cases of public prosecution, if the accused's crime has caused any material loss to the victim, it shall also be stated that if there is any incidental civil action.

F. Ending part. The name of the people's court to which the indictment is served, the legal position and name of the person handling the case, the date (Year/Month/Day) on which the indictment is made, and the official seal of the people's procuratorate shall be affixed to it.

G. Additional items. In this part, the residential address or place of custody of the accused, the list of witnesses and their residential addresses or the addresses of their entities, the residential address of the forensic identification and evaluation expert or the address of his/her entity, the number of volumes and pages of files transferred with the case, and the evidence and illicit property transferred with the case.

For a case of public prosecution initiated by a people's procuratorate, the indictment, case file and evidence shall be transferred to the people's court. The people's procuratorate shall, in accordance with the provisions on trial jurisdiction, bring a public prosecution to the people's court at the same level. When initiating a public prosecution, a people's procuratorate may suggest a people's court to apply the summary procedure; however, the people's court shall decide whether the summary procedure is to be applied.

3.4. Non-Prosecution

(1) Concept, Nature and Effect of Non-Prosecution

The term "non-prosecution" refers to a people's procuratorate's decision not to transfer a criminal suspect to a people's court for trial and to pursue his/her criminal liability after having examined a case transferred by a public security organ for prosecution after the close of investigation or a case's investigation was concluded by itself, because it is believed that the conduct of a criminal suspect does not meet the conditions for prosecution or it is unnecessary to initiate a prosecution. Non-prosecution is one of the results of handling by a people's procuratorate after examining a case in accordance with the law. The nature of non-prosecution is a litigation disposition taken by the people's procuratorate against a criminal suspect that should not be pursued, need not be pursued or cannot be pursued for criminal liability as determined by itself, and has the legal effect of terminating the criminal procedure. For the criminal suspect, the non-prosecution decision means that he/she is legally innocent.

(2) Types of and Conditions of Application of Non-Prosecution

In accordance with the provisions of the Criminal Procedure Law, there are five types of non-prosecution in China's criminal procedures: statutory non-prosecution, discretionary non-prosecution, non-prosecution due to insufficient evidence, conditional non-prosecution and special non-prosecution.

A. Statutory non-prosecution. It means the decision not to initiate a prosecution that the people's procuratorate shall make if the criminal suspect has no facts of a crime or is not subject to criminal liability as provided in Article 16 of the Criminal Procedure Law. According to Articles 16 and 177 of the Criminal Procedure Law, the statutory non-prosecution shall fall under any of the following circumstances: where the criminal suspect has no criminal fact; where the act committed by the criminal suspect is obviously minor, causing no serious harm and is therefore not deemed a crime; where the limitation period for criminal prosecution has expired; if the criminal suspect's crime is exempted from criminal punishment after a special amnesty decree; if the crime is to be handled only upon a complaint according to the Criminal Law, but there is no complaint or the complaint has been withdrawn; if the criminal suspect or the accused is deceased; or if other laws provide an exemption from criminal punishment.

B. Discretionary non-prosecution. It is also called "relative non-prosecution", referring to a decision that the people's procuratorate may make on non-prosecution of a case in which the criminal suspect's crime circumstances are deemed minor, and the criminal suspect needs not be subject to criminal punishment or shall be exempted from criminal punishment in accordance with the Criminal Law. The circumstances under which criminal punishment may be exempted in accordance with the Criminal Law mainly include: the criminal suspect has committed a crime outside the territory of the People's Republic of China and shall bear criminal liability in accordance with the Criminal Law of the People's Republic of China, but has been subject to criminal punishment in a foreign country; the criminal suspect is deaf and mute or a blind person commits a crime; the criminal suspect commits a crime due to excessive self-defense or urgent danger avoidance exceeding the necessary limit, which results in undue harm; the criminal suspect prepares tools or creates conditions for a crime; the criminal suspect automatically discontinues or automatically and effectively prevents the criminal consequences from occurring in the course of a crime, or plays a secondary or auxiliary role in a joint crime; the criminal suspect is coerced or induced to commit a crime; the criminal suspect voluntarily surrenders or renders meritorious service after voluntary surrenders.

C. Non-prosecution due to insufficient evidence. It means that if the people's procuratorate, after supplementary investigation has been conducted, still believes that evidence is insufficient and the case is not eligible for prosecution, the people's procuratorate may make the decision not to initiate a prosecution upon discussion and decision by the procuratorial committee. Where a case, after two supplementary investigation into it, falls under any of the following circumstances, and it cannot be confirmed that the criminal suspect has committed a crime or the criminal suspect shall be pursued for criminal liability, the case shall be deemed as having insufficient evidence and thus does not meet the conditions for prosecution: the evidence on which the decision is based is doubtful and cannot be verified; there is no necessary evidence to prove the facts constituting any essential element of a crime; the contradictions among pieces of evidence cannot be excluded reasonably; or other alternative conclusions can be drawn from the evidence and cannot be excluded.

D. Conditional non-prosecution. According to Article 282 of the Criminal Procedure Law, conditional non-prosecution refers to where a juvenile may be sentenced to fixed-term imprisonment of one year or a lighter punishment if he/she is suspected of committing a crime of infringement upon the personal right, democratic right, property right or obstructing the management of public order as prescribed in Chapters IV, V and VI of the Specific Provisions of the Criminal Law, if the prosecution conditions are met but the juvenile has shown repentance, a people's procuratorate may make the decision of conditional non-prosecution after examination for prosecution. During the probation period for conditional non-prosecution, a people's procuratorate shall supervise and inspect a juvenile suspect who is not prosecuted under conditions. The guardian of the juvenile suspect shall strengthen control and education of the criminal suspect and cooperate with the people's procuratorate in supervision and inspection. The probation period for conditional non-prosecution shall range from six months to one year, starting from the day when the people's procuratorate makes a conditional non-prosecution decision. A juvenile suspect who is not prosecuted under conditions shall comply with the following provisions: abiding by laws and administrative regulations and obeying supervision; reporting his/her activities as required by the inspection authority; obtaining the approval of the inspection authority before leaving the city or county where he/she resides or relocating to another place; and receiving correction and education as required by the inspection authority. Where the juvenile suspect or his/her legal representative raises any objection to the conditional non-prosecution decision of the people's procuratorate, the people's procuratorate shall make the decision of prosecution. If a juvenile suspect under conditional non-prosecution is discovered to be under any of the following circumstances during the probation period, a people's procuratorate shall revoke the conditional non-prosecution decision and initiate a public prosecution: the juvenile suspect commits a new crime, or it is discovered that another crime committed before the conditional non-prosecution decision was made needs to be prosecuted; the juvenile suspect seriously violates the provisions on public security administration or the provisions of the inspection authority on supervising and administering conditional non-prosecution. Where a juvenile suspect who is not prosecuted under conditions does not fall into any of the above circumstances during the probation period, upon expiration of the probation period, the people's procuratorate shall make a non-prosecution decision.

E. Special non-prosecution. Special non-prosecution was a new type of non-prosecution created when the Criminal Procedure Law was amended in 2018. Article 182 of the Criminal Procedure Law stipulates that, where a criminal suspect voluntarily and truthfully confesses to the facts of the suspected crime or has any major meritorious act, or the case involves any major national interest, with the approval of the Supreme People's Procuratorate, the public security authority may dismiss the case, and the people's procuratorate may decide not to initiate prosecution or decide not to prosecute one or more crimes in the multiple crimes suspected.

(3) Non-Prosecution Procedure

After making a non-prosecution decision, a people's procuratorate shall prepare a non-prosecution decision in writing. A non-prosecution decision is a decisive legal document for a people's procuratorate to confirm, on behalf of the State, that a criminal suspect is not subject to criminal liability, and shall have the legal effect of terminating criminal proceedings. Their main contents include: the basic information of the person against whom no prosecution is to be initiated, cause of action and source of the case, case facts, legal basis and reasons for not initiating a prosecution, disposal of money and property involved in the case, and relevant matters to be notified.

The decision not to initiate a prosecution shall be announced publicly by the people's procuratorate. The written decision of not to initiate a prosecution shall become effective as of the date of public announcement. The written decision shall be delivered to the person who is not to be prosecuted and his/her entity, and the person may appeal to the people's procuratorate if he/she is not satisfied with the decision. If the person who is not prosecuted is in custody, he/she shall be released immediately. With respect to a case transferred by a public security organ for prosecution, the decision shall be served upon the public security organ. If the case involves a victim, the written decision shall be served upon the victim or his close relative or his litigation representative and he/she shall be informed that if he/she refuses to accept the decision regarding non-prosecution, he/she may present a petition to a people's procuratorate or bring a private prosecution to a people's court.

3.5. Initiation of Private Prosecution

Compared with public prosecution, private prosecution in criminal procedure refers to a criminal proceeding directly brought by an individual who has the right to initiate a private prosecution to the people's court having jurisdiction. In China, cases of private prosecution refer to the cases that may be directly prosecuted at the people's courts by the victims or their legal representatives or close relatives and that can be directly accepted by the people's courts.

(1) Conditions for Initiating a Private Prosecution

The initiation of a private prosecution by a private prosecutor will not be accepted by the people's court unless the following conditions are met:

First, the case is within the scope of private prosecution as determined in the Criminal Procedure Law;

Second, the case is under the jurisdiction of the people's court accepting the case;

Third, private prosecutors enjoy the right of private prosecution. Normally, private prosecution cases shall be filed by victims. If the victims die, lose the capacity for conduct, or are unable to file complaints due to coercion, intimidation or other reasons, or if the victims are persons with limited capacity for conduct, or because of old age, illness, blindness, deafness, muteness or other reasons, are unable to file complaints in person, the complaints can be filed by their legal representatives or close relatives on their behalf.

Fourth, there are definite accused persons, specific litigation claims and the evidence that can prove the criminal facts of the accused.

(2) Procedures for Initiating Private Prosecution

When bringing a private prosecution, the private prosecutor shall submit a criminal complaint to the people's court; if he/she brings an incidental civil action, he/she shall also submit the complaint of civil action incidental to the criminal action. In order to facilitate the private prosecutor to file his/her complaint, the Criminal Procedure Law provides that if the private prosecutor has difficulty in writing the complaint, he/she may file his/her complaint orally, and the personnel of the people's court shall make a written record of his/her complaint and read it out to the private prosecutor; and the private prosecutor shall sign or seal his/her complaint after confirming it to be correct.

The complaint or records of the private prosecution shall include the following contents: **a.** the name, gender, age, nationality, place of birth, education level, occupation, employer, residential address and contact information of the private prosecutor and the accused; **b.** the time, place, means, details, harmful consequences, etc. of the crime committed by the accused; **c.** the name, source, etc. of the evidence; **d.** specific claims; **e.** the people's court to which the complaint is sent and the time of complaint submission.

CHAPTER SIX

TRIAL STAGES

Generally speaking, criminal cases will go through the first and second instances in the trial stage, but some special cases will also go through special stages of review of death sentences and trial supervision.

1. First Instance

1.1. Overview

The term "procedures at first instance" refers to the steps, manners and methods that shall be followed by the people's court in the first trial of a case in which a public prosecution was initiated by a people's procuratorate or a private prosecution was initiated by a private prosecutor.

Criminal cases of first instance may be divided into cases of public prosecution and cases of private prosecution according to different prosecution subjects. Cases of public prosecution refer to the cases initiated by the people's procuratorates to the people's courts; cases of private prosecution refer to the cases that are initiated by the victims or their legal representatives to the people's courts and directly accepted by the people's courts. The procedures at first instance can be divided into three categories: ordinary procedures at first instance, summary procedures and expedited procedures. Among them, ordinary procedures at first instance include the procedures at first instance for cases of public prosecution and private prosecution. The summary procedures and expedited procedures are simplified procedures at first instance.

1.2. Procedures at First Instance for Cases of Public Prosecution

The term "procedures at first instance for cases of public prosecution" refers to the steps, manners and methods that shall be followed by the people's court in the first trial of a case in which a public prosecution was initiated by a people's procuratorate. The procedures at first instance for cases of public prosecution include pre-trial examination, pre-trial preparation, court trial, and other litigation steps.

(1) Pre-Trial Examination for Cases of Public Prosecution

The term "pre-trial examination for cases of public prosecution" refers to the activities that the people's court conducts pre-trial examination of a case in which a public prosecution was initiated by a people's procuratorate in order to determine whether to try the case in a court session. Article 186 of the Criminal Procedure Law provides that: "After examining a public prosecution initiated, a people's court shall decide to hold a court session to hear the case if the charges in the indictment are based on clear facts." This provision shows that the examination of cases of public prosecution is the necessary step before cases of public prosecution formally enter the procedures at first instance.

The examination of cases of public prosecution shall be mainly subject to procedural examination, and shall include: **a.** whether the case is under the jurisdiction of this court; **b.** whether the indictment has stated the identity of the defendant, whether he/she has been or is being subject to criminal punishment, the type of compulsory measures taken, the place of detention, the time, place, means, consequences of the crime, and other circumstances that may affect the conviction and sentencing; **c.** whether the evidence materials proving the facts of the accused's crime are transferred, including the decision on approval of taking technical investigation measures and the evidence materials collected; **d.** whether the illegal income or other property involved in the case of the defendant is sealed, seized or frozen, and whether the evidence materials able to prove that relevant property shall be recovered according to law are attached; **e.** whether the victim's name, address, and contact information are listed; whether the lists of witnesses and forensic identification and evaluation experts are attached; whether the application has been filed to courts for witnesses, forensic identification and evaluation experts and persons of special knowledge to appear in court, and whether the name, gender, age, occupation, address, and contact information of relevant persons are attached; **f.** whether the parties have appointed defenders or agents ad litem, or where the parties have accepted legal aid, whether the names, addresses, and contact information of the defenders and agents ad litem have been listed; **g.** whether an incidental civil action is brought, whether the names, addresses, and contact information of the parties to the incidental civil action are listed, and whether the relevant evidence materials are attached; **h.** whether the various legal formalities and litigation documents for the procedures for investigation, examination and prosecution are complete; **i.** whether there are circumstances under which criminal liability shall be exempted from as prescribed in the Criminal Procedure Law.

The people's court shall, after receiving the indictment from the people's procuratorate, designate judges to review the above contents of the case. After review, the case shall be respectively handled in light of the different circumstances of the case: **a.** the case that shall only be handled upon complaint shall be returned to the people's procuratorate, and the victim shall be notified of his/her right to bring private prosecution; **b.** if the case is not under the jurisdiction of this court or the defendant is not found, it shall be returned to the people's procuratorate; **c.** the people's procuratorate shall be notified to provide additional materials within three days if supplementary materials are required; **d.** after the defendant is declared innocent due to insufficient evidence, if the people's procuratorate brings a new prosecution on the basis of new facts and evidence, the people's court shall accept the case in accordance with the law; **e.** the case that the people's court has allowed the people's procuratorate to withdraw shall be returned to the people's procuratorate if there is no new fact or evidence for a new prosecution to be brought; **f.** under any of the circumstances specified in Section 2 to Section 6 of Article 16 of the Criminal Procedure Law, the people's court shall rule to terminate the trial or return the case to the people's procuratorate. The review on whether or not to accept a case of public prosecution shall be completed within seven days.

(2) Pre-Trial Preparation for Cases of Public Prosecution

Prior to a court session, the people's court shall: **a.** determine the presiding judge and the members of the collegial panel; **b.** serve the copy of the indictment upon the defendant and the defender ten days before commencement of the court session; **c.** notify the parties, legal representatives, defenders, and litigation representatives of the list of witnesses and forensic identification and evaluation experts and the evidence to be presented in court five days before commencement of the court session; where a witness, forensic identification and evaluation expert, or person with expertise is to be applied for appearing in court, the name, gender, age, occupation, address, and contact information of the person concerned shall be indicated; **d.** notify the people's procuratorate of the time and place of the court session three days before commencement of the court session; **e.** serve the summons upon the parties concerned and the notice of appearance in court to notify the defender, litigation representative, legal representative, witness, and forensic identification and evaluation expert, etc. three days before commencement of the court session; the notice of appearance in court can also be served by telephone call, text message, fax, email or other means with acknowledgement of receipt by the party concerned; and **f.** for a case to be heard in public, announce the cause of action, the name of the defendant, and the time and place of the court session three days before commencement of the court session. The information about the above work shall be recorded.

Prior to a court hearing, the people's court may convene a pre-trial conference. The judges may learn the information from the prosecution and the defense on the following issues and listen to their opinions: **a.** whether there is any objection to the jurisdiction of the case; **b.** whether to apply for the disqualification of the persons concerned; **c.** whether to apply for obtaining the evidence materials collected by the public security organ or the people's procuratorate during the investigation, review and prosecution period which have not accompanied the case and which can prove the innocence or mitigation of offences of the defendant; **d.** whether to provide new evidence; **e.** whether to raise objection to the list of witnesses, forensic identification and evaluation experts and experts appearing in court; **f.** whether to apply for the exclusion of illegal evidence; **g.** whether to apply for a private hearing; and **h.** other issues related to the trial. The judges may inquire whether the prosecution and the defense have any objection to the evidence materials. If there is any objection to the evidence, emphasis shall be put on the investigation of that evidence during the court hearing; if there is no objection, the provision and cross-examination of evidence may be simplified during the court hearing. If the victim or his/her legal representative or close relative brings an incidental civil action, such action may be mediated. A written record shall be made for the information of the pretrial conference.

(3) Court Hearing

Court hearing procedures can be generally divided into five stages: opening of the court hearing, court investigation, court debate, final statement of the defendant, deliberation and declaration of judgment.

A. Opening of the court hearing. Before a court hearing, the court clerk shall make sure whether the public prosecutor, parties, witnesses and other litigation participants are present in courtroom; the court rules shall be read out; the public prosecutor and relevant litigation participants shall be invited to enter the courtroom; the presiding judge and the judges (the people's jurors) shall be invited to enter into the courtroom; and the court clerk shall report to the presiding judge that the pre-trial preparations have been completed. The presiding judge shall announce the opening of the court hearing and summon the defendant to appear in court. The presiding judge shall announce the source and cause of action of the case, the names of the parties to the incidental civil action and whether to hear the case in public; if the case is heard in private, the reasons shall be announced. The presiding judge shall announce the name list of the members of the collegial panel, the court clerks, the public prosecutors, the defenders, the forensic identification and evaluation experts, the interpreters and other litigation participants. The presiding judge shall inform the parties and their legal representatives, defenders and agents ad litem of their litigation rights according to law in the course of court hearing, and ask them whether to apply for disqualification.

B. Court investigation. Court investigation refers to the litigation activity in which the collegial panel presides over the investigation and verification of the facts and evidence of a case in the presence of the public prosecutor, parties and other litigation participants. Court investigation is an important stage during which a case enters into substantive trial and the central stage of a court trial. During a court investigation, the court shall not only investigate the facts relating to the conviction, but also ascertain the extent of a specific statutory sentence applicable to the defendant and other statutory or discretionary sentencing circumstances for heavier, lighter, mitigated or exempted punishment. The procedures for court investigation are as follows: **a.** After the presiding judge announces the commencement of court investigation, the public prosecutor shall read out the indictment first; if there is an incidental civil action, the plaintiff of the incidental civil action or his legal representative or litigation representative shall read out the complaint for the incidental civil action. **b.** After the public prosecutor has read out the complaint, the defendant and the victim may make statements regarding the crime accused in the indictment respectively under the direction of the presiding judge. **c.** The public prosecutor may interrogate the defendant regarding the crime accused in the indictment. **d.** Upon permission of the presiding judge, the victim and his/her legal representatives, agents ad litem, the plaintiff and his/her legal representatives, agents ad litem of the incidental civil action, the defendant's legal representatives and defenders, the defendant and his/her legal representatives and agents ad litem of the incidental civil action may question the defendant, and the prosecutor and the defender may question the victim and the plaintiff of the incidental civil action. **e.** After the interrogation and questioning of the parties, the public prosecutor may request the presiding judge to summon the witnesses or forensic identification and evaluation experts to testify in court, or to show evidence. When the prosecutor and the defender apply for the witnesses to appear in court and show evidence, the names and sources of the evidence and the facts to be proved shall be explained. The court shall grant permission if it deems necessary. All evidence provided by the prosecutor and the defender to courts shall be cross-examined, identified and debated in court.

C. Court debate. Court debate is a kind of litigation activity whereby the prosecutor and the defender, on the basis of the court investigation, argue and refute with each other on such issues as whether the defendant's conduct constitutes a crime, the nature of the crime, the seriousness of the crime, whether the evidence is solid and sufficient, and how to apply the penalty. Where the collegial panel deems that the facts of the case are clear, the presiding judge shall announce the conclusion of the court investigation, and commence court debate on such issues as the facts for conviction and sentencing, evidence and applicable law. Court debate shall be presided over by the presiding judge and conducted in the following order: statement by the public prosecutor; statement by the victim and his/her litigation representative; self-defense by the defendant; defense by the defender; debate by the prosecutor and the defender. The debate of the incidental civil action shall be conducted after the debate of the criminal action. The order of debate shall be: first, the plaintiff of the incidental civil action and his/her litigation representative shall make statements, and then the defendant of the incidental civil action and his/her litigation representative shall respond. During the court debate, the presiding judge shall listen to the opinions of the prosecutor and the defender. Where the collegial panel finds any new fact relating to conviction or sentencing, and court investigation is necessary, the presiding judge may announce suspension of debate and resume the court investigation, and continue the debate after investigation of the new fact. After several rounds of debate, if the presiding judge considers that there are no new issues or opinions raised in the statements of the prosecutor and the defender, and there is no need to continue the debate, he/she shall terminate the statements of both parties and declare that the debate has ended.

D. Final statement of the defendant. Article 198 of the Criminal Procedure Law provides that, after the presiding judge declares the end of debate, the defendant shall have the right to present a closing statement. As the final statement of the defendant is an independent stage of the court trial, as long as it does not exceed the scope of the present case, the time limit for his/her speech shall not be set, and the speech shall not be interrupted at will. If the statement is in contempt of the court or the public prosecutor, damaging the interests of others and the public, or irrelevant to the case, a stop shall be given to the statement. In a case heard in public, if the final statement of the defendant involves national secrets or personal privacy, a stop shall also be given to the statement. If the defendant submits new facts or evidence in his/her final statement, and the collegial panel considers it may affect the correctness of the judgment, the court investigation shall be resumed; if the defendant submits new reasons for defense, and the collegial panel considers it necessary, the court debate may be resumed.

E. Deliberation and declaration of judgment. After the defendant makes his/her final statement, the presiding judge shall announce an adjournment, and the collegial panel shall conduct its deliberations. When deliberating a case, the collegial panel shall, on the basis of the ascertained facts, evidence and relevant legal provisions, and on the basis of full consideration of the opinions of the prosecutor and the defender, determine whether the defendant is guilty, what crime he/she has committed, whether there are circumstances for heavier, lighter, mitigated or exempted punishment, whether to impose criminal punishment, what punishment to be imposed, how to solve the problems in the incidental civil action, how to dispose of the sealed, seized or frozen property and proceeds thereof, etc., and shall render a judgment and ruling in accordance with law. If the facts of a case are clear, the evidence is solid and sufficient, and the defendant is found guilty in accordance with law, a guilty sentence shall be rendered accordingly; if the defendant is found innocent in accordance with law, an acquittal sentence shall be rendered accordingly; if the evidence is insufficient, thus the defendant cannot be found guilty accordingly, an acquittal sentence shall be rendered stating that the charges are denied for insufficient evidence. After the collegial panel has rendered a judgment through deliberation, it shall declare the judgment. There are two forms of declaration of judgment: declaration of judgment in court and declaration of judgment on a fixed date. If the judgment is declared in court, the written judgment shall be served within five days. If the judgment is declared on a fixed date, the time and place of declaration of judgment shall be announced in advance before the declaration of judgment, and the parties shall be summoned and the public prosecutor, legal representative, defender and litigation representative shall be notified; after the declaration of judgment, the written judgment shall be immediately served. The written judgment shall be served upon the people's procuratorate, the parties, legal representative, defender and litigation representative, and may be served upon the close relative of the defendant. In all cases, judgments shall be declared publicly. The absence of the public prosecutor, defender, litigation representative, victim, private prosecutor or the plaintiff of the incidental civil action in court shall not affect the declaration of judgment. When declaring a judgment or ruling of first instance, a local people's court at any level shall notify the defendant, private prosecutor or his legal representative that he/she has the right to appeal, in writing or orally, to the court or directly to the original people's court of first instance at the next higher level against the judgment or ruling within the statutory time limit.

(4) Time Limit for the Trial of First Instance of a Case of Public Prosecution

Article 208 of the Criminal Procedure Law provides that: a people's court shall announce a sentence for a case of public prosecution within two months, or three months at the latest, after accepting the case. For a case with the possibility of a death penalty or a case with an incidental civil action or under any of the circumstances as set forth in Article 158 of this Law, the period of trial may be extended for three months with the approval of the people's court at the next higher level; and, if more extension is needed under special circumstances, the extension shall be reported to the Supreme People's Court for approval. Where the jurisdiction of a people's court over a case is changed, the period of trial of the case shall be counted from the day when the people's court having jurisdiction receives the case after the change. For a case under supplementary investigation by a people's procuratorate, the people's court shall count anew the period of trial of the case after the supplementary investigation has bee completed and the case has been transferred to the people's court.

1.3. Procedure at First Instance for Cases of Private Prosecution

Procedure at first instance of a case of private prosecution refers to the procedure for the first trial of a case initiated by a private prosecutor in a people's court. The procedure at first instance of a case of private prosecution is basically the same as that of first instance of a case of public prosecution in general. Among them, the scope of cases of private prosecution as well as the conditions and procedures for initiating private prosecution have been introduced in the foregoing paragraphs; we will only elaborate some characteristics of the acceptance and trial of cases of private prosecution.

(1) Acceptance of Cases of Private Prosecution

After receiving a privately-prosecuted complaint or an oral complaint, the people's court shall examine the case pursuant to the conditions for acceptance. If it finds any of the following circumstances, the people's court shall persuade the private prosecutor to withdraw the private prosecution or render a ruling to dismiss the private prosecution; if the private prosecutor does not withdraw the private prosecution, the people's court shall refuse to accept the private prosecution: **a.** where the conditions for initiating private prosecution are not met; **b.** where the evidence is insufficient; **c.** where there is lack of evidence; **d.** where the limitation period for criminal prosecution has expired; **e.** where the defendant is deceased; **f.** where the defendant's whereabouts are unknown; **g.** where the private prosecutor, after withdrawing the complaint, files a complaint with respect to the same fact, unless the case is withdrawn due to insufficient evidence; **h.** where, after closing the case through mediation of the people's court, the private prosecutor renounces the mediation and files a complaint with respect to the same fact again.

If the people's court, upon examination, deems that the case meets the conditions for acceptance, it shall make a decision of case filing and notify the private prosecutor or the person prosecuting on behalf of him/her in writing.

(2) Hearing of Cases of Private Prosecution

Because of the particularity of cases of private prosecution, the trial procedure of such cases also has some characteristics different from the ordinary procedure at first instance of cases of public prosecution:

For cases to be handled only upon complaint, summary procedure may be applied if the victims prosecute the cases for which there is evidence to prove that such cases are minor.

For cases to be handled only upon complaint and minor criminal cases for which the victims have evidence to prove, when such cases are minor, the people's court may mediate on the basis of ascertaining the facts and distinguishing right from wrong. If an agreement is reached through mediation, the people's court shall prepare a written mediation agreement in the criminal case of private prosecution, which shall be signed by the judges/jurors and court clerks, and affixed with the seal of the people's court. The written mediation agreement shall become legally effective after it is received and signed by both parties. If no agreement is reached through mediation or if a party renounces the mediation before signing for receipt of the written mediation agreement, the people's court shall make a judgment. Mediation shall not apply to cases of private prosecution converted from public prosecution.

For cases of private prosecution, the private prosecutor may reach a settlement with the defendant or withdraw his/her prosecution before a judgment is announced. If the private prosecutor requests to withdraw his/her prosecution, and the people's court considers upon examination that the request is indeed voluntary, the people's court shall approve the request. If the private prosecutor, having been served twice with summons according to law, refuses to appear in court without justifiable reasons, or if he/she leaves from a court session without permission of the court, the case may be considered withdrawn by him/her.

During the trial of a case of private prosecution, if the defendant's whereabouts are unknown, the trial may be suspended. After the defendant is brought to justice, the trial shall be resumed, and compulsory measures shall be taken against the defendant according to law when necessary.

In the process of the proceedings, the defendant or his/her legal representative of a case handled only upon complaint and a minor case for which the victim has evidence to prove may file a counterclaim against the private prosecutor. A counterclaim must meet the following conditions: first, the defendant of the counterclaim must be the private prosecutor of the case; second, the content of the counterclaim must be acts related to the case; and third, the counterclaim must be cases to be handled only upon complaint or minor cases for which the people's procuratorate has not initiated a prosecution while the victims have evidence to prove.

Time limit for the trial of first instance of a case of private prosecution. Article 212 of the Criminal Procedure Law provides that: "The period for a people's court to try a case of private prosecution shall be governed by paragraph 1 or 2, Article 208 of this Law if the defendant is in custody; or a sentence shall be announced within six months after the case is accepted if the defendant is not in custody."

1.4. Summary Procedure

Summary procedure refers to a relatively simplified trial procedure that is applied by a primary people's court to hear certain criminal cases in which the facts are clear, and the defendant admits his/her crimes and raises no objection to the facts of the crime accused in indictment.

(1) Characteristics of Summary Procedure

First, only applicable to the procedure at first instance. Summary procedure does not apply to the procedure at second instance, the procedure for review of death sentences or the procedure for trial supervision.

Second, only applicable to primary people's courts. Summary procedure does not apply to major, complex or difficult criminal cases that fall within the jurisdiction of intermediate people's courts, higher people's courts and the Supreme People's Court.

Third, the specific content of summary procedure is the relative simplification of the general procedure at first instance, such as simplification of trial organization and trial procedure, etc. These simplifications are expressly provided for in the Criminal Procedure Law.

Fourth, the trial period is shorter than that of general procedure. Article 220 of the Criminal Procedure Law provides that: "For a case under summary procedures, a people's court shall close the case within 20 days after accepting the case; or, if the defendant may be sentenced to fixed-term imprisonment of more than three years, the above period may be extended to one and a half months."

(2) Conditions to the Application of Summary Procedure

Article 214 of the Criminal Procedure Law provides that: "A case under the jurisdiction of a primary people's court may be heard under summary procedures, if the following conditions are met: (1) the facts of a case are clear and evidence is sufficient; (2) the defendant confesses his/her crime and raises no objection to the charges; and (3) the defendant raises no objection to the application of summary procedures." At the same time, Article 215 provides that: "Under any of the following circumstances, summary procedures shall not apply: (1) the defendant suffers vision, hearing, or speech impairment or is a mental patient who has not completely lost the ability to recognize or control his/her behavior; (2) the case has a significant social impact; (3) in a joint crime, some defendants plead not guilty or raises an objection to the application of summary procedures; or (4) the application of summary procedures is otherwise inappropriate." Pursuant to Article 360 of the Interpretation of the Criminal Procedure Law, if the defendant is blind, deaf or dumb; if the defendant is a mental patient who has not completely lost the ability to recognize or control his own behavior; if the case has a significant social impact; if some defendants in a joint crime case plead not guilty or raise an objection to the application of summary procedure; if the defender pleads unguilty; or if the defendant pleads guilty but the court believes upon review that the case may not constitute a crime, summary procedure shall not apply.

(3) Application of Summary Procedure and Trial

If, after accepting a case of public prosecution, the primary people's court believes that the facts of the case are clear and the evidence is sufficient upon review, it shall, when serving the copy of the indictment upon the defendant, ask for the defendant's opinions on the charges and inform him/her of the legal provisions on the application of summary procedure. If the defendant has no objection to the charges and agrees to the application of summary procedure, the people's court may decide to apply summary procedure and notify the people's procuratorate and the defender before trial. For a case for which the people's procuratorate suggests the application of summary procedure, it shall be handled in accordance with the above provisions; if the case does not meet the application conditions of summary procedure, the people's procuratorate shall be notified thereof.

For a case to which summary procedure applies, attention shall be paid to the following aspects in the trial stage:

A. Simplification of the form of trial organization. Article 216 of the Criminal Procedure Law provides that: "In a case under summary procedures, if the defendant may be sentenced to fixed-term imprisonment of three years or a lighter punishment, the case may be tried by a collegial panel or a sole judge; and if the defendant may be sentenced to fixed-term imprisonment of more than three years, a collegial panel must be formed to try the case."

B. Requinement of the procurators' apperance. In a case of public prosecution, the people's procuratorate shall send procurators to appear in court.

C. Simplification of the procedures of court investigation and court debate. Article 219 of the Criminal Procedure Law provides that: "The trial of a case under summary procedures shall not be subject to the provisions of Section 1 of this chapter regarding the time limit for service of process and the procedures for questioning the defendant, witnesses, and identification or evaluation experts, adducing evidence, and debating in court. However, before a sentence is announced, the closing statement of the defendant shall be heard."

D. Possibility of summary procedure be changed into general procedure when necessary. According to Article 368 of the Interpretations of the Criminal Procedure Law, the trial of a case under summary procedure shall be changed into general procedure if: the defendant's acts may not constitute any crime; the defendant may not bear any criminal liability; the defendant denies in court the crime charged in the indictment; the facts of the case are unclear or the evidence is insufficient; or there are other circumstances under which the summary procedure shall not be applied or is inappropriate to apply. For a case changed into general procedure, the time limit for trial shall be recalculated as of the date when the decision to change it into general procedure is made.

E. Simplification of the declaration of judgments. For a case to which summary procedure applies, a judgment shall generally be declared in court, and the written judgment shall be served upon the defendant and the people's procuratorate that initiated the public prosecution within five days.

1.5. Expedited Procedure

Expedited procedure was a new procedure added into the 2018 amendment to the Criminal Procedure Law, and was a simpler ordinary trial procedure more than the summary procedure.

(1) Scope of Application of Expedited Procedure

Article 222 of the Criminal Procedure Law provides that: "The expedited procedure may apply to a case under the jurisdiction of a primary people's court where the defendant may be sentenced to fixed-term imprisonment of not more than three years, provided that the facts of the case are clear, the evidence is solid and sufficient, and the defendant admits guilt, accepts punishment, and agrees with the application of the expedited procedure."

Article 223 provides that: "Under any of the following circumstances, the expedited procedure shall not apply: (1) The defendant suffers vision, hearing, or speech impairment or is a mental patient who has not completely lost the ability to recognize or control his/her behavior. (2) The defendant is a juvenile. (3) The case has a significant social impact. (4) In a joint crime case, some defendants raised any objection to the facts of the crime which they are charged with, the charges, the sentencing recommendation, or the application of the expedited procedure. (5) The defendant fails to reach a mediation or settlement agreement with the victim or his/her legal representative on compensation in an incidental civil action and other matters. (6) The application of the expedited procedure is otherwise inappropriate."

(2) Trial of Expedited Procedure

In accordance with Articles 222 to 226 of the Criminal Procedure Law, when a people's procuratorate initiates a public prosecution, it may recommend that the people's court apply the expedited procedure. The people's court may also decide to apply at its own discretion. And the case shall be tried by a sole judge.

The trial of a case under the expedited procedure shall not be subject to the provisions of Section 1 of this chapter regarding the time limit for service of process, and court investigation and debating in court are generally not conducted; however, before a sentence is announced, the opinion of the defender and the closing statement of the defendant shall be heard. For a case under the expedited procedure, a people's court shall close the case within ten days after accepting the case; or if the defendant may be sentenced to fixed-term imprisonment of more than one year, the above period may be extended to fifteen days. For a case tried under the expedited procedure, the sentence shall be announced in court.

Where, during the trial of a case, a people's court discovers that the defendant's conduct does not constitute a crime or the defendant shall not be held criminally liable, the defendant admits guilt and accepts punishment against his/her will, the defendant denies the facts of the crime which he/she is charged with or the application of the expedited procedure to the trial of the case is otherwise inappropriate, the people's court shall try the case anew in accordance with the provisions of Section 1 or Section 3 of this chapter.

2. Second Instance

2.1. General Overview

(1) Concept of Procedure at Second Instance

The procedure at second instance is also referred to as the procedure of appeal. It includes steps, methods and ways which shall be followed by the people's court of second instance in hearing a case regarding the facts ascertained and the law applicable in the judgment or ruling of the people's court of first instance that has not become legally effective, according to the appeal by the appellant or protest by the people's procuratorate. It is an independent stage in the criminal procedure.

(2) Characteristics of Procedure at Second Instance

A. The procedure of the second instance may not necessarily be the

second trial of the same case. The second trial of the same case may be the second instance, the first instance, or even a trial supervision procedure.

B. The procedure of the second instance is not a compulsory procedure in the trial of criminal cases. Whether a case has gone through the second instance procedure or not depends on whether the appellant or the procuratorial authority has appealed or protested according to law.

C. The people's courts at all levels other than the primary people's courts may become the people's courts at higher levels. Any appeal or protest filed against the first-instance judgment or ruling made by the court at a lower level shall be subject to the procedure at second instance.

(3) The Tasks of Procedure at Second Instance

The tasks of the procedure at the second instance are: the people's court of the second instance shall conduct a comprehensive examination and trial of the facts ascertained in the judgment or ruling of the first instance, whether the evidence is solid and sufficient, whether the application of law is correct, and whether the procedure is lawful, and make a ruling or judgment according to law, so as to maintain the correct judgment or ruling of the first instance and correct the wrong judgment or ruling of the first instance.

2.2. The Initiation of Procedure at Second Instance

(1) The Subject of Procedure at Second Instance

According to Articles 227 and 228 of the Criminal Procedure Law, against a sentence or ruling of a local people's court at any level as a court of first instance, a defendant, a private prosecutor, or a legal representative thereof shall have the right to appeal in writing or verbally to the people's court at the next higher level. A defender or close relative of a defendant may, with the consent of the defendant, file an appeal for the defendant. Deeming that there is any definite errors in a sentence or ruling of a people's court at the same level as a court of first instance, a local people's procuratorate shall file a protest with the people's court at the next higher level. In order to ensure that the defendant can exercise the right to appeal, this article clearly provides that: "A defendant shall not be deprived of the right to appeal under any pretext." In addition, Article 229 of the Criminal Procedure Law provides that: "Against a sentence of a local people's court at any level as a court of first instance, a victim or his/her legal representative shall, within five days after receiving a written sentence, have the right to request that the people's procuratorate files a protest. The people's procuratorate shall, within five days after receiving the request of the victim or his or her legal representative, make a decision on whether to file a protest and make a reply to the requesting party."

(2) The Reasons for Appeal or Protest

The Criminal Procedure Law provides no limitation on the grounds for appeal. Therefore, the appellant shall be allowed to appeal within the statutory time limit, regardless of whether the grounds are good or not. According to Article 228 of the Criminal Procedure Law, the people's procuratorate can lodge a protest only when it has sufficient grounds to determine that the original judgment or ruling is "definitely wrong". In practice, the grounds for appeal or protest can be summed up as follows: **a.** the determination of facts in the judgment or ruling is wrong, or lacks solid and sufficient evidence; **b.** the application of laws, conviction and sentencing in the judgment or ruling is wrong; **c.** the litigation rights to which the parties are legally entitled are infringed upon, which may affect the correctness of the judgment or ruling.

(3) Time Limit for Appeal or Protest

Article 230 of the Criminal Procedure Law provides that: "The time limit for filing an appeal against a sentence shall be 10 days, and the time limit for filing an appeal against a ruling shall be five days, starting from the next day of receipt of a written sentence or ruling."

(4) Methods and Procedures for Appeal or Protest

Generally, an appeal shall be lodged in writing. An appellant who has difficulty in writing an appeal may lodge an appeal orally. The people's court of first instance shall make a written record of the reasons and requests stated by him/her. After the record has been read by the appellant or has been read out to him/her, the appellant shall sign or seal the record. An appellant may appeal through the people's court of original instance or directly to the people's court of second instance.

With regard to the methods for lodging a protest, Article 232 of the Criminal Procedure Law provides that: "Against a sentence or ruling of a people's court at the same level as a court of first instance, a local people's procuratorate shall file a written protest through the original trial court and send a copy thereof to the people's procuratorate at the next higher level. The original trial court shall transfer the written protest along with the case file and evidence to the people's court at the next higher level and serve a copy of the written protest upon the parties. Deeming the protest inappropriate, the people's procuratorate at a higher level may withdraw the protest from the people's court at the same level and notify the people's procuratorate at a lower level."

2.3. Trial in the Procedure at Second Instance

(1) Examination of Appeal or Protest Cases

The people's court of second instance shall examine the files of appeal or protest cases transferred by the people's court of first instance to determine whether the following contents are included: **a.** letter of transfer of appeal (protest) cases; **b.** petition for appeal or protest; **c.** copies of written judgment or ruling of first instance; and **d.** all case materials and evidence. If the above materials are complete, the people's court of second instance shall accept the case; if the materials are incomplete or do not meet the requirements, the people's court of first instance shall be notified to make timely supplements.

Article 233 of the Criminal Procedure Law provides that: "The people's court of second instance shall conduct a comprehensive review of the facts found and law applied in the sentence of the people's court of first instance, without limitations to the extent of appeal. Where not all defendants in a case of joint crime file an appeal, the entire case shall be reviewed and handled." Therefore, the principle of comprehensive examination shall be adhered to in the procedure at second instance. A comprehensive examination of an appeal or protest case shall focus on the following contents:

a. Whether the facts ascertained in the judgment of first instance are clear, whether the evidence is solid and sufficient, and whether there is any contradiction between the evidence.

b. Whether the law applied in the judgment of first instance is correct, and whether the sentencing is appropriate.

c. Whether there is any violation of the legal procedures in the investigation, prosecution and the procedure at first instance.

d. Whether any new fact or evidence is presented in the appeal or protest.

e. The confessions and arguments of the defendant.

f. The defense opinions of the defender and the adoption thereof.

g. Whether the judgment or ruling of the incidental civil action is appropriate.

h. The opinions of the collegial panel and the judicial committee of the court of first instance, and so on.

On the basis of a comprehensive examination, the people's court of second instance shall make a comprehensive treatment of the case, that is, whether the reasons for appeal or protest are sufficient, whether the judgment or ruling of first instance is correct, and whether the procedure is lawful, so that all the erroneous judgments or rulings concerning the defendants that appealed or not appealed, whether pointed out and not pointed out in the petition of appeal or protest, are corrected.

(2) Trial Methods and Procedures of Cases of Second Instance

Article 234 of the Criminal Procedure Law provides that: "A people's court of second instance shall form a collegial panel to hear the following case in a court session: (1) an appellate case where a defendant or a private prosecutor or the legal representative thereof has raised any objection to the facts and evidence determined in the trial at first instance, which may affect conviction and sentencing; (2) an appellate case where the defendant is sentenced to the death penalty; (3) a case protested by the people's procuratorate; and (4) any other case which shall be heard in a court session. Where a people's court of second instance decides not to hold a court session to hear a case, it shall arraign the defendant and hear the opinions of other parties, defenders, and litigation representatives. A people's court of second instance may hold a court session to hear an appellate case at the place of occurrence of the case or the place where the original trial court is located." Article 235 of the Criminal Procedure Law provides that: "For a case protested by a people's procuratorate or a case of public prosecution heard by a people's court of second instance in a court session, the people's procuratorate at the same level shall send procurators to appear before court. The people's court of second instance shall, after deciding to hold a court session to hear a case, notify the people's procuratorate in a timely manner to consult the case file. The people's procuratorate shall complete consultation of the case file within one month. The time for the people's procuratorate to consult the case file shall not be counted in the period of trial."

During the court investigation stage, after the presiding judge or the judge reads out the judgment or ruling of first instance, the appellant shall state the reasons for appeal or the procurator shall read out the written protest. The focus of court investigation shall be on the reasons for appeal or protest, with a comprehensive investigation of the facts and verification of evidence.

During the court debate stage, with respect to a case of appeal, the appellant and the defender shall first make statements, then the procurator and the other party shall make statements; with respect to a case of protest, the procurator shall first make statements, then the defendant and the defender shall make statements, then the debate shall be carried out successively. The defendant in a joint crime case who does not file an appeal or is not against shall also be asked to participate in court investigation and debate. The victims shall have the right to participate in the court trial. At the end of the debate, the appellant (the defendant) shall have the right to make a final statement; then the collegial panel shall deliberate on it and render a judgment.

With respect to a case not to be heard in a court session, the collegial panel of a people's court of second instance shall, after consulting the case files, interrogating the defendant and hearing the opinions of other parties, defenders, and agents ad litem, render a judgment or ruling.

(3) Handling of Cases of Second Instance

According to Article 236 of the Criminal Procedure Law, "After hearing an appellate case against a sentence of a people's court of first instance, the people's court of second instance shall handle it as follows: (1) if the original sentence is correct in fact finding and application of law and is appropriate in sentencing, the people's court of second instance shall render a ruling to dismiss the appeal and uphold the original sentence; (2) if the original sentence is correct in fact finding but erroneous in application of law or is inappropriate in sentencing, the people's court of second instance shall modify the original sentence; or (3) if the facts are unclear or evidence is insufficient in the original judgment, the people's court of second instance may modify the original sentence after the case facts are ascertained, or render a ruling to revoke the original sentence and remand the case to the original trial court for retrial. Where a defendant or the people's procuratorate appeals after the original trial court renders a sentence for a case remanded for retrial under item (3) of the preceding paragraph, the people's court of second instance shall render a sentence or ruling in accordance with law and may not remand the case again to the original trial court for retrial."

Article 238 provides that: "Where a people's court of second instance discovers that a people's court of first instance has committed any of the following violations of statutory procedures when hearing a case, it shall render a ruling to revoke the original sentence and remand the case to the original trial court for retrial: (1) the provisions of this Law regarding open trial are violated; (2) the disqualification provisions are violated; (3) a party is deprived of statutory procedural rights or such rights of a party are restricted, which may affect a fair trial; (4) the composition of a trial organization is illegal; or (5) statutory procedures are otherwise violated, which may affect a fair trial."

All judgments or rulings rendered by the people's court of second instance, except for death penalty cases, shall be final and shall come into force once announced. The appellant and his legal representative, etc. shall not appeal again, and the people's procuratorate shall not lodge a protest pursuant to the procedures of second instance. The people's court of second instance may announce its judgment or ruling by itself or entrust the people's court of original instance to announce on its behalf.

(4) Time Limit for the Trial of Cases of Second Instance

According to Article 243 of the Criminal Procedure Law, after accepting an appellate case, a people's court of second instance shall close the trial of the case within two months. For a case with the possibility of a death penalty or a case with an incidental civil action or under any of the circumstances as set forth in Article 158 of this Law, the period of trial may be extended for two months with the approval or decision of the higher people's court of a province, autonomous region, or municipality directly under the Central Government; and, if more extension is needed under special circumstances, the extension shall be reported to the Supreme People's Court for approval. The period for the Supreme People's Court to try an appellate case shall be decided by the Supreme People's Court.

2.4. Principle of No Aggravation of Punishment in Appeal

The principle of no aggravation of punishment in appeal in China refers to a trial principle that when the people's court of second instance hears a case only appealed by the defendant, it shall not aggravate the criminal punishment on the defendant for any reason. The specific meaning of this principle is:

First, appeal is the lawful right of the defendant, and whether the reasons for appeal are proper or not, the original sentence shall not be aggravated in the judgment of second instance on the ground that the defendant disagrees with the judgment or has a bad attitude.

Second, for a case which only the defendant appeals, when the court of second instance confirms the necessity of changing the sentence after trial, even if the original sentence is too light, the criminal punishment on the defendant shall not be aggravated.

Third, for a case which only the defendant appeals, the court of second instance shall not, on the ground of unclear facts and insufficient evidence, remand a case with only too light sentencing for a new trial, nor direct the court of first instance to aggravate the criminal punishment on the defendant. In a case remanded by the people's court of second instance for retrial, the people's court which originally retried the case may not aggravate the criminal punishment on the defendant, unless there is any new crime and the people's procuratorate has initiated a supplementary prosecution.

The fact that no aggravation of punishment may be imposed upon appeal does not mean that in any case the court of second instance may not aggravate the criminal punishment on the defendant. Article 237 of the Criminal Procedure Law provides that, for a case protested by a people's procuratorate or appealed by a private prosecutor, if the judgment of first instance is indeed too light, the people's court of second instance may change the sentence to aggravate the criminal punishment on the defendant.

3. Review of Death Sentences

3.1. Concept and Characteristics of Procedure for Review of Death Sentences

Procedure for review of death sentences refers to the special trial procedure conducted by the people's court in the review and approval of a case in which a death penalty is imposed. This special procedure embodies legislators' extremely cautious attitude towards death penalty cases, which can prevent and correct the deviations and mistakes that may occur in death penalty cases to the greatest extent, unify the standards for the application of death penalty, and implement the guidelines of imposing fewer death penalties, exerting caution in making death sentences, and avoiding mistakes in death penalty cases. Procedure for review of death sentences has the following characteristics:

A. Specific objects of trial. Procedure for death sentence review only applies to cases in which the death penalty is imposed, including the cases in which death penalty is imposed with immediate execution and death penalty with a two-year suspension.

B. Final procedure in death penalty cases. The judgments on ordinary criminal cases shall become legally effective after they go through the procedure at first and second instance. In addition to the procedures of first and second instance, death penalty cases must also go through the procedure of death sentence review. Only the death penalty which has been reviewed and approved will become legally effective. In this sense, the procedure for review of death sentences is an exception to the system of two instances.

C. The procedure of review of death sentences is initiated proactively. That is different from the principle of "no complaint, no hearing" that must be followed in other trial procedures, and the procedure of review of death sentences is automatically initiated without complaint.

D. The power to review the death penalty is exclusive. The Supreme People's Court has the power to review death penalty cases and the higher people's courts have the power to review cases of death penalty with a two-year suspension.

3.2. Submission for Review of Death Sentences

For a case of first instance heard by the intermediate people's court in which the defendant has been sentenced to the death penalty, if the defendant does not appeal and the people's procuratorate does not protest, such a case shall be submitted to the higher people's court for review within ten days upon expiry of the time limit for appeal or protest. Where the higher people's court agrees with the death penalty, it shall submit the case to the Supreme People's Court for approval within ten days after it renders its ruling; if it disagrees, the higher people's court shall bring the case up for trial or remand the case for retrial in accordance with the procedure at second instance.

For a case of first instance heard by the intermediate people's court in which the defendant has been sentenced to the death penalty, if the defendant appeals or the people's procuratorate protests, but the higher people's court rules to uphold the judgment, the case shall be submitted to the Supreme People's Court for approval within ten days after it renders its ruling.

For a case of first instance heard by the higher people's court in which the defendant has been sentenced to the death penalty, if the defendant does not appeal and the people's procuratorate does not protest, such a case shall be submitted to the Supreme People's Court for approval within ten days upon expiry of the time limit for appeal or protest.

3.3. Materials and Requirements for Submitting Death Penalty Cases for Review

For each death penalty case submitted for review, one submission shall be made for each case. The materials to be submitted shall include five copies of the report on submission for review, the written documents of judgment of first and second instance and the comprehensive report on the case, and all case files and evidence. For cases that have been remanded for retrial, the files of the ordinary. first and second instance shall be submitted at the same time.

The report on submission for review shall include the following contents: cause of action, summary of the case, trial process, and judgment.

The comprehensive report on the death penalty case shall include the following contents: **a.** Basic information about the defendant and the victim. Where the defendant has a criminal record or has been subject to any administrative penalty, such a record or history shall be stated. **b.** Case origin and process of trial. Where the case has been remanded for retrial, the reasons for remanding for retrial, the time of remanding and the case number, etc. of such a retrial shall be stated. **c.** Investigation of the case. The situation of catching the defendant and detecting the case through technical investigation measures, and the situation related to the voluntary surrender and meritorious service shall be stated. **d.** Trial of first instance, including the opinions of the prosecutor and the defender, the facts of crime determined in the first instance, the opinions of the collegial panel and the judicial committee. **e.** Trial of second instance or review of the higher people's court, including the reasons for appeal, opinions of the procuratorate, the facts determined in the trial of second instance or the review of the higher people's court, the admissibility of evidence and the reasons therefor, the opinions of the prosecutor and the defender and the admissibility thereof. **f.** Issues that need to be stated, including the conviction and sentencing of other offenders of the same case in the joint crime case, whether the case has significant social impact, and the reactions of the parties concerned, etc. **g.** Handling opinions, which shall state the opinions of the collegial panel and the judicial committee.

Files and evidence of cases shall, in light of the specific situation of a case, include the following contents: **a.** photocopies of detention warrant, arrest warrant, and search warrant; **b.** list of seized money, stolen goods and other physical evidence on the case; **c.** prosecution opinions or the report of the investigation conclusion of the people's procuratorate; **d.** indictment of prosecution of the people's procuratorate; **e.** reports of case examination, records of court examination, records of deliberations of the collegial panel, and records of discussions and decisions of the judicial committee; **f.** petitions for appeal and protest; **g.** judgments, rulings, records of announcements, and acknowledgements of service of the people's courts; **h.** all kinds of affirmative and negative evidence that can prove the specific situation of a case and have been verified to be true, including material evidence or pictures thereof, documentary evidence, testimony of witnesses, statements of victims, confessions and arguments of the defendant, expert opinions, and records of inquests and examination, etc.

3.4. Procedures for Review of Death Sentences

Review of death sentences by the Supreme People's Court shall be conducted by a collegial panel composed of three judges. In general, the following activities shall be conducted for the review of death penalty cases:

(1) Interrogation of the Defendant

Interrogation of the defendant is not only conducive to providing him/her with an opportunity to defend himself/herself finally, but also helpful for finding out the true situation of the case, discovering and correcting the wrongful judgment, and effectively safeguarding the defendant's right of defense. Therefore, with respect to death penalty cases, the defendant shall be interrogated and his/her defense opinions shall be heard in his/her presence.

(2) Examination and Verification of Case Files

A comprehensive examination of case files may reveal whether the facts are clearly ascertained in the original judgment, whether the evidence is solid and sufficient, whether the determination of the nature of the case is accurate, whether the legal procedures are complete, and whether the sentence of the death penalty against the defendant is correct, so as to correctly handle the case in light of the arraignment of the defendant. When reviewing case files, the following contents shall be comprehensively examined: **a.** the age of the defendant, and whether the defendant has the capacity for liability, and whether she is a pregnant woman; **b.** whether the main facts ascertained in the original judgment are clear, and whether the evidence is solid and sufficient; **c.** the circumstances, consequence and extent of harm of the crime; **d.** whether the application of law in the original judgment is correct, and whether the sentence of death penalty must be imposed immediately; and **e.** whether there are statutory and discretionary circumstances for lighter or mitigated punishment, and so on.

(3) Hearing the Opinions of the Defender

Article 251 of the Criminal Procedure Law provides that: "The Supreme People's Court reviewing a death sentence shall arraign the defendant and, if the defense lawyer files a request for presenting an opinion, hear the opinion of the defense lawyer."

(4) Considering Opinions of the Supreme People's Procuratorate

During the review of a death penalty case, the Supreme People's Procuratorate may present an opinion to the Supreme People's Court.

(5) Preparation of a Review and Hearing Report

After a comprehensive examination of a death penalty case submitted for review, the collegial panel shall conduct the deliberations and work out a report on the review and hearing. The report on the review and hearing shall include: **a.** the case origin and process of the case hearing; **b.** the profiles of the defendant and the victim; **c.** the investigation of the case; **d.** key points of the original judgment and the opinions of the prosecutor and the defender; **e.** the analysis and determination of the facts and evidence after the review; **f.** the deliberations of the collegial panel and the opinions of the judicial committee after the discussion; and **g.** other issues that need to be explained.

(6) Informing the Supreme People's Procuratorate of the Review Results of Death Penalty

The Criminal Procedure Law requires the Supreme People's Court to notify the Supreme People's Procuratorate of the review results of the death penalty case. The system aims to strengthen the procuratorial organ's legal supervision of the review procedures of death penalty cases.

3.5. Handling of Death Penalty Cases after the Review

After the review, the Supreme People's Court shall handle the cases respectively in one of the following manners:

a. If the original judgment is correct in the determination of facts and the application of law, and the sentencing is appropriate and the procedures are lawful, it shall render a ruling of approval.

b. If the original judgment is flawed in the determination of any specific fact or the application of law, but it is not inappropriate to sentence the defendant to the death penalty, it may render a judgment or ruling of approval after correction.

c. If the original judgment is based on unclear facts and insufficient evidence, it may render a ruling of disapproval, revoke the original judgment, and remand the case for retrial.

d. If, during the review, new facts or evidence that affect conviction and sentencing arise, it may render a ruling of disapproval, revoke the original judgment, and remand the case for retrial.

e. If the original judgment is based on correct facts, but it is inappropriate to sentence the defendant to death penalty according to the law, it may render a ruling of disapproval, revoke the original judgment, and remand the case for retrial.

f. If the original trial is in violation of the statutory procedures, which may affect the impartiality of the trial, it may render a ruling of disapproval, and revoke the original judgment, and remand the case for retrial.

For cases of combined punishment for more than two crimes committed by a person who is sentenced to death, if the Supreme People's Court finds upon such reviews that the facts in the judgment or verdict of the death penalty for some of these crimes are unclear and the evidence is insufficient, it may render a ruling of disapproval of the whole case, revoke the original judgment, and remand the case for retrial; if the Supreme People's Court finds upon such reviews that the facts in the judgment or verdict of death penalty for some of these crimes are correct while it should not be sentenced to death according to the law, it may change the judgment or verdict, and render a ruling of death penalty for other crimes that should be punished by death penalty. For cases of death penalty involving more than two defendants, if the Supreme People's Court finds upon review that the facts in the judgment or verdict of death penalty for some of the defendants are unclear and the evidence is insufficient, it shall render a ruling of disapproval of the whole case, revoke the original judgment, and remand the case for retrial; if the Supreme People's Court finds that facts in the judgment or verdict of death penalty for some of the defendants are correct, but it is inappropriate to give them death penalty according to the law, it may change the judgment of death penalty on such defendants, and make a ruling of approval of death penalty for other defendants that should be sentenced to death.

If the Supreme People's Court renders a ruling of disapproval of death penalty, it may remand the case to the people's court of second or first instance for retrial in accordance with the situation of the case. Where the people's court of first instance retries the case, it shall hear the case in a court hearing. If the people's court of second instance retries the case, it may directly revise the judgment; if a court session must be held to confirm the facts or verify the evidence, or correct any illegal act in the ordinary trial procedure, the case shall be heard in a court hearing. If, after the higher people's court submits the case to the Supreme People's Court for approval of the death penalty in accordance with the review procedure, the Supreme People's Court renders a ruling of disapproval, and remands the case to the higher people's court for retrial, the higher people's court may directly retry the case or remand the case for retrial in accordance with the procedure of second instance.

For the case which the Supreme People's Court renders a ruling of the disapproval of the death penalty and remands for retrial, the original people's court shall form a new collegial panel to hear such cases.

4. Trial Supervision

4.1. Concept and Characteristics of Trial Supervision Procedure

Trial supervision procedure refers to the procedure whereby the people's court or the people's procuratorate discovers any definite errors in the determination of facts or application of law in a legally effective judgment or ruling, and initiate the procedure to retry the case in accordance with the law.

Trial supervision procedure has the following characteristics: first, from the nature of the litigation, trial supervision procedure is a remedial procedure. As a general rule of criminal procedure, a legally effective judgment or ruling shall have res judicata once it is announced, and shall not be arbitrarily modified or revoked without going through legal procedures. However, in judicial practice, the established judgment or ruling is not absolutely correct. Due to subjective and objective reasons, some judgments or rulings may be wrong, resulting in the contradiction between the certainty of the judgment and the truthfulness of the case. In order to solve this contradiction, trial supervision procedure is established by legislation. Trial supervision procedure is therefore a remedial procedure established to correct miscarriages of justice. Second, from the perspective of the litigation process, trial supervision procedure is not a necessary procedure in every criminal case. Trial supervision procedure is not only applicable to special objects, but also, unlike the first or second instance procedures, even if there is a complaint (such as a prosecution or an appeal or protest), there may not be the retrial of the case. It is also different from the procedure review of death sentence, where the death penalty (including death penalty with a two-year suspension) must be reported level by level for approval. Whether this procedure is initiated or not does not depend on the appeal of the parties, and some cases may not necessarily be retried even after repeated appeals and requests, let alone reported for retrial level by level unconditionally. Therefore, from this point of view, trial supervision procedure cannot become a necessary procedure in every criminal case.

4.2. Sources of Materials for Initiating Trial Supervision Procedure

Sources of materials for instituting trial supervision procedure refer to channels for producing relevant evidence and materials when errors are found in legally effective judgments or rulings. It mainly includes: **a.** Petitions of the parties and their legal representatives, close relatives and relevant outsiders. **b.** Proposals for correcting wrongful judgments by People's Congresses at all levels. **c.** Letters and visits of the people. **d.** Judicial authorities' discovery of erroneous cases through case handling or reviewing. **e.** Opinions reflected by governmental institutions, groups, enterprises, public agencies, news media and networks on the effective judgments or rulings.

(1) Reasons for Petition and Their Effect

Reasons for petition must be given. According to Article 253 of the Criminal Procedure Law, where a petition of a party or his/her legal representative or close relative meets any of the following conditions, the people's court shall conduct a retrial: **a.** there is new evidence to prove that the facts are erroneously determined in the original sentence or ruling, which may affect conviction and sentencing; **b.** the evidence on which conviction and sentencing are based is not solid and sufficient or shall be excluded in accordance with the law, or the material evidence on the facts of the case contradicts each other; **c.** the application of law in the original sentence or ruling is incorrect; **d.** the statutory procedures are violated, which may affect a fair trial; or **e.** a judge committed embezzlement, bribery, or fraud for personal gains or bended the law when trying the case. As long as any of the reasons mentioned above for petition is satisfied, the people's court shall retry the case under trial supervision procedure.

Effect of petition refers to the effect on whether or not a legally effective judgment or original ruling shall be suspended for enforcement after the petition is made due to the party's disagreement with the judgment or ruling. Article 257 of the Criminal Procedure Law provides that, "for a case tried under the trial supervision procedure, a people's court may decide to suspend the execution of the original sentence or ruling." Article 464 of the Interpretation of the Criminal Procedure Law provides that, for a case decided to be retried under trial supervision procedure, the people's court shall make a written decision on retrial, and the execution of the original judgment or ruling shall not be suspended during the retrial. However, if the defendant may be found innocent after retrial, or may be found to have a lighter sentence, resulting in the expiration of his/her term of sentence after retrial, the people's court may decide to suspend the execution of the original judgment or ruling. When necessary, the people's court may take such measures as bail and residential confinement against the defendant.

(2) Acceptance, Examination and Handling of Petition

For the acceptance of petition, the first step shall be to accept the petition materials. Second, the issue of jurisdiction shall be resolved. The petition shall be examined and handled by the people's court of final instance. However, for a case in which the people's court of second instance approves the withdrawal of appeal, if the petitioner files a petition against the judgment of first instance, the people's court of first instance may examine and handle the petition. For a petition that has not been examined and handled by the people's court of final instance, the people's court at the next higher level may notify the petitioner to file a petition with the people's court of final instance, or directly deliver the petition to the people's court of final instance for examination and handling and notify the petitioner; if the case is difficult, complex and significant, the people's court at the next higher level may also examine and handle it directly. For a case which has not been examined and handled by the people's court of final instance or the people's court at next higher level but directly files a petition to the people's court at next higher level, the people's court at next higher level may notify the petitioner to file a petition to the people's court at next lower level. The petition against the death penalty case may be directly examined and handled by the people's court that originally approves the review of death sentence, or delivered to the people's court of first instance for examination and handling.

For a petition that has been placed on file for examination, the people's court shall make a decision within three months, which may not exceed six months at the latest. After accepting a petition, the people's court shall persuade the petitioner to withdraw the petition if it finds upon examination that there is none of the circumstances as provided in Article 253 of the Criminal Procedure Law; if the petitioner still insists on the petition, it shall dismiss the petition in writing. If the petitioner still refuses to accept the dismissal, he/she may file a petition to the people's court at next higher level. If the people's court at next higher level holds that the petition does not meet the provisions of the law, it shall persuade the petitioner to withdraw the petition; if the petitioner still insists on the petition, it shall dismiss the petition or notify the petitioner that the case shall not be reheard.

After examining a petition that has been accepted, if the people's procuratorate believes there are indeed errors in the effective judgment or ruling of the people's courtand a protest needs to be lodged, it shall be reported to the chief procurator who shall submit it to the procuratorial committee for discussion and decision.

For a case in which the people's procuratorate lodges a protest in accordance with the procedure of trial supervision, the people's court shall file it within one month upon receipt of the written protest. However, under any of the following circumstances, the case shall be handled in light of different circumstances: **a.** If the case is not within the jurisdiction of the people's procuratorate, the case shall be returned to the people's procuratorate. **b.** If it is impossible to serve the written protest upon the defendant of the original trial according to the address provided in the written protest, the people's procuratorate shall be notified to re-provide the address of the defendant of the original trial within three days; if it fails to do so within the time limit, the case shall be returned to the people's procuratorate. **c.** If the protest is lodged on the ground that there is new evidence, but the relevant evidence materials are not attached or the relevant evidence is not pointing to the facts of the original prosecution, the people's procuratorate shall be notified to provide supplementary materials within three days; if it fails to do so within the time limit, the case shall be returned to the people's procuratorate. For a protest case the people's court decides to return, if the people's procuratorate lodges the protest again after supplementing relevant materials, and it is examined that the protest meets the conditions for acceptance, the people's court shall accept the case.

4.3. Initiation of Trial Supervision Procedure

(1) Subject of Initiating Trial Supervision Procedure

The subjects that have the right to initiate trial supervision procedure can only be the following institutions, personnel and organizations:

A. The presidents of people's courts and judicial committees at all levels. Section 1, Article 254 of the Criminal Procedure Law provides that: "Where the president of a people's court at any level discovers that there are any definite errors in fact finding or application of law in an effective sentence or ruling of the court, the sentence or ruling must be submitted to the judicial committee for handling."

B. The Supreme People's Court and the people's courts at higher levels. Section 2 of this article provides that: "Where the Supreme People's Court discovers any definite errors in an effective sentence or ruling of a people's court at any level or a people's court at a higher level discovers any definite errors in an effective sentence or ruling of a people's court at a lower level, it shall have the authority to directly retry the case or order a people's court at a lower level to retry the case."

C. The Supreme People's Procuratorate and the people's procuratorates at higher levels. Section 3 of this article provides that: "Where the Supreme People's Procuratorate discovers any definite errors in an effective sentence or ruling of a people's court at any level or a people's procuratorate at a higher level discovers any definite errors in an effective sentence or ruling of a people's court at a lower level, it shall have the authority to file an appeal under the trial supervision procedures with the people's court at the same level."

(2) Grounds for Initiating Trial Supervision Procedure

Article 254 of the Criminal Procedure Law provides that: "Where the president of a people's court at any level discovers that there are any definite errors in fact finding or application of law in an effective sentence or ruling of the court, the sentence or ruling must be submitted to the judicial committee for handling." The errors in ascertaining facts in the original judgment include unclear facts and unreliable and insufficient evidence. Firstly, errors in the application of laws refer to the errors in the application of substantive laws, namely, the Criminal Law. Secondly, errors in the application of procedural laws, namely, the Criminal Procedure Law, mainly refer to the serious violations of criminal procedures by the people's court.

4.4. Retrying Cases in Accordance With Trial Supervision Procedure

(1) Methods of Retrial

Retrying cases in accordance with trial supervision procedure is for the purpose of correcting effective erroneous judgments, so a particularly prudent attitude should be taken. Both the res judicata of the original judgment and the correction of misjudged cases have to be achieved. Therefore, the methods of trial thereof should be mainly based on hearing, and supplemented by trial with no hearing.

The following cases shall be heard in a court session: **a.** trial in accordance with procedures at first instance; **b.** trial of facts or evidence in accordance with procedure at second instance; **c.** trial of the case in which people's procuratorate lodged a protest in accordance with trial supervision procedure; **d.** trial may aggravate the criminal punishment on the defendant of the original instance; **e.** other circumstances under which a court hearing shall be held.

The following cases may not be heard in a court session: **a.** The facts in the original judgment or ruling are clear, the evidence is solid and sufficient, but the application of law is wrong and the punishment is too heavy. **b.** The judgment or ruling was made before the Criminal Procedure Law came into effect in 1979. **c.** The defendant of the case of original instance or private prosecutor of the case of original instance is dead or has lost capacity for conduct. **d.** The defendant of the case of original instance is serving a sentence in a remote area where the traffic is quite inconvenient, and it is really difficult for the defendant of the case of original instance to be taken to court, when the people's procuratorate protests and the people's court has obtained the consent of the people's procuratorate. **e.** The people's court decides to retry the case in accordance with trial supervision procedure, and the people's procuratorate fails to assign procurators to appear in court after being notified twice.

(2) Procedure of Retrial

Article 256 of the Criminal Procedure Law provides that: "Where a people's court retries a case under the trial supervision procedure, a new collegial panel shall be formed if the retrial is conducted by the original trial court. If the case is originally tried by a people's court of first instance, it shall be retried under procedures at first instance and the sentence or ruling rendered may be appealed. If the case is originally tried by a people's court of second instance or is a case directly retried under the trial supervision procedures by a people's court at a higher level, it shall be retried under procedures at second instance and the sentence or ruling rendered shall be final. When a people's court retries a case in a court session, the people's procuratorate at the same level shall send procurators to appear before the court."

Article 257 of the Criminal Procedure Law provides that: "For a case which a people's court decides to retry, any necessary compulsory measure against a defendant shall be decided by the people's court; or, for a case to be retried upon appeal of a people's procuratorate under the trial supervision procedures, any necessary compulsory measure against a defendant shall be decided by the people's procuratorate."

(3) Time Limit for Retrial

Article 258 of the Criminal Procedure Law provides that: "The trial of a case by a people's court under the trial supervision procedures shall be closed within three months from the day when the court decides to directly retry the case or when a retrial decision is made, and, if any extension of the period is necessary, the period shall not exceed six months. The preceding paragraph shall apply to the period for a people's court accepting an appeal under the trial supervision procedures to retry the case appealed; and if it is necessary to order a people's court at a lower level to retry the case, a decision shall be made within one month from the day when the court accepts the appeal, and the preceding paragraph shall apply to the period for the people's court at a lower level to retry the case."

(4) Disposition After Retrial

After retrying a case in accordance with the procedure of trial supervision, the people's court shall, on the basis of the different circumstances of the case and the judicial interpretations of the Supreme People's Court, handle it as follows: **a.** Where the original judgment or ruling was correct in the determination of facts and the application of law and appropriate in terms of punishment, the people's court shall dismiss the petition or protest and affirm the original judgment or ruling. **b.** Where the original judgment or ruling was correct in the determination of facts and the application of law, but there are flaws in the determination of facts and the application of law, the people's court shall order to correct and affirm the original judgment or ruling. **c.** Where the original judgment or ruling was correct in the determination of facts but the application of law was incorrect, or the punishment was inappropriately given, the original judgment or ruling shall be rescinded and the judgment shall be amended in accordance with law. **d.** Where the facts in the original judgment or ruling were not clear or the evidence is insufficient in the original judgment or ruling, the people's court may revise the judgment after ascertaining the facts, or it may rescind the original judgment and remand the case to the people's court of original instance for retrial.

In addition, where the facts in the original judgment or ruling are unclear or the evidence is insufficient, and the facts have been ascertained after the trial, the people's court shall make the judgment according to the ascertained facts in accordance with the law; where the facts cannot be ascertained clearly and the evidence is insufficient, and the defendant cannot be found guilty, the people's court shall revoke the original judgment or ruling, and announce the defendant to be innocent. Where the defendant in the original trial against whom the protest is lodged is dead or dies during the trial, the people's court shall make a ruling to terminate the trial. However, if the facts can be ascertained clearly and the defendant in the original trial is confirmed to be innocent, the people's court shall change the original judgment. For parties who are declared innocent upon retrial, the people's court shall inform them that they may apply for state compensation in accordance with the law after the judgment takes effect when announcing the judgment.

It shall be pointed out that in general, the retrial may not aggravate the criminal punishment on the defendant in the original trial, except for those protested by the people's procuratorate. Where the retrial decision or protest is only against part of the defendants in the original trial, the criminal punishment of other defendants in the original trial of the same case may not be aggravated.

CHAPTER SEVEN

EXECUTION

The execution in criminal proceedings refers to the litigation activities involving the people's court, the people's procuratorate, the public security authority and other criminal penalty executing authorities to put the contents affirmed in legally effective judgments and rulings into effect in accordance with the law and settle the problems such as modification of execution that appear during the implementation.

1. Death Sentence With Immediate Execution

1.1. Execution

Death sentence is a punishment that deprives a convict of his/her life, so a death sentence shall be made or executed with great caution. In order to assure proper application of the death sentence and prevent wrongful execution in terms of litigation proceedings, the Criminal Procedure Law and relevant judicial interpretations provide strict and detailed provisions on the procedures for the death sentence with immediate execution, which mainly include:

(1) Issuance of the Order to Execute the Death Sentence

Pursuant to Article 261 of the Criminal Procedure Law, "for a death sentence with immediate execution rendered or approved by the Supreme People's Court, the president of the Supreme People's Court shall sign and issue an order to execute the death sentence." The order to execute a death sentence shall be filled out in a uniform format, signed by the president of the Supreme People's Court and affixed with the stamp of the Supreme People's Court.

(2) Organs and Time Limit for Execution of the Death Sentence

The order to execute a death sentence issued by the Supreme People's Court shall be handed over by the High People's Court to a people's court of first instance for execution. The people's court of first instance shall deliver the death sentence to be executed within seven days upon receipt of the order. If a convict sentenced to death with a two-year suspension intentionally commits a crime during the suspension period of the death sentence and the Supreme People's Court has approved the execution of the death sentence thereof, the execution shall be carried out by the intermediate people's court in the place where the convict serves his/her sentence.

(3) Supervision of Execution of the Death Sentence

Upon receipt of the notice of on-site supervision by the people's court at the same level over execution of the death sentence, the people's procuratorate shall immediately send officers to supervise the execution, including: **a.** ascertaining whether the people's court at the same level has received a judgment or ruling issued by the Supreme People's Court approving the death sentence as well as an order to execute the death sentence; **b.** examining the legality of the place, method of execution and the execution activities to be carried out; **c.** if, prior to execution of the death sentence, it is discovered that the execution shall be stopped or suspended as stipulated in the Criminal Procedure Law, the people's procuratorate shall advise the people's court to stop the execution immediately; **d.** taking photos and video recordings in the course of execution of a death sentence if necessary; **e.** checking whether the convict is dead after execution of the death sentence, filling out the on-site supervision record of execution, followed by signing and filing.

(4) Procedures for Execution of the Death Sentence

According to Article 263 of the Criminal Procedure Law, "execution of the death sentence shall be directed by the judge of the people's court. Prior to the execution, the judge directing execution shall confirm the identity of the convict, including but not limited to checking the name, gender, age, occupation, time of detention and arrest, so as to further ascertain whether the convict is the one to be executed in order to prevent wrongful execution; a judge directing execution shall verify the identity of the convict, ask the convict for any last words or letters, and then deliver the convict to the executioner for execution of the death sentence."

(5) The Convict is Entitled to Meet With Close Relatives Before Execution of the Death Sentence

In accordance with Article 505 of the Interpretation on the Application of the Criminal Procedure Law, "prior to execution of the death sentence, the people's court of first instance shall inform the convict of his/her right to meet with his/her close relatives. If the convict applies for meeting with his/her close relatives and providing specific contact information, the people's court shall notify close relatives of the convict. If it is indeed impossible to reach close relatives of the convict, or close relatives of the convict refuse to meet the convict, the convict shall be informed thereof. The people's court may grant permission to the convict for leaving his/her last words by means of audio recording, video recording or other means upon his/her application."

(6) Methods and Places for Execution of the Death Sentence

According to Article 507 of the Interpretation on the Application of the Criminal Procedure Law, "a death sentence shall be executed by such means as shooting or injection. Where a death sentence is executed by means other than shooting or injection, a prior approval shall be obtained from the Supreme People's Court. A death sentence may be executed on the execution ground or in a designated place of custody."

(7) After Execution of the Death Sentence

After a death sentence is executed, a forensic expert shall verify that the convict is indeed dead, and the court clerk present shall make a written record. The people's court that is in charge of execution shall submit a report on the execution of a death sentence, including photos taken prior and post-execution, to the Supreme People's Court through administrative levels within fifteen days. After execution of the death sentence, the court shall notify the family members of the convict, make a detailed list of the relics and heritages belonging to the convict that has been clearly checked out, followed by handing them over to the family members. The people's court that is in charge of execution shall attach the receipt to the file for reference.

1.2. Stop Execution

For the purpose of prevention of wrongful execution, "stop execution" and "suspension of execution" are stipulated in the execution procedures after the execution orders of death sentences have already taken legal effect in the Criminal Procedure Law.

For "stop execution", according to Article 262 of the Criminal Procedure Law, "after receiving an order from the Supreme People's Court to execute a death sentence, a people's court at a lower level shall deliver the convict for execution within seven days. However, under any of the following circumstances, the people's court at a lower level shall suspend execution and immediately report it to the Supreme People's Court for a ruling: (1) it is discovered before execution that the sentence may be erroneous; (2) before execution, the convict exposes any major crimes of others or has other major meritorious acts, and the sentence may be changed; or (3) the convict is pregnant."

1.3. Suspension of Execution

As for "suspension of execution", in accordance with Article 263 of the Criminal Procedure Law, "a judge directing execution shall verify the identity of the convict, ask the convict for any last words or letters, and then deliver the convict to the executioner for execution of the death sentence. If it is discovered before execution that there may be any errors, execution shall be suspended, and it shall be reported to the Supreme People's Court for a ruling." According to Article 500 of the Interpretation on the Application of the Criminal Procedure Law, "if the people's court at a lower level finds any of the following circumstances after receiving an order to execute the death sentence or before execution, the court shall suspend the execution and immediately report the request for suspension of execution of the death sentence and relevant materials to the Supreme People's Court: **a.** the convict may have committed other crimes; **b.** presence of other criminal suspects in a joint crime may affect the sentencing of the convict; **c.** execution of death sentences for other convicts who jointly commit crimes have been suspended or stopped, which may affect the sentencing of the convict; **d.** the convict exposes any major crimes of others or has other major meritorious acts, and the sentence may be changed; **e.** the convict is pregnant; **f.** other errors in the judgment or ruling that may affect the conviction and sentencing."

1.4. Procedures and Disposal for Stopping Execution or Suspension of Execution of the Death Sentence

Procedures for stopping execution or suspension of execution of the death sentence are as follows: **a.** If a people's court at a lower level discovers that a case was under a statutory circumstance of "possible error" after receiving the order from the Supreme People's Court to execute a death sentence or before the execution, it shall suspend the execution and immediately report the request for suspension of execution and relevant materials to the Supreme People's Court. If the Supreme People's Court finds any of the above circumstances after issuance of the order to execute a death sentence or before the execution, it shall immediately order the people's court at a lower level to stop executing the death sentence and hand over the relevant materials to the people's court at a lower level. **b.** Upon receipt of the order issued by the Supreme People's Court to suspend the execution, the people's court at a lower level shall immediately investigate and verify the particulars for suspension of execution together with the departments concerned, and shall promptly report the findings and opinions of the investigation to the Supreme People's Court for examination and verification. **c.** If, after examination, the Supreme People's Court considers that the conviction and sentencing of the convict will not be affected, it shall order the people's court at a lower level to continue carrying out the death sentence; if the Supreme People's Court considers that it may affect the conviction and sentencing, it shall order the people's court at a lower level to stop execution of the death sentence. The original collegial panel of the Supreme People's Court that approved the death sentence shall be responsible for examining the investigation results and relevant materials submitted by the people's court at a lower level to request the suspension of execution of a death sentence. If necessary, a new collegial panel shall be formed according to law to conduct the examination.

The Supreme People's Court, after reviewing the death penalty case in which execution has been stopped or suspended, shall make the following decisions: **a.** If it is confirmed that the convict is pregnant, or was under the age of 18 at the time of the crime committed, or was over the age of 75 at the time of the trial (except where death was caused by especially cruel means), the sentence shall be modified according to law. **b.** If it is confirmed that the convict has committed other crimes and shall be prosecuted according to law, a decision shall be made not to approve the death sentence, the original judgment shall be revoked and the sentence shall be remanded for a new trial. **c.** If it is confirmed that mistakes were made in the original judgment or ruling, or that the convict has major meritorious acts, and the sentence needs to be modified, a ruling shall be made to disapprove the death sentence, the original judgment shall be revoked and the sentence shall be remanded for a new trial. **d.** If it is confirmed that the original judgment or ruling was free from error and that the convict has no other major meritorious acts, or that the major meritorious act does not affect the execution of the original judgment or ruling, the court shall order the continuation of the execution of the death sentence, and the president of the Supreme People's Court shall issue a new order for execution of the death sentence.

2. Punishment Against Liberty

The execution of punishment against liberty includes two parts: execution and modification of execution. The execution can be divided into execution and probation of various types of punishment against liberty, and modification of execution includes temporarily serving a sentence outside an incarceration facility, commutation and parole.

2.1. Execution of Various Types of Punishment Against Liberty

(1) Execution of Sentences of Death Penalty With a Two-Year Suspension, Life Imprisonment, Fixed-Term Imprisonment and Limited Incarceration

Pursuant to Article 264 of the Criminal Procedure Law, "where a convict is delivered for execution of a criminal penalty, the people's court delivering the convict for execution shall serve the relevant legal documents upon the public security authority, prison, or other executing authority within ten days after the sentence takes effect. A convict sentenced to the death penalty with a two-year suspension, life imprisonment, or fixed-term imprisonment shall be delivered by the public security authority to a prison for execution of the criminal penalty. Where a convict is sentenced to fixed-term imprisonment but the remaining term of the penalty is not more than three months before the convict is delivered for execution, the sentence shall be executed by a jail instead. For a convict sentenced to limited incarceration, the sentence shall be executed by the public security authority. The criminal penalty on a juvenile delinquent shall be executed in a reformatory for juvenile delinquents." For those convicts who do not need to be held in the relevant prison, the judgment, ruling and decision instrument thereof shall be handed over to community correction institutions for execution.

For those convicts who need to be taken into custody for execution of criminal penalty but have not been detained before the judgment or ruling becomes effective, the people's court shall, in accordance with the effective judgment or ruling, transfer the convicts to the jail for custody and complete the execution procedures according to law. When taking a convict into custody, the executing authority shall give the convict a physical examination. If the convict is not fit for execution in prison or other places of execution, he/she may temporarily not be put in prison; however, if it causes danger to the society for the convict to temporarily serve his/her sentence outside an incarceration facility, he/she shall be taken back to prison.

After taking a convict into custody, the executing authority shall notify the family members of the convict within five days from the date of taking him/her into custody of the charged crime, term of sentence and address of execution, etc. If the convict dies, or escapes during his/her sentence and is not arrested for over two months, or if there is a change after arrest, the executing authority shall submit a written report to the people's court which delivers him/her for execution and the people's procuratorate that supervises the execution.

The term of a convict sentenced to fixed-term imprisonment or limited incarceration shall be counted from the date of execution of the judgment. If he/she is detained or arrested before the judgment, one day in custody equals one day of the term of imprisonment; if a convict is placed under residential confinement at a designated residence, two days of residential confinement equals one day of the term of imprisonment. Upon completion of the sentence, the executing authority shall release the convict immediately and a certificate of release shall be issued to the convict.

(2) Execution of Supervision Without Incarceration

Supervision without incarceration is a kind of punishment in which the convict who committed an obviously minor crime is not held in custody but shall be subject to community correction under the management and supervision of community correction institutions. Supervision without incarceration is an independent form of punishment. The application of this kind of punishment is of great significance for reducing the pressure of prison, promoting the convicts to live on their own and preventing them from having negative influence on each other in prison.

Under the circumstance that a convict is sentenced to supervision without incarceration, and is in custody at the time of sentencing, the people's court of first instance shall notify the public security authority to modify the coercive measures. After the sentence made by a people's court becomes effective, relevant legal documents shall be handed over to the community correction institution for execution.

Any convict who is sentenced to supervision without incarceration shall observe the following during the term in which his/her sentence is being executed: **a.** observe laws and administrative rules and regulations, and subject to supervision; **b.** exercise no right of freedom of speech, of the press, of assembly, of association, of procession or of demonstration without the approval of the authority executing the supervision without incarceration; **c.** report on his/her own activities as required by the authority executing the supervision without incarceration; **d.** observe the regulations for receiving visitors stipulated by the authority executing the supervision without incarceration; and **e.** file an application for approval with the authority executing the supervision without incarceration for any departure from the city or county he/she lives in or for any change in residence. In addition, a convict sentenced to supervision without incarceration may be prohibited from engaging in certain activities, entering certain areas or places or contacting certain persons, otherwise, the convict shall be penalized by the public security authority in accordance with the Law on Administrative Penalties for Public Security. The convict sentenced to supervision without incarceration is entitled to receive equal pay for equal work if they participate in labor during the term of execution.

Execution and termination of supervision without incarceration shall be announced to the public. Upon the expiration of the term of supervision without incarceration, the executing authority shall promptly terminate the restriction of the convict; where deprivation of political rights was sentenced as an accessory penalty, the executing authority shall announce the restoration of political rights at the same time. The term of a convict sentenced to supervision without incarceration shall be counted from the date of execution of the judgment. If he/she is held in custody before execution of the judgment, one day in custody equals two days of the term of supervision without incarceration.

2.2. Probation

Probation is a system that allows a convict who meets the statutory conditions and is sentenced to fixed-term imprisonment of no more than three years or limited incarceration not to be executed if he/she will not commit a new crime during the suspension of execution for a certain period of time. Probation is not an independent kind of punishment, but a special way of execution.

If the people's court of first instance has imposed a sentence of limited incarceration or fixed-term imprisonment with a probation, the convict cannot be handed over for execution before the judgment has taken effect. However, where the convict is granted probation during custody, the people's court of first instance shall first modify the coercive measures to having the convict released upon bail pending trial or subjecting him/her to residential confinement, and notify the public security authority. For a convict sentenced to fixed-term imprisonment or limited incarceration with a probation, the probation period of suspension shall be announced at the same time. According to Article 73 of the Criminal Law, "the probation period for suspension of limited incarceration is to be not less than the term originally decided and not more than one year, but it may not be less than two months. The probation period for suspension of fixed-term imprisonment is to be not less than the term originally decided and not more than five years, but it may not be less than one year. The probation period for suspension is to be counted as commencing on the date the judgment becomes final."

Any convict who is granted probation shall observe the following: **a.** observe laws and administrative rules and regulations, and subject to supervision; **b.** report on his/her own activities as required by the observation authority; **c.** observe the regulations for receiving visitors stipulated by the observing authority; **d.** file an application for approval with the observation authority for any departure from the city or county he/she lives in or for any change in residence; **e.** not engage in certain activities, entering certain areas or places or contacting certain persons. Where a convict is granted probation without deprivation of political rights as an accessory penalty, his/her political rights shall not be restricted during the probation period, and the convict is entitled to receive equal pay for equal work if they participate in labor during the term of execution. If the convict does not violate the above provisions during the probation period, the original sentence shall not be executed after the probation period has expired, and the sentence shall be publicly announced; if, during the probationary period for suspension of sentence, the convict who is granted probation commits a crime again or it is discovered that before the judgment is announced, he/she has committed another offence for which he/she is not sentenced, the probation shall be revoked and another judgment shall be rendered for the newly committed or discovered offence, the punishment to be executed shall be decided on the basis of the punishments for the old offence and the new offence and according to principles for combined penalties for several crimes.

Where a convict who is granted probation violates any provision of laws, administrative regulations or supervision and management regulations of probation during probation, if the circumstances are serious, the probation shall be revoked and the original sentence shall be executed. The probationary period for suspension of sentence already executed shall not be converted into the term of imprisonment, while the date of detention prior to the execution of the judgment shall be converted into the term of imprisonment.

2.3. Temporarily Serving a Sentence Outside an Incarceration Facility

Temporarily serving a sentence outside an incarceration facility refers to an alternative method of temporarily placing convicts sentenced to life imprisonment, fixed-term imprisonment or limited incarceration outside an incarceration facility to community correction institutions for execution when they are not suitable for execution in the incarceration facility due to certain special legal circumstances. It not only changes the place of execution, but also changes the way of execution.

(1) Applicable Objects and Conditions for Temporarily Serving a Sentence Outside an Incarceration Facility

Pursuant to Article 265 of the Criminal Procedure Law, under any of the following circumstances, "a convict sentenced to fixed-term imprisonment or limited incarceration may temporarily serve his/her sentence outside an incarceration facility: (1) the convict suffers a serious illness and needs to be released on bail for medical treatment; (2) the convict is a pregnant woman or a woman who is breastfeeding her own baby; or (3) the convict cannot take care of himself/herself, and it will not cause any danger to the society for the convict to temporarily serve his/her sentence outside an incarceration facility. Under item (2) of the preceding paragraph, a convict sentenced to life imprisonment may temporarily serve her sentence outside an incarceration facility. If the release of a convict on bail for medical treatment may cause any danger to the society or a convict suffers any self-inflicted injury or disability, the convict may not be released on bail for medical treatment."

(2) Decision Authority and Approval Authority for Temporarily Serving a Sentence Outside an Incarceration Facility

In accordance with Article 265 of the Criminal Procedure Law, "before a convict is handed over for execution of a criminal penalty, whether the convict temporarily serves his/her sentence outside an incarceration facility shall be decided by the people's court which hands over the convict for execution of a criminal penalty; after a convict is handed over for execution of a criminal penalty, regarding a convict's temporarily serving a sentence outside an incarceration facility, the prison or jail shall prepare a written opinion, which shall be reported to the prison administrative authority at or above the provincial level or the public security authority at or above the level of a districted city for approval."

(3) Procedures for Temporarily Serving a Sentence Outside an Incarceration Facility

If the convict may be sentenced to imprisonment before being handed over for execution but meets the conditions for temporarily serving a sentence outside an incarceration facility, the convict and his/her defenders have the right to file an application for temporarily serving a sentence outside an incarceration facility, and the jail may notify the people's court of the relevant information. The people's court shall examine the case and make a decision on whether to approve temporarily serving a sentence outside an incarceration facility before handing the convict over for execution. Where it is decided to approve a convict's temporarily serving a sentence outside an incarceration facility, the people's court shall make a written decision and notify the judicial administrative authority at the county level where the convict resides to send officers to handle the formalities for handover, and send a copy of the written decision to the people's procuratorate and the public security authority; if a convict is found to be applicable to temporarily serving a sentence outside an incarceration facility in the course of serving his/her sentence, the executing authority shall submit a written opinion and report it to the prison administration authority of the province, autonomous region or municipality directly under the central government or to the public security authority at or above the municipal level divided into districts for approval. If such an approval is granted, the approving authority shall notify the public security authority and the people's court that originally tried the case of its decision on approval, and send a copy to the people's procuratorate.

Deeming the temporarily serving a sentence outside an incarceration facility improper, the people's procuratorate shall, within one month from the date of receiving the notification, submit a written opinion to the deciding or approving authority, and the deciding or approving authority shall reexamine its decision immediately after receiving the written opinion of the people's procuratorate.

In accordance with Article 516 of the Interpretation on the Application of the Criminal Procedure Law, a convict granted temporarily serving a sentence outside an incarceration facility shall be put in prison for execution under any of the following circumstances: **a.** failing to meet the conditions for temporarily serving a sentence outside an incarceration facility; **b.** leaving the city or county where he/she lives without approval, refusing to correct after warning, or refusing to report his/her whereabouts, and not subject to supervision; **c.** those who have been punished for violating supervision and administration regulations but still do not rectify; **d.** refusing to correct after being warned twice by the executing authority; **e.** failing to submit the condition review as required during the bail for medical treatment period and refusing to correct after being warned; **f.** the circumstances allowing a convict's serving a sentence outside an incarceration facility disappear and the convict's term of sentence has not expired; **g.** the guarantor loses the guarantee conditions or is disqualified as a guarantor due to non-performance of obligations and is unable to put forward a new guarantor within the prescribed time limit; **h.** other serious circumstances in violation of laws, administrative regulations and supervision and management regulations.

Where a convict who temporarily serves a sentence outside an incarceration facility as decided by a people's court shall be taken back to prison, a decision shall be made by the people's court. Once the written decision on execution of the convict is made, it shall take effect immediately. The written decision and relevant legal documents shall be served upon the public security authority, prison, and other judicial administrative authority where the convict resides, and a copy shall be sent to the people's procuratorate at the same time.

Where a convict who does not meet the conditions is permitted to temporarily serve a sentence outside an incarceration facility by illegal means such as bribery, the time served outside an incarceration facility shall not be counted in the executed period of punishment. If a convict escapes during the period of temporarily serving a sentence outside an incarceration facility, the period of escape shall not be counted in the executed period of punishment.

2.4. Commutation and Parole

(1) Concept of Commutation and Parole

Commutation refers to the system whereby the people's court, according to law, appropriately mitigates the original punishment of a convict sentenced to supervision without incarceration, limited incarceration, fixed-term imprisonment or life imprisonment if, during the period of execution, he/she conscientiously observes prison regulations, shows genuine repentance or performs meritorious services. Parole refers to a system of conditional early release of convicts sentenced to fixed-term imprisonment or life imprisonment who, after serving a certain period of time for reform, show genuine repentance and have no danger of committing another crime.

(2) Object of Commutation and Parole

The object of commutation must be convicts sentenced to supervision without incarceration, limited incarceration, fixed-term imprisonment or life imprisonment. The commutation of a death sentence with a two-year suspension is carried out in accordance with special provisions of the law and is a component part of the system of death penalty with a two-year suspension and does not fall within the scope of application of the commutation system.

The subject of parole must be convicts sentenced to fixed-term imprisonment or life imprisonment. No parole may be granted to a repeat offender or a convict sentenced to fixed-term imprisonment of more than ten years or life imprisonment for murder, rape, robbery, abduction, arson, explosion, dissemination of hazardous substances or organized violent offence. A convict sentenced to death with a two-year suspension because of the foregoing circumstances or crimes may not be granted parole even if his/her sentence is commuted to life imprisonment or fixed-term imprisonment.

(3) Conditions of Application to Commutation and Parole

With respect to conditions of application to commutation, the punishment of a convict sentenced to supervision without incarceration, limited incarceration, fixed-term imprisonment or life imprisonment may be commuted if, while serving his/her sentence, he/she conscientiously observes prison regulations, accepts education and reform through labor and shows true repentance or performs meritorious services; the punishment shall be commuted if a convict performs major meritorious services.

As for conditions of application to parole, there are two requirements that must be satisfied simultaneously: firstly, a certain sentence shall be actually executed, i. e., a convict sentenced to fixed-term imprisonment has served not less than half of the term of his original sentence, or a convict sentenced to life imprisonment has actually served not less than thirteen years of imprisonment; secondly, the convict shall earnestly observe the prison rules, accept reform through education and show true repentance and is not likely to commit any offence again. Under special circumstances, with the approval of the Supreme People's Court, a parole may be granted without being subject to the above restrictions on the term served.

(4) Trial of Commutation and Parole Cases

With respect to commutation of the sentence of a convict sentenced to death with a two-year suspension, the higher people's court in the place where the convict is to serve his/her sentence shall make a ruling on the commutation of the sentence on the basis of the recommendation which has been examined and approved by the administrative authority of prison at the same level; with respect to commutation or parole of a convict sentenced to life imprisonment, the higher people's court in the place where the convict is to serve his/her sentence shall make a ruling within one month after receiving the written recommendation for commutation or parole which has been examined and approved by the administrative authority of prison at the same level, and an extension of one month may be given if the case is complicated or the circumstances are special; with respect to the commutation or parole of a convict sentenced to fixed-term imprisonment or commuted to fixed-term imprisonment, the intermediate people's court in the place where the convict is serving his/her sentence shall make a ruling within one month after receiving the recommendation for commutation or parole submitted by the executing authority, and an extension of one month may be given if the case is complicated or the circumstances are special; with respect to the commutation of the sentence of a convict sentenced to limited incarceration or supervision without incarceration, the intermediate people's court in the place where the convict is serving his/her sentence shall make a ruling within one month after receiving the written recommendation for commutation or parole which has been examined and approved by the executing authority at the same level.

When trying a commutation or parole case, the execution of the property penalty and the incidental civil judgment shall be examined, as well as whether and how much the illegal income has been returned or the victim compensated. If a convict actively performs the obligations determined in the judgment, he/she may be deemed to have shown repentance and be treated leniently when his/her sentence is being tried for commutation or parole; if a convict does have the ability to perform the judgment but fails to do so, strict restrictions shall be imposed on him/her.

A collegial panel shall be formed when trying a commutation or parole case, although it may be tried in written form, a court session shall be held for the following cases: **a.** a commutation of sentence is requested because the convict has rendered great meritorious service; **b.** the starting time, interval or range of commutation requested does not conform to general provisions; **c.** cases with significant social impact or high social concern; **d.** receipt of complaints during the public announcement; **e.** the people's procuratorate has raised objections; **f.** other cases that need to be heard in court.

After the people's court has made a ruling on commutation or parole, it shall, within seven days, serve the ruling upon the executing authority requesting commutation or parole, the people's procuratorate at the same level and the criminal himself/herself. If the people's procuratorate considers that the ruling on commutation or parole is improper and puts forward its written opinions for correction within the statutory time limit, the people's court shall, after receiving the opinions, form a new collegial panel to try the case and make a ruling within one month. If the people's court find out any definite errors in its effective ruling on commutation or parole, it shall form a new collegial panel to try the case; if it is found that an effective ruling on commutation or parole made by a people's court at a lower level contains definite errors, it may instruct the people's court at a lower level to form a new collegial panel for the trial.

(5) Investigation and Disposition of the Paroled Convict

According to Article 269 of the Criminal Procedure Law, "a convict who is sentenced to supervision without incarceration, is granted probation or parole, or temporarily serves a sentence outside an incarceration facility shall be subject to community correction, which shall be executed by a community correction institution." If a convict who is granted parole commits another offence during the probation period for parole or is discovered to have committed other offences for which no punishment is imposed before the judgment is announced, and the parole shall be revoked, the people's court that is trying the new offence shall revoke the parole declared in the original judgment or ruling, and notify in writing the people's court that tried the case and the executing authority.

During the probation period for parole, if a convict falls under any of the following circumstances, the people's court that made the original judgment or ruling on parole shall, within one month after receiving the recommendation of the executing authority, make a ruling on cancellation of parole: **a.** serious violation of restraining order; **b.** failing to register within prescribed time without justifiable reasons or not subject to supervision during the period of acceptance of community correction for more than one month; **c.** those who have been punished for violating supervision and administration regulations but still failing to make corrections; **d.** refusing to correct after being warned three times by the executing authority; **e.** other serious cases in violation of relevant laws, administrative regulations and supervision and management regulations.

The ruling of the people's court revoking parole shall take effect immediately. The people's court shall deliver the written order on revocation of parole to the judicial administrative authority at the county level where the convict resides, which shall hand over the convict for execution in accordance with relevant provisions. A copy of the revocation of the parole order shall simultaneously be sent to the people's procuratorate and the public security authority at the same level where the convict resides.

If none of the circumstances mentioned above occurs during the probation period for parole, the original sentence of the convict who is granted parole shall be deemed to have been fully served upon expiration of parole, which shall be announced to the public.

3. Punishment Against Property

Punishment against property is to deprive the convict of property as the punishment content, including two kinds: fine and confiscation of property.

3.1. Execution of Fine

Fine is a penalty method for the people's court to judge the convicted individuals or entities to pay a certain amount of money to the state. The judgment of paying fines shall be executed by the responsible department of the people's court of first instance. A convicted individual or entity sentenced to a fine shall pay it in a lump sum or in installments within the time limit specified in the judgment. If a fine is not paid or paid in full upon the expiration of that time limit, the payment shall be compelled. Where a fine is still unable to be made in full, the people's court shall recover the enforceable property of the person subject to enforcement at any time when such property is found, including after the main sentence has been carried out when the fine is imposed as a supplementary punishment. If a convict has true difficulties in paying the fine due to an irresistible disaster or other reasons, he/she may apply to the people's court for deferment of payment, or for the reduction or exemption of the fine as appropriate. Upon verification, the people's court may, at its discretion, order the deferment of the payment or the reduction or exemption of the amount of the fine determined in the original judgment. The fine paid by a convict shall be turned over to the state treasury without delay in accordance with the provisions, no authorities, organizations or individuals may misappropriate or dispose of such property without permission.

3.2. Execution of Confiscation of Property

Confiscation of property refers to the confiscation of part or all of the property personally owned by a convict to the state without compensation. All judgments on confiscation of property, whether imposed as a supplementary punishment or independently, shall be executed by a people's court; when necessary, the people's court may execute such judgments jointly with a public security authority. In order to prevent the transfer of property by convicts or others from affecting the execution of the judgment on confiscation of property before execution, the people's court of first instance may seize, impound and freeze the defendant's property first. The confiscation of property shall be limited to part or all of the property personally owned by the convict. Where confiscation of all the property of a convict is imposed, the amount necessary for the daily expenses of the convict himself/herself and the family members supported by him/her shall be spared, property that the convict's family members own or should own shall not be subject to confiscation. Where it is necessary to use part of the confiscated property to repay the legitimate debts that the convict incurred before the confiscation, the debts shall be repaid at the request of the creditors. As for the confiscated property, the people's court shall turn it over to the state treasury or financial department in time in accordance with relevant provisions, and no authorities, organizations or individuals shall use, exchange, auction at a lower price or divide such property without permission.

CHAPTER EIGHT

SPECIAL PROCEDURE

There are several special procedures in Chinese criminal proceedings, namely, incidental civil action procedure, procedures for juvenile criminal cases, procedures for public prosecution cases where parties have reached settlement, procedure for trial in absentia, confiscation procedures for illegal income in cases where the criminal suspect or defendant escapes or dies, and procedures for involuntary medical treatment of mental patients legally exempted from criminal liabilities.

1. Incidental Civil Action

1.1. Concept and Characteristics of Incidental Civil Action

Incidental civil actions refer to the litigation activities carried out during the process of criminal proceedings for incidental settlement of the problem of compensation for the material losses caused by the criminal acts of the accused while solving the criminal liability of the accused.

An incidental civil action has the following characteristics:

First, the particularity of the nature of the incidental civil action. The incidental civil action is to resolve economic compensation in terms of the nature of its solution, which is the same as the damage compensation in civil action. So it is in nature a kind of civil action. But it is different from the general civil action, because this kind of compensation is caused by the crime and is brought in the course of the criminal action and handled by the trial organization trying the criminal case, so it is a part of the criminal action and a special civil action.

Second, the legal basis of incidental civil action is complex. Because incidental civil action solves the civil liability for compensation caused by the criminal act, the legal basis of incidental civil action is complex. In substantive law, the determination of the facts of damage shall not only comply with the provisions of the Criminal Law, but also be subject to the adjustment of civil laws and regulations; in procedural law, the provisions of the Civil Procedure Law shall apply unless otherwise specified in the Criminal Procedure Law.

Finally, the ancillary nature of incidental civil action procedure. The incidental civil action is based on the establishment of the criminal case and must be brought in the course of the criminal action. The judgment of the incidental civil action shall not contradict with the judgment of the criminal part. The limitation of action, the time limit for appeal and the competent court of the incidental civil action all depend on the circumstances of the criminal case. Therefore, the incidental civil action is dependent on the criminal action in terms of handling procedure and must be based on criminal procedures. If the criminal action does not exist, the incidental civil action cannot be brought.

1.2. Conditions for Establishing the Incidental Civil Action

(1) The Incidental Civil Action Must Have the Prerequisite of the Establishment of the Criminal Action.

If criminal actions are not established, incidental civil actions will lose the basis for their existence. If the accused's act is not a criminal act, but an act protected by law, such as justifiable defense, emergency avoidance of danger, etc., the damage caused by these acts cannot, of course, be brought in an incidental civil action.

(2) The Plaintiff Must Have the Capacity to Bring an Incidental Civil Action.

The plaintiffs of the incidental civil action are complicated as follows:

A citizen who suffers material damage as a result of a criminal act. Any citizen who suffers material damage as a result of a criminal act committed by the accused has the right to bring an incidental civil action during the course of criminal proceedings.

Any enterprise, public institution, organ, organization, etc. that has suffered material damage due to infringement by any criminal.

If the victim is a juvenile or a mentally ill person, his/her legal representative or guardian may bring an incidental civil action on his/her behalf. At this time, the plaintiff should still be the victim, but victim's litigation rights and obligations as the plaintiff are exercised by the legal representative or guardian.

Where the victim is dead or has lost his/her capacity for conduct, his/her legal representative or close relative shall have the right to bring an incidental civil action.

In the case of loss of state property or collective property, the people's procuratorate may bring an incidental civil action when initiating a public prosecution.

(3) An Incidental Civil Action Must Have a Definite Accused Person and a Specific Claim.

The defendant in the incidental civil action is generally the accused in the criminal action. However, under some special circumstances, the defendant in the incidental civil action who shall compensate for material losses is not the accused in the criminal action mainly under the following circumstances:

A. The guardian of the criminal defendant. The civil liability of the guardian is caused by his/her specific guardianship relationship and failure to fulfill the guardianship responsibility. In such cases, the defendant in incidental civil action should be the criminal defendant, but the liability for compensation should be borne by the guardian.

B. Other persons who jointly committed the harmful act but have not been pursued for criminal liability. Such a circumstance mainly refers to that, for a crime jointly committed by several persons, some defendants are handed over to the people's court for trial for pursue of criminal liability, and some are under administrative detention or the people's procuratorate decides not to prosecute. Under such circumstances, all other persons of the case who have been dealt with otherwise may be defendants in the incidental civil action.

C. Inheritor of the estate of the criminal sentenced to death or inheritor of the estate of the defendant who died before the end of the trial of the case in a joint criminal case. In both cases, the economic compensation to the victim shall be deemed as the debt owed by the deceased criminal defendant prior to his/her death and shall fall under the repayment scope of estate. However, if such a successor declares himself/herself disclaiming the inheritance, he/she may not continue to be a defendant.

D. Other entities and individuals that shall bear civil compensation liabilities for criminal act by the criminal defendant in accordance with the law.

Where the plaintiff files an incidental civil action, he/she shall not only have a definite defendant, but also have a concrete claim, namely, put forward the specific amount of compensation, and shall have a factual basis for the material losses caused by the fact of injury and shall bear the burden of proof.

(4) The Cause of Action of the Incidental Civil Action Is That the Criminal Act of the Accused Causes Material Loss to the Victim

First of all, the loss which the victim suffered is material. The so-called material loss, as opposed to spiritual loss, is the loss that can be measured in monetary terms. According to the Interpretation of Criminal Procedure Law, where, as a result of violation by crime, an incidental civil action is filed or a separate civil action is filed to demand compensation for spiritual damage, people's courts shall generally not accept the filing. Secondly, the material loss is directly caused by the criminal act of the accused. That is to say, the criminal behavior of the accused and the material loss must have a causal relationship and there is an internal link.

Therefore, Article 192 of the Interpretations of the Criminal Procedure Law defines the scope of compensation for incidental civil actions. Where criminal acts have caused physical damage to victims, compensation shall be made for reasonable expenses payable for treatment and recovery including medical care expenses, nursing care expenses and travelling expenses, and for reduced income as a result of loss of working time. Where disability of the victim is caused, compensation shall also be made for expenses for disability living support devices and other expenses. Where the death of the victims is caused, compensation shall also be made for funeral expenses and other expenses. Where the driving of motor vehicles causes the death or injury of persons or causes serious losses of public or private property, which constitutes a crime, the responsibility for compensation shall be determined in accordance with Article 76 of the Law of the People's Republic of China on Road Traffic Safety. Where the parties in incidental civil actions reach mediation or settlement agreement on matters of civil compensation, the scope and amount of compensation shall not be subject to the limitation of the above provisions.

1.3. Procedures for Incidental Civil Actions

(1) Commencement of Incidental Civil Actions

The starting time of bringing up an incidental civil action should be after the criminal case is opened, and then the incidental civil action can be brought up. The ending time of bringing up incidental civil action is the announcement of the judgment of first instance. Once the judgment of first instance has been announced, the incidental civil action part loses the basis of the combined trial with the criminal part. Therefore, Article 198 of the Interpretations of the Criminal Procedure Law provides that if no incidental civil action is brought during the first instance but is brought during the second instance, the people's court of second instance may conduct mediation in accordance with the law; if the mediation fails, the parties concerned shall be informed that they may bring an independent civil action after the criminal judgment or ruling becomes effective.

In general, the incidental civil statement of claim shall be submitted; where there is any difficulty in writing the statement of claim, the incidental civil action may be filed orally. Either in writing or orally, the basic personal information of the plaintiff and defendant shall be specified in the incidental civil action such as the name, age, occupation and residential address, the criminal facts accused, the material losses caused by the criminal act and the relevant evidence, and the specific compensation claim, etc. shall be stated. Where the people's procuratorate brings an incidental civil action together with the public prosecution, the litigation must only be in written form.

(2) Trial of Incidental Civil Action

Article 104 of the Criminal Procedure Law stipulates the principle of combining criminal and civil actions in a trial of incidental civil action, that is: "An incidental civil action shall be heard concurrently with the criminal case. An incidental civil action may be heard by the same judicial organization after the trial of the criminal case only to prevent the excessive delay of the trial of the criminal case." When tried separately, it should be ensured that: First, the criminal part shall be tried first, and then the civil part shall be tried, and the civil part cannot be tried first. Second, the same organization that hears the criminal case shall continue to hear the part of incidental civil action, and no new collegial panel shall be formed. However, in practice, if a judge hearing the criminal case is really unable to continue to participate in the trial of the incidental civil action due to death or serious illness, other judges may replace him/her. Third, the determination of facts in the incidental civil action part shall not contradict with the criminal judgment; fourth, the postponement of the trial of the incidental civil action part shall not affect the effectiveness of the criminal judgment in general. In addition, Article 103 of Criminal Procedure Law also stipulates the mediation and judgment in the incidental civil action, namely, "When trying an incidental civil case, a people's court may conduct mediation or render a judgment or ruling based on the material loss."

According to Chapter VI of the Interpretation of the Criminal Procedure Law, the trial procedures of the incidental civil action are as follows:

First, after accepting the criminal case, the people's court may notify the victim or his/her legal representative or close relative of his/her right to bring the incidental civil action if the conditions for bringing the incidental civil action are met. After receiving a statement of claim for an incidental civil action or an oral statement of claim, a people's court shall review the statement of claim and decide whether to open the case within seven days. If the requirements for acceptance are met, the people's court shall accept the case; otherwise, the people's court shall rule not to accept the case.

Second, the people's court shall, within five days after accepting the incidental civil action, serve the duplicates of the statement of claim of the incidental civil action upon the defendant of the incidental civil action and the legal representative, and shall make transcripts thereof. In serving duplicates of any incidental civil statement of claim, people's courts shall, in accordance with the time limit for trial of criminal cases, set the time for the defendant and the legal representative to submit civil pleading.

Third, before a court session to try a case, the people's court shall serve summons upon the plaintiff and the defendant in the incidental civil action and summon them to appear in court. If the plaintiff refuses to appear in court without justified reasons or leaves the court session halfway without permission of the court, the case shall be considered withdrawn; if the defendant refuses to appear in court without justified reasons or leaves the court session halfway without permission of the court, the trial of the part of incidental civil action in the case may go in absentia.

Fourth, the parties to the incidental civil action shall be responsible for providing evidence for their claims in court.

Fifth, in trying cases of incidental civil actions, people's courts may, in accordance with the principles of voluntariness and lawfulness, make mediation. Where an agreement is reached through mediation, a mediation decision shall be produced. Any mediation decision shall be of legal effect after being signed for by the parties of both sides. Where an agreement has been reached through mediation and has been fulfilled immediately, the production of a mediation decision may be omitted, but transcripts hereon shall be made. Any transcripts hereon will be of legal effect after signature or seal by both sides of the parties, judges and court clerks. Where no agreement is reached through mediation or where parties go back on their agreement before signing for the mediation decision, judgment in the incidental civil action shall be made along with judgment in the relevant criminal action. Where the people's court determines that the acts of the defendant in a public prosecution case do not constitute a crime, for any brought incidental civil action but no agreement is reached upon mediation, the people's court shall render a judgment on the incidental civil action at the same time. For a case of public prosecution that the people's court allows the people's procuratorate to withdraw, the people's court may conduct mediation for any brought incidental civil action; where mediation is not appropriate or no agreement is reached upon mediation, the people's court shall dismiss the case, and notify the plaintiff to the incidental civil action that he/she may bring a civil action independently.

Sixth, where relatives or friends of defendants in incidental civil actions voluntarily make compensation instead, permission may be granted. In trying cases of criminal actions with incidental civil actions, people's courts shall determine the repentance of defendants in keeping with the extent of their compensation for the material losses of victims, and shall take it into consideration in deciding criminal punishment to them.

Seventh, people's courts do not charge court fees for trying cases of incidental civil actions.

2. Procedures for Juvenile Criminal Cases

In China, a juvenile criminal case refers to a case in which the accused has reached the age of 14 but is under the age of 18 when committing the accused crime. The procedure for a juvenile criminal case refers to a special criminal procedure that is specially applicable to such procedures as investigation, prosecution, trial and enforcement of a juvenile criminal case.

2.1. Special Principles of Proceedings in Juvenile Criminal Cases

(1) Principle of Education First and Punishment Second

The principle of education first and punishment second plays an important guiding role in the proceedings of the entire juvenile criminal case, and is the leading thought in the handling of juvenile criminal cases. All other litigation principles of the juvenile criminal case are carried out according to this principle. Article 277 of the Criminal Procedure Law stipulates that, "For juvenile criminals, the policy of education, reformation, and redemption shall apply, and the principle of education assisted by punishment shall be followed." This principle requires that the public security and judicial organs should insist on education first and punishment second, and to educate and save juveniles in all stages of juvenile criminal proceedings. Public security and judicial personnel should take into consideration the physical and mental characteristics of juveniles, respect their personal dignity and safeguard their lawful rights and interests. They shall educate the accused juveniles to recognize their own mistakes and crimes and their seriousness and harmfulness, awaken their consciousness of repentance, and educate them to re-behave.

(2) Principle of Separating Case Handling

Separating case handling means, a juvenile criminal case shall be handled at a time and place separately from a case involving a crime committed by an adult. Article 280 of the Criminal Procedure Law stipulates that, juveniles and adults who are detained or arrested or are serving criminal penalties shall be held in custody, managed, and educated separately. Article 459 of the Rules of Criminal Procedure for People's Procuratorates stipulates that, when handling a case of a joint crime committed by a juvenile and an adult, a people's procuratorate shall generally prosecute the juvenile and the adult separately. If the separate handling of the case is inappropriate, special protective measures such as privacy protection and fast-track handling shall be adopted for the juvenile. The reason for the separation of cases is that the juveniles are immature in all aspects. If they are imprisoned, tried or served their sentences together with adults, they may not only be improperly educated, but may also be adversely affected by adults, which is not conducive to the reform of the juveniles.

(3) Principle of Not Trying the Case Openly

According to Article 285 of the Criminal Procedure Law and Articles 557 and 559 of the Interpretation of the Criminal Procedure Law, a case may not be tried openly if the defendant has not attained the age of 18 at the time of trial. However, with the consent of the juvenile defendant or his/her legal representative, the juvenile defendant's school and a juvenile protection organization may send representatives to be present. The number and scope of representatives to be present shall be decided by the court. With the consent of the court, a representative to be present may participate in the court education for the juvenile defendant. No person may be organized to observe the court session if a case has to be heard in public in accordance with the law but the criminal record may need to be sealed up. If there is any person observing the court session, he/she shall be informed not to disseminate case information. When hearing the juvenile criminal case, the names, domiciles or photos of the juveniles as well as other materials that may be used to deduce the identity of the juveniles may not be disclosed to the public. The case files for consultation, extraction or reproduction involving juveniles may not be publicized or disseminated. Not to hear the cases involving juveniles openly is conducive to protecting the reputation, self-esteem and personal dignity of the juvenile defendants, preventing unnecessary mental trauma and excessive pressure caused to them by public lawsuits, and is conducive to their acceptance of education.

2.2. Special Features of the Procedure for Juvenile Criminal Cases

(1) The Exact Date of Birth of the Criminal Suspect or Defendant Must Be Ascertained

For juvenile criminal cases, whether at the stage of case filing, investigation, prosecution and trial, the determination of the exact time of birth of the criminal suspect or defendant shall be focused on because the factor of age is likely to determine whether the criminal liability shall be pursued for. In accordance with Article 4 of Interpretation of the Supreme People's Court on Some Issues Concerning the Specific Application of Law in the Trial of Juvenile Criminal Case, where there is no sufficient evidence proving that the defendant has reached the age for statutory criminal liability when the accused's crime is committed and which really cannot be verified, it shall be assumed that he/she has not reached the corresponding age for statutory criminal liability. Where there is sufficient relevant evidence proving that the defendant has reached the age for statutory criminal liability when the accused crime is committed but the specific birth date of the defendant cannot be accurately found out, he/she shall be regarded as having reached the corresponding age for statutory criminal liability.

(2) Handled by Special Agency or Dedicated Personnel

Article 277 of the Criminal Procedure Law stipulates that, when handling juvenile criminal cases, a people's court, a people's procuratorate, and a public security authority shall ensure that juveniles are able to exercise their procedural rights, ensure that they receive legal assistance, and assign judges, prosecutors, and investigators who are familiar with the physical and psychological characteristics of juveniles to handle such cases.

(3) Social Investigation of Juvenile Suspects and Defendants

In the handling of juvenile criminal cases, in addition to the same work as that in the adult cases, such as ascertaining the facts of the case, collecting evidence and identifying the criminal offender, the litigation activities shall be more comprehensive and meticulous. Article 279 of Criminal Procedure Law stipulates that, when handling juvenile criminal cases, a people's court, a people's procuratorate, and a public security authority may, according to the actual circumstances, investigate the growth, cause of crime, guardianship, education, and other aspects of the juvenile suspect or defendant. When preparing the litigation documents, the public security and judicial officers shall, in addition to specifying the case source, time and place of occurrence, facts of crime, existing evidential materials, legal basis and handling opinions, emphatically specify the exact birth time of the criminal suspect or defendant (year, month, day), living environment, psychological and personality characteristics, the reasons for committing crime and so on. These should be as detailed and comprehensive as possible.

(4) Safeguarding Special Litigation Rights of Juvenile Suspects and Defendants

A. The presence of appropriate adults. Where a juvenile under the age of 18 commits a crime, the legal representative of the juvenile suspect or defendant shall be notified to be present at the time of interrogation and trial. If such notification is impossible, the legal representative is unable to be present, or the legal representative is an accomplice, any other adult relative of the juvenile suspect or defendant, or a representative of his/her school or employer, a basic organization at the place of his/her residence, or a juvenile protection organization may be notified to be present, and relevant circumstances shall be recorded. The present legal representative may exercise the litigation rights of the juvenile suspect or defendant on his/her behalf. Deeming that case-handling personnel have infringed the juvenile's lawful rights and interests in the course of interrogation or trial, present legal representatives or other persons may present an objection. During the trial of a juvenile criminal case, after the juvenile defendant makes his/her final statement, his/her legal representative may make a supplementary statement.

B. Compulsory defense. If a juvenile suspect or defendant has not had a defender, a people's court, a people's procuratorate, or a public security authority shall notify a legal aid agency to designate a lawyer to defend him/her.

C. Sealing of criminal records. If a person is under the age of 18 when committing a crime and is sentenced to a punishment below five-year fixed-term imprisonment, the relevant criminal records shall be sealed for preservation. The sealed criminal records may not be provided to any entity or individual, unless as needed for a judicial authority to handle cases or for consultation by relevant entities according to relevant State provisions. Entities making inquiry in accordance with the law shall keep information on the crime records sealed up for safekeeping confidential.

(5) Strictly Limit the Application of Compulsory Measure

The arrest of a juvenile suspect shall be strictly restricted and minimized.

When examining of the arrest of a juvenile suspect, the people's procuratorate shall comprehensively measure the danger to the society based on the facts of the crime that the juvenile suspect is charged, the subjective viciousness of the juvenile suspect and the existence of guardianship or social assistance and education conditions. The arrest of a juvenile suspect shall not be approved if the offense is minor and the conditions for effective guardianship or social help and education measures are complied with, causes no danger or comparatively small danger to the society, and the failure to arrest the juvenile suspect will not impede the normal proceedings of legal proceedings. The public security authority shall change the compulsory measures in a timely manner in accordance with the law, provided that the juvenile suspect shall obey the administration after detention and arrest, the modification of the compulsory measures will not cause danger to the society and the normal litigation proceedings can be ensured.

(6) Conditional Non-Prosecution System

Article 282 of the Criminal Procedure Law stipulates that, when a juvenile is suspected of a crime in Chapters IV, V, and VI of the Specific Provisions of the Criminal Law and may be sentenced to fixed-term imprisonment of one year or a lighter punishment, if the prosecution conditions are met but the juvenile suspect has shown repentance, a people's procuratorate may make a conditional non-prosecution decision. Before making a conditional non-prosecution decision, the people's procuratorate shall hear the opinions of the public security authority and the victim. Where the juvenile suspect or his/her legal representative raises any objection to the conditional non-prosecution decision of the people's procuratorate, the people's procuratorate shall make a decision to initiate a public prosecution.

The probation period for conditional non-prosecution shall range from six months to one year, starting from the date when the people's procuratorate arrives at the decision of conditional non-prosecution. During the probation period for conditional non-prosecution, a people's procuratorate shall supervise and inspect a juvenile suspect who is not prosecuted under conditions. The guardian of the juvenile suspect shall strengthen control and education of the juvenile suspect and cooperate with the people's procuratorate in supervision and inspection.

A juvenile suspect who is not prosecuted under conditions shall comply with the following during the probation period: **a.** abiding by laws and administrative regulations, and obeying supervision; **b.** reporting his/her activities as required by inspection organs; **c.** obtaining the approval of the inspection organ for any departure from the city or county where he/she lives or for any change in residence; **d.** receiving correction and education in accordance with the requirements of inspection organs.

For a juvenile suspect who is not prosecuted under conditions, a people's procuratorate shall revoke the conditional non-prosecution decision and initiate a public prosecution under any of the following circumstances during the probation period: **a.** he/she has committed a new crime, or it is discovered that another crime committed before the conditional non-prosecution decision was made needs to be prosecuted; **b.** he/she has seriously violated the provisions on public security administration or the provisions of the inspecting organ on supervising and administering conditional non-prosecution. If the juvenile suspect under conditional non-prosecution does not fall into any of the above circumstances during the probation period, upon expiration of the probation period, the people's procuratorate shall make a non-prosecution decision.

3. Procedures for Public Prosecution Cases Where Parties Have Reached Settlement

Procedures for public prosecution cases where parties have reached settlement were one of the four special procedures newly established in the 2012 revision to the Criminal Procedure Law. This procedure means that in a public prosecution case within the statutory scope, the criminal suspect or defendant shows sincere repentance, obtains the victim's forgiveness by making compensation, an apology, etc., and both parties voluntarily reach an agreement, then the public security authority, people's procuratorate or people's court can adopt such a procedure of making lenient treatment to the criminal suspect or defendant in different ways.

3.1. Scope of Application of Settlement by Parties in Public Prosecution Cases

Article 288 of the Criminal Procedure Law stipulates the scope of procedures for public prosecution cases where parties have reached settlement by way of explicit enumeration and prohibition:

First, the case is caused by civil disputes and is suspected of committing a crime as prescribed in Chapters IV and V of the Specific Provisions of the Criminal Law and is punishable by fixed-term imprisonment of three years or a lighter penalty. Such cases must meet the following three conditions: First, "arising from civil disputes". In general, civil disputes refer to the disputes between citizens concerning personal and property rights and interests as well as other disputes arising from daily life. Second, "criminal cases suspected of committing crimes in Chapters IV and V of the Specific Provisions of the Criminal Law". That is, "crimes of infringing upon citizens' personal rights and democratic rights" and "crimes of infringing upon property". Third, "may be sentenced to three years in prison or imposed a lighter penalty." According to the mainstream criminal law theory, the punishment under three years fixed-term imprisonment is a misdemeanor. The purpose of limiting the parties' settlement to the misdemeanor is to give full play to its positive role and avoid its negative influence as far as possible. All the above three conditions must be met at the same time.

Second, a negligent criminal case, excluding the crime of dereliction of duty, which is punishable by fixed-term imprisonment of not more than seven years. This kind of cases shall also meet the following three conditions: First, "negligent crime". The so-called "negligent crime" refers to the crime that one should foresee the result of possible harm to the society by his/her act, but fails to do so because of negligence, or believes easily that it can be avoided after having foreseen the result, therefore the result comes. Criminal liability shall be borne for negligent crimes only when the law so provides. Second, "the offender may be sentenced to fixed-term imprisonment of seven years or below." The maximum punishment for most negligent crimes is seven-year imprisonment, which corresponds to the punishment for negligent crimes. Third, the crime of dereliction of duty is excluded. The crime of dereliction of duty violates the impartiality, honesty and diligence of the official duty, obstructs the normal function of the State organs, is a serious damage to the interests of the State and the people, and therefore does not belong to the scope of settlement between the parties.

Third, if the criminal suspect or defendant committed any intentional crime in the past five years, the settlement procedure shall not apply. In other words, even if the case falls within the scope of the above two types of cases, if the criminal suspect or defendant committed any intentional crime in the past five years, no matter whether he/she was subject to a criminal penalty or not, the settlement procedure shall be prohibited. In such cases, the criminal suspect or defendant's social harm, personal danger and subjective viciousness are greater, which belong to the circumstances shall be subject to heavier punishment. Therefore, settlement system that would allow lighter punishment to the criminal suspect or defendant shall not be applied to such cases.

3.2. Procedures for Settlement Cases

(1) The Subjects of Settlement

In China, the subjects of settlementin public prosecution cases are the criminal suspect, defendant and the victim. They negotiate and reach a settlement. If the victim is deceased, his/her legal representative or close relative may reach a settlement with the criminal suspect or defendant. If the victim is a person with no capacity of conduct or with limited capacity of conduct, his/her legal representative may reach a settlement on behalf of him/her. If the criminal suspect or defendant is a person with limited capacity of conduct, his/her legal representative may settle on behalf of him/her. If the criminal suspect or defendant is in custody, with the consent of him/her, his/her legal representative or close relative may reach a settlement on behalf of him/her.

(2) Conditions for Settlement of the Parties

First of all, the criminal suspect or defendant shall show voluntary and sincere repentance, which is the prerequisite for the parties to reach a settlement. Repentance refers to the situation that the criminal pleads guilty and repents after committing a crime and before the court makes a judgment. Secondly, the facts of the crime must be clear, the evidence is solid and sufficient. Otherwise, even the criminal suspect or defendant pleads guilty on the surface, but in fact, the case may be misjudged.

(3) Method of Settlement of the Parties

First of all, the criminal suspect or defendant shall obtain the forgiveness of the victim by making compensation, an apology, etc. Compensation includes compensation for material damage and spiritual damage. The main form of compensation is economic compensation. Apologies can be made either in writing or orally. Secondly, the victim must settle voluntarily. Here, it emphasizes that the victim voluntarily settles on the basis of the forgiveness of the suspect or defendant, and prevents the phenomenon of forcing the victim to settle. Even if the suspect or defendant is willing to settle, but the victim is not willing to settle, settlement shall not be allowed. Finaly, the public security and judicial organ may intervene in the examination of the settlement only when the two parties have reached a settlement.

(4) Person Reviewing Settlement

The subjects of review are public security authorities, people's procuratorates and people's courts. The public security authorities, the people's procuratorates, and the people's courts have the duty to examine the settlement reached by the parties to determine whether or not they are valid. As the criminal proceedings are carried out in stages, if the parties reach a settlement of their own accordingly, the public security authority shall be responsible for examination at the investigation stage, the people's procuratorate shall be responsible for examination at the examination for the prosecution stage, and the people's court shall be responsible for examination at the trial stage.

(5) Examination Process and Content

The public security and judicial organ shall hear the opinions of the parties and other relevant persons, and preside over making the settlement agreement of the parties based on that. The content of the examination is "the voluntariness and legality of the settlement". "Voluntariness" means that the content of settlement reflects the true will of both parties, rather than the outcome through various coercive means of the opposing party or the third party. "Legality" means that the settlement must comply with the law, including the substantive legality and the procedural legality. Any settlement between the parties that violates the voluntariness or legality of the parties is null and void.

After examination, the public security and judicial organ will preside over the making of the settlement agreement if it believes the settlement is consistent with the principle of voluntariness and legality. The settlement agreement shall be a litigation document with legal effect, and shall be legally binding on both parties.

(6) Handling after Settlement Agreements Are Reached at Each Stage of Criminal Procedure

A. The investigation stage. In a case of public prosecution, if the criminal suspect commits a crime and shall be pursued for criminal liability, the public security authority has no power to make a decision on withdrawing the case at the investigation stage. Therefore, the public security authority shall not withdraw the case or take other direct measures to handle the case in which the parties concerned have reached a settlement, but may only transfer the case to the people's procuratorate for prosecution, and propose leniency suggestions in the prosecution opinions.

B. Examination for the prosecution phase. People's procuratorates give lenient punishments as follows: First, for a settled ordinary case between the parties concerned, the people's procuratorate may record in the public prosecution that the parties concerned have reached a settlement, and suggest that the people's court give lenient punishment to the defendant and transfer the settlement agreement of the parties with the case file. Second, for a settlement case where the circumstances of crime committed by the criminal suspect are minor and no criminal punishment is required, the people's procuratorate may decide not to initiate a prosecution at its discretion.

C. The trial stage. Where a criminal suspect or defendant and a victim reach a settlement during the stage of investigation, examination for prosecution, or trial, a people's court may render a lenient punishment to the defendant. A defendant who commits a crime with minor circumstances and little social harm, or a defendant who commits a serious crime but has statutory or discretionary circumstances for lenient punishment and a defendant with relatively small subjective viciousness and little personal threat may be given a lighter or mitigated punishment or be exempted from punishment; an act that caused danger to the society to a certain extent but with obviously slight circumstances and minor harm shall not be dealt with as a crime; with respect to a person who may not be subject to imprisonment according to the law, he/she shall be subject to probation, public surveillance, a fine only or any other non-imprisonment punishment to the largest extent.

4. Procedure for Trial in Absentia

The Criminal Procedure Law, revised in 2018, established the procedure for trial in absentia for the first time. This refers to the special trial procedure of a case conducted by the court when a defendant who meets the statutory conditions that he/she has fled abroad and is unable to attend the court hearing. The reason why this procedure should be set up is mainly out of the realistic need of punishing the escaped criminals in accordance with the law. On the one hand, we should pursue the escaped criminals abroad for their criminal liability; on the other hand, we should effectively protect their litigation rights and safeguard the procedural justice.

4.1. Application Scope and Jurisdiction of Procedure for Trial in Absentia

In accordance with Articles 291, 296 and 297 of the Criminal Procedure Law, where the criminal suspect or defendant is outside China in a case regarding a crime of embezzlement or bribery, or in a case regarding a crime of seriously compromising state security or terrorist activities that requires a timely trial as confirmed by the Supreme People's Procuratorate, if the supervisory authority or public security authority transfers the case for prosecution, and the people's procuratorate deems that the facts of the crime have been substantiated, the evidence is solid and sufficient and the criminal suspect or defendant shall be held criminally liable in accordance with the law, it may file a public prosecution with the people's court. After examination, the people's court shall decide to hold a court session to hear the case if the facts of the crime alleged in the criminal indictment are clear and the conditions for the application of the procedure for trial in absentia are met. Where the defendant is unable to appear before court for suffering a serious illness, and trial is suspended for more than six months, if the defendant is still unable to appear before court, and the defendant or his/her legal representative or close relative applies for or agrees to the resumption of the trial, the people's court may try the case in absentia without the defendant's presence in court, and render a judgment in accordance with the law. Where the defendant dies, the people's court shall rule to terminate the trial. However, if there is any evidence proving the innocence of the defendant, and the people's court confirms his/her innocence by trial in absentia, it shall render a judgment in accordance with the law. Where the defendant dies in a case retried by a people's court under the trial supervision procedures, the people's court may try the case in absentia, and render a judgment in accordance with the law. A case as mentioned in the preceding paragraph shall be tried by a collegial panel of the intermediate people's court at the place of commission of the crime, at the place of residence of the defendant before his/her departure from China, or designated by the Supreme People's Court.

4.2. Service of Cases Tried in Absentia

In accordance with Article 292 of the Criminal Procedure Law, a people's court shall, in a manner of judicial assistance specified in the relevant international treaties or proposed through diplomatic channels or in any other manner permitted by the laws of the place where the defendant is located, serve the summons and a copy of the criminal indictment of the people's procuratorate upon the defendant. If the defendant fails to appear in court as required after the summons and the copy of the criminal indictment are served upon him/her, the people's court shall hear the case in a court session, render a judgment in accordance with the law, and handle the illegal income and other property involved in the case.

4.3. Protection of the Rights of the Prosecuted

Articles 293 and 294 of the Criminal Procedure Law provide that, where a people's court tries a case in absentia, the defendant shall have the right to have a defender, and a close relative of the defendant may have a defender on behalf of the defendant. If the defendant and his/her close relatives do not have such a defender, the people's court shall serve a notice on a legal aid agency requiring the designation of a lawyer to defend him/her. A people's court shall serve a written sentence upon a defendant, his/her close relative, and the defender. The defendant or his/her close relative shall have the right to appeal the sentence to the people's court at the next higher level. The defender may file the appeal with the consent of the defendant or his/her close relative.

4.4. Handling After the Defendant Appears Before Court

Article 295 of the Criminal Procedure Law provides that, where the defendant voluntarily surrenders himself/herself or is captured during the trial period, the people's court shall try the case anew. Where a convict appears before court after a judgment or ruling takes effect, the people's court shall deliver the convict for execution of the criminal penalty. The people's court shall, before delivering the convict for execution of the criminal penalty, inform the convict that he/she has the right to raise an objection to the judgment or ruling. If the convict raises any objection to the judgment or ruling, the people's court shall try the case anew. Where there are some definite errors in the handling of the convict's property based on an effective judgment or ruling, the property shall be returned, and the compensation shall be made.

5. Confiscation Procedure for Illegal Income in Cases Where the Criminal Suspect or Defendant Escapes or Dies

This is a special procedure for the disposal of illegal proceeds and other property involved where the criminal suspect escapes or dies.

5.1. Conditions to Application of Confiscation Procedure for Illegal Income

Article 298 of the Criminal Procedure Law provides that, where, in a case regarding a serious crime such as embezzlement, bribery, or terrorist activities, a criminal suspect or defendant escapes and cannot be present in court after being wanted for a year, or a criminal suspect or defendant dies, if his/her illegal income and other property involved in the case shall be recovered in accordance with the Criminal Law, a people's procuratorate may file an application with a people's court for confiscation of illegal income.

5.2. Objects of Confiscation in the Procedure for Confiscation of Illegal Income

The objects of confiscation under the procedure for confiscation of illegal income are the illegal income of criminal suspects and defendants and other involved property. The term "illegal income" as mentioned herein refers to all property obtained through committing criminal activities, including money or articles, such as money or articles obtained through embezzlement and bribery. In general, "other involved property" refers to crime-related money and articles, tools for committing crimes, illegally held contraband, etc. other than illegal income. Before submitting the written opinion on confiscation of illegal income to the people's procuratorate, the public security authority may seize, impound or freeze the illegal income and other involved property of the criminal suspect or defendant involved in the case. When necessary, the people's court may also seize, impound or freeze the property the confiscation of which has been applied for.

5.3. Launching of Procedure for Confiscation of Illegal Income

In judicial practice, procedures for confiscation of illegal income shall be launched according to the litigation stage.

At the stage of investigation, where the circumstance meets conditions for confiscation of illegal income, the public security authority shall, upon approval of the chief of the public security authority at or above the county level, prepare the written opinion on confiscation of illegal income, which shall be transferred to the people's procuratorate at the same level together with relevant evidential materials; in the process of investigation of self-investigation cases, the people's procuratorates shall also initiate the procedures for confiscation of illegal income ex officio.

Where, at the stage of examination for prosecution, a people's procuratorate finds that a case meets the provisions on the procedures for confiscating illegal income, it may directly initiate the procedures for confiscating illegal income and file an application for confiscating illegal income to the people's court.

If, at the trial stage, the criminal suspect or defendant escapes, the people's court shall suspend the trial; if the criminal suspect or defendant dies, the people's court shall terminate the trial. If the conditions for confiscation of illegal income are met, the people's procuratorate shall file an application for confiscation of illegal income, otherwise the people's court shall not directly make a ruling on confiscation of illegal income.

5.4. Jurisdiction and Announcement of Procedure for Confiscation of Illegal Income

Article 299 of the Criminal Procedure Law provides that, an application for confiscation of illegal income shall be heard by a collegial panel formed by the intermediate people's court at the place of crime or the place of residence of a criminal suspect or defendant. After accepting an application for confiscation of illegal income, a people's court shall make a public announcement. The public announcement period shall be six months. The close relatives of a criminal suspect or defendant and other interested parties shall have the right to apply for participating in the procedure, and may have litigation representatives to participate in the procedure. A people's court shall hear an application for confiscation of illegal income upon expiration of the public announcement period. If any interested party participates in the procedure, the people's court shall hold a court session to hear the application.

5.5. Ruling in Procedure for Confiscation of Illegal Income

Article 300 of the Criminal Procedure Law provides that, a people's court shall render a ruling confiscating illegal income and other property involved in cases that are confirmed at trial, except those legally returned to the victims; or, for property which shall not be recovered, shall render a ruling to dismiss the application and terminate the seizure, impound, or freezing measure taken. Against a ruling rendered by a people's court under the preceding paragraph, the close relatives of a criminal suspect or defendant, other interested parties, or the people's procuratorate may appeal.

5.6. Handling and Remedies after the Accused Appear in Court

Article 301 of the Criminal Procedure Law provides that, where a fugitive criminal suspect or defendant voluntarily surrenders himself/herself or is captured during the trial period, a people's court shall terminate the trial. Where the property of a criminal suspect or defendant is erroneously confiscated, such property shall be returned, and compensation shall be made.

6. Procedures for Involuntary Medical Treatment of Mental Patients Legally Exempted From Criminal Liabilities

The procedure for involuntary medical treatment refers to the special procedure for taking involuntary medical treatment measures against the mental patients who do not bear any criminal liabilities and are dangerous to the society. Because the mental patients lose the ability of discernment and control, they do not bear criminal liabilities when they commit crimes. However, in order to maintain social order, prevent their activities from further endangering the safety of the person and property of others, and from the perspective of fully protecting the health of the mental patients, it is necessary for the State to impose certain restrictions on their personal freedom and take involuntary medical treatment measures. Therefore, the purpose of involuntary medical treatment is not to punish nor educate the perpetrator, but to provide a special social defense.

6.1. Application Objects of the Procedure for Involuntary Medical Treatment

Article 302 of the Criminal Procedure Law provides that, a mental patient who has committed any violent behavior compromising public security or seriously endangering the personal safety of citizens and is legally exempted from criminal liability after identification under statutory procedures shall be subject to involuntary medical treatment if the mental patient may continue to endanger the society. In accordance with such provisions, a person subject to involuntary medical treatment in China shall meet the preconditions, medical conditions and conditions of danger to the society simultaneously.

6.2. Procedures for Involuntary Medical Treatment

(1) Initiation of Involuntary Medical Treatment Procedures

If a public security authority finds that a mental patient meets the conditions for involuntary medical treatment, it shall, within seven days, prepare a written opinion on involuntary medical treatment, which shall be transferred to the people's procuratorate together with the relevant evidential materials and expert opinions upon approval by the person in charge of the public security authority at or above the county level. The people's procuratorate shall make a decision on whether to file an application for involuntary medical treatment within thirty days upon receipt of the written opinion on involuntary medical treatment transferred by the public security authority. For a mental patient that meets the condition for involuntary medical treatment who is transferred by a public security authority or is so discovered in the process of examination for prosecution, a people's procuratorate shall file an application for involuntary medical treatment with a people's court after making a decision not to initiate a prosecution. The application for involuntary medical treatment shall be filed by the primary people's procuratorate at the place where the respondent carries out the violence and shall be under the jurisdiction of the primary people's court at the place where the respondent carries out the violence. However, if such an application is more appropriate to be put forward by the people's procuratorate at the place where the respondent resides, such a proposal may be put forward by the primary people's procuratorate at the place where the respondent resides, and the primary people's court at the place where the respondent resides has jurisdiction.

Under special circumstances, the court may also directly decide to start the involuntary medical treatment procedure. In some ordinary criminal cases, the procuratorate initiates a public prosecution to pursue for the criminal liability of the defendant. However, if the court, during the trial of the case, determines that the defendant has "committed violence, endangered public security or seriously endangered the personal safety of any citizen", the court shall rule that the defendant shall not bear any criminal liability if, upon appraisal, the defendant is a mentally ill person who bears no criminal liability in accordance with the law. If the court holds that the defendant meets the conditions of "having the possibility to continue endangering the society", it may directly decide to take compulsory medical measures against the defendant.

Before a court makes an involuntary medical treatment decision, for the mental patient who has committed violent behavior, upon approval by the person in charge of the public security authority at or above the county level, a public security authority may take interim protective restraint measures against him/her to prevent him/her from endangering public security or the personal safety of other persons. For example, to send the patient to a mental hospital or a specialized institution for nursing or medical treatment. If the mental patient is no longer likely to continue endangering the society and will not endanger the society after the lifting of the restraint, the public security authority shall lift protective restraint measures in a timely manner. Where the public security authority fails to take temporary protective restraint measures that shall be taken, the people's procuratorate concerned shall suggest the public security authority to take temporary protective restraint measures.

(2) Deciding Authority on Involuntary Medical Treatment

Although the procedure of involuntary medical treatment is different from the ordinary criminal procedure, it is still related to the restriction and deprivation of personal freedom. Therefore, in order to protect the personal freedom of citizens from unlawful infringement, involuntary medical treatment procedure is included in the scope of criminal litigation, and in most cases, it is necessary for a neutral third party, that is people's courts, to make a decision in accordance with the litigation principles and system.

For the application for involuntary medical treatment filed by the people's procuratorate, the people's court shall complete the examination and handle within seven days: in case of no jurisdiction of the people's court, the application shall be returned to the people's procuratorate; in case of incomplete materials, the people's procuratorate shall be notified to make supplements within three days; where the case falls within the scope of procedure for involuntary medical treatment and it is under the jurisdiction of the court, and the materials are complete, it shall accept the case. Where the people's court decides to implement involuntary medical treatment, it shall serve the written decision on involuntary medical treatment and the notice on execution of involuntary medical treatment upon the public security authority within five days upon decision, and the public security authority shall deliver the person decided to his/her involuntary medical treatment. Where a people's procuratorate considers that the decision on involuntary medical treatment or the decision on overruling the application for involuntary medical treatment made by a people's court is improper, it shall, within twenty days upon receipt of the duplicate of the written decision, issue written opinions on correction to the people's court.

(3) Trial of Cases of Involuntary Medical Treatment

A. Trial organizations. The law provides that for involuntary medical treatment cases, the court shall form a collegial panel to try.

B. Notification procedures. Article 304 of the Criminal Procedure Law provides that, in the trial of a case regarding involuntary medical treatment, a people's court shall notify the legal representative of the respondent or defendant to be present.

C. Compulsory representation. Involuntary medical treatment cases involve professional knowledge of law and psychiatry, and due to the actor's incapacity or limited capacity of conduct, professional help is more needed in litigation. In order to protect the legitimate rights and interests of them, the Criminal Procedure Law requires that where the respondent or the defendant has not appointed litigation representatives, the court shall notify a legal aid institution to designate a lawyer to provide legal assistance for him/her.

D. Manner of trial. A collegial panel shall be formed to hear cases of involuntary medical treatment and open a court session. However, if the legal representative of the respondent or defendant requests not to hold a court session to hear the case, the people's court may agree not to hold a court session to hear the case upon examination. Where a court holds a court session to hear a case regarding involuntary medical treatment, the people's procuratorate shall send procurators to appear before court.

E. Trial procedures and handling after trial. After the presiding judge announces the commencement of court investigation, the procurator shall first read out the application, and then the legal representative and the litigation representative of the respondent shall give their opinions. The court shall investigate in sequence whether the respondent has carried out acts of violence endangering the public security or seriously endangering the personal safety of any citizen, whether the respondent is a mental patient who is legally exempted from any criminal liability, and whether there is any possibility that the respondent will continue to endanger the society. During the course of trial, if the respondent requests to appear in court, and the people's court considers that the respondent can appear in court after examining his/her physical and mental state, the people's court shall allow him/her to do so. The respondent appearing in court may present his/her opinions during the stage of court investigation and debate. A people's court shall make a decision within one month with respect to a case of involuntary medical treatment. Where the people's court deems that the respondent meets the conditions for involuntary medical treatment upon trial, it shall render a decision on involuntary medical treatment of the respondent; where the people's court deems that the respondent is a mental patient legally exempted from criminal liabilities but does not meet the conditions for involuntary medical treatment, it shall render a decision on overruling the application for involuntary medical treatment; where the respondent has caused harmful results, his/her family or guardian shall be ordered to take strict custody of him/her and give him/her medical treatment; where the respondent is considered to have full or partial capacity for criminal liability and shall be pursued for criminal liability in accordance with the law, the people's court shall render a decision on overruling the application for involuntary medical treatment and return the case to the people's procuratorate for handling in accordance with the law.

Where a party is dissatisfied with the decision on involuntary medical treatment made by the people's court, that party and his/her legal representative or close relative may apply to the people's court at the next higher level for reconsideration within five days upon receipt of the decision, but the enforcement of the decision on involuntary medical treatment shall not be suspended during the reconsideration. The people's court at the next higher level shall form a collegial panel to hear the application for reconsideration of the decision on involuntary medical treatment and make a reconsideration decision within one month; where it believes that the person decided to be subject to involuntary medical treatment meets the conditions for involuntary medical treatment, it shall reject the application for reconsideration and sustain the original decision; where it considers that the person decided to be subject to involuntary medical treatment does not meet the conditions for involuntary medical treatment, it shall revoke the original decision; where it considers that the original trial violates the statutory procedure, which may affect the fair trial, it shall revoke the original decision and remand the case to the original people's court for retrial.

6.3. Review and Supervision of Involuntary Medical Treatment

In order to protect the personal freedom of citizens from illegal infringement, the institution implementing involuntary medical treatment shall re-examine the mental condition of person subject to involuntary medical treatment on a regular basis. If it is found that the person poses no danger to the society, the measures for involuntary medical treatment shall be lifted to restore the personal freedom of the person and allow him/her return to the society. The person subject to involuntary medical treatment and his/her close relative shall have the right to file an application for termination of involuntary medical treatment to the people's court making the decision on involuntary medical treatment. The people's court shall form a collegial panel to examine the diagnosis opinions on termination of involuntary medical treatment measures, and respectively handle the case in accordance with the following circumstances within one month: Where the person subject to involuntary medical treatment no longer poses danger to others and does not need to continue involuntary medical treatment, the people's court shall render a decision on termination of involuntary medical treatment and may order family of the person subject to involuntary medical treatment to take strict supervision on him/her and provide medical treatment to him/her; and where the person subject to involuntary medical treatment still poses danger to personal safety, and needs to continue the involuntary medical treatment, the people's court shall render a decision on continuing the involuntary medical treatment.

The people's procuratorate shall supervise the decision and execution of involuntary medical treatment, and the people's procuratorate has the right to supervise whether the people's court makes a decision on involuntary medical treatment in accordance with law, whether the legal rights of the person subject to involuntary medical treatment have been infringed upon during the execution period, etc. If any illegal circumstance is found, the people's procuratorate shall put forward opinions on correction in a timely manner.